By the same author
The Vendée and surrounding area

Northern France

What to do and see within 90 minutes of Calais

ANGELA BIRD

Malnoue Publications

This book would not have happened without the enthusiasm of:
Charles Arnold and Hugh Brune, of Portfolio Books, who set me on the road;
Adrian Hulf, who brought it all to life with pictures and maps; and
Jon Bird, Sue Codrington and Miranda Robinson, who heroically examined every word.

My thanks to them all, as well as to:
Paul Reed who cast his expert eye over much World War I material;
and the friends and family members who enlivened my research trips, provided
photographs, and answered countless requests for obscure information.

Design and cartography Adrian Hulf

Cover picture:
Lighthouse at Petit-Fort-Philippe, near Gravelines (Nord)
© Luke Smith 2007

Malnoue Publications, London
malnouepublications@angelabird.plus.com/

© Angela Bird 2007
All rights reserved for all countries
ISBN-13: 978-0-9545803-1-5
ISBN-10: 0-9545803-1-1

Printed by D2 Print Pte Ltd (Singapore)

Contents

Names in bold type indicate larger towns.

*While every care has been taken in compiling
this book, neither the author nor the
publisher can accept responsibility for any
inaccuracies, and visitors are advised to check
details in advance before making a special
journey. Prices, usually based on 2006 rates,
are given as a guide only and do not
constitute a guaranteed admission charge.
The author welcomes any comments,
corrections or suggestions to:
malnouepublications@angelabird.plus.com/*

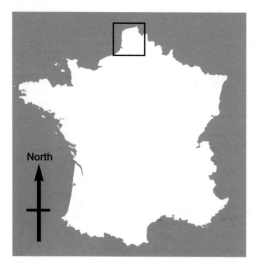

North

Northern France
What to do and see within 90 minutes of Calais

This guide is divided into six geographical areas. Below
are the various symbols used on maps and other pages.

ARRAS	major town
Béthune	smaller town
Amettes	small town, or village
Somme	county/*département*
☆	Top 30 site (see p33)
═══	road
≡≡≡	motorway
✈	airport
⌇	county boundary
⌐	river/canal
▬	lake
▦	woodland
※	marshland

┄┄	ferry/tunnel service
⛳	golf course
ⓘ	tourist office
✚	hospital
🅿	car park
⊏⊐	church
♿	disabled access
☂	wet-day visit
⚲	Sunday-morning visit
●	long season
◑	medium season
○	short season
╫╫╫╫	railway

*Maps are for guidance only, and do not show all roads and villages. They should be used in
conjunction with current Michelin or IGN maps.*

Tunnel

Straits of Dover

Ferry

Wimereux ☆

BOULOGNE ☆

Hardelot

Étaples

LE
TOUQUET ✈

Berck-
sur-Mer   D 303

*Bird
reserve*

*English
Channel*   Rue

Le Crotoy

Cayeux-
sur-Mer   St-Valé
sur-So

D 940

D 9

Eu

D 1015

Blangy-
sur-Bresle

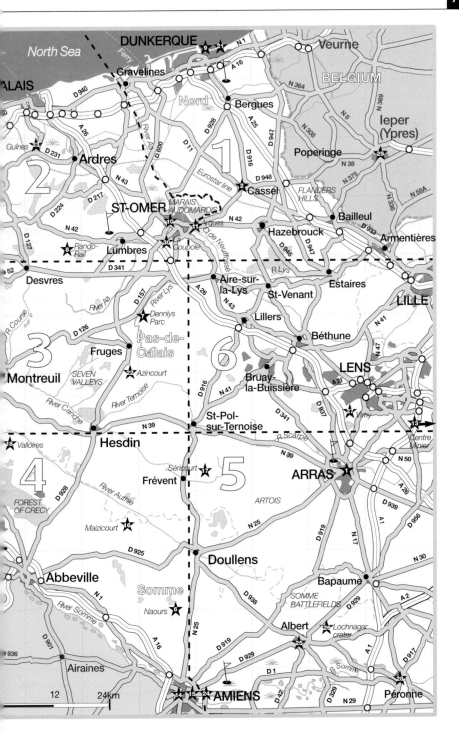

Introduction

We have all said it: "Northern France? Oh, flat/industrial/boring/bleak; we just dash through it on the way to somewhere more interesting."

But just stop for a minute. Turn off the motorway: drive into a village on market day; find picturesque valleys and staggering views; look for German blockhouses, the battlefield of Agincourt or the Field of the Cloth of Gold; pay tribute to the fallen of the Artois and the Somme; try dishes with unpronounceable names, and beers from a hundred local brews; ride on a steam train, watch for storks, or admire carvings on village churches and Gothic cathedrals.

The lovely—and underrated—Côte d'Opale, or Opal Coast, lies just 22 miles from the shores of Kent. It runs some 150km from the Belgian frontier to the estuary of the river Somme, fringing the *départements* of the Nord, the Pas-de-Calais and the Somme. It may not be as chic as the Côte d'Azur (roadside stalls sell cauliflowers, chicory and potatoes rather than melons, tomatoes and aubergines). However, within minutes of landing, you can be dabbling your toes at charming resorts like Wimereux; boating along quiet waterways near St-Omer; or touching history on the beaches of Dunkerque. The wide sands are ideal for families; brisk breezes make them a paradise for sand-yachters and kite-fliers, too. Museums feature local industries, vanished ways of life, warfare, archaeology, fine art, and aspects of the region's complex history.

The dense *autoroute* system shrinks the distances, so whichever port you arrive at you will be amazed how quickly you can reach your chosen destination. You really can drive from Dunkerque to Abbeville or from Calais to the Somme battlefields in 90 minutes—though the book's title is not intended to be a challenge! Dawdling through the villages is a joy, and the motorway-free centre of the region is full of fascinating gardens, caves and stately homes.

This book covers parts of three *départements*, or counties: the western half of the Nord, most of the Pas-de-Calais and the northern section of the Somme. The first two fall into the region of Nord/Pas-de-Calais; the Somme is part of the Picardie region. You will also come across the names of historic provinces, such as Flandre (Flanders) and Artois (most of the area from Flanders down to the Authie river, and east as far as Arras), and of smaller touristic areas such as Audomarois, Canche-Authie, Deux-Caps, Ponthieu or Gohelle that vie with and sometimes overlap one another. I have simplified presentation by dividing the book into six geographical areas, each with a distinct character.

With the end of coal, steel and textile production, northern France has turned to tourism to complement its surviving industries of fishing and agriculture. The British are made gratifyingly welcome by locals, who recall wartime solidarity between our nations, praise our politeness, and admire our continuing respect for the war dead.

Tourism here is nothing new. Tenth-century pilgrims took the Via Francigena (see page 25) from Canterbury to Rome; the 18th-century rich began their "grand tour" by stepping from the packet boat at Calais; and Charles Dickens wrote enthusiastically about holidays spent near Boulogne in the 1850s. By the 1930s, new resorts among the sand dunes—first Le Touquet, then Hardelot—were drawing high society from across the Channel. Long-term residents settled here, too. Nelson's bereft Lady Hamilton, the financially-strapped "Beau" Brummel, and hundreds of Nottingham lacemakers were among those who made Calais their home.

There is no shortage of activities, with many signposted footpaths, marked cycleways and perfectly-groomed golf courses. In return for a climb, you will enjoy spectacular vistas from belfries, cliffs, slag-heaps and the Flanders Hills.

I shall direct you to unusual museums, events and market days and throw in a seasoning of things that I find irresistible like flea-markets, crafts shops, and local customs and food. I shall tell

FUN AND FESTIVITIES IN THE NORTH

The **Fêtes des Géants**, carnivals with giant figures (see page 10), take place all year in northern France and Belgium, especially in February, and between May and September.

In late April, during the **Journées des Villes Fortifiées**, there are guided tours of Bergues, Gravelines, Montreuil and other fortified towns. June starts off with the **Semaine des Jardins**, when some unusual private gardens are open for visits. Around the middle of the month are the **Journées du Patrimoine du Pays**, when craftsmen demonstrate time-honoured building skills; the date usually coincides with the **Journée des Moulins** on which windmills and watermills open their doors. Bonfires are often lit to celebrate the **Fête de la Saint-Jean** (Feast of St John the Baptist) around 24 June, while the end of the month sees the week-long **Fête de la Musique**, with concerts held indoors and out.

The **Fête Nationale** (Bastille Day) is marked by parades and fireworks on 13 or 14 July. From mid July to mid August

is the peak French holiday period; countless annual events—especially in holiday areas—show off local food and culture. In mid-September, on the **Journées du Patrimoine** (the nation-wide Heritage Weekend) you have a chance to visit historic properties at reduced rates, including some normally closed to the public (information from tourist offices in early September, or on www. journeesdupatrimoine. culture.fr).

The crack of gunshot announces the start of the season for *la chasse* (shooting), usually in late August. Wildfowling is first, over rivers and lakes, followed in September by more general shooting in the countryside. From then till late February, on Sundays and on varying weekdays, it is probably wise

to resist taking woodland or country walks, or at least to wear brightly-coloured clothes and make sure you are noticed. Early October sees the **Journées Portes Ouvertes Entreprises**, when local businesses demonstrate everything from sea-fishing to coffee-roasting. In the same month, the annual **Portes Ouvertes des Ateliers d'Artistes** gives a chance to visit artists' studios in town and country. The new herring season is celebrated in Étaples with the **Hareng Roi** festival (pictured, above) in November.

Christmas markets are popular in the north, and in December you can expect to find **Marchés de Noël** in most towns, sometimes for a month (such as at Arras), sometimes for a single weekend. The most elegant Christmas lights are those near the **Place de l'Hermitage** in Le Touquet. Even more captivating is the **Cathédrale en Couleurs**, a magical lighting show that during late December restores their original bright colours to the hundreds of statues on the front of Amiens cathedral.

---

you where to parade with giants, try the region's *potjefleesch*, and nibble its home-made biscuits.

I have visited and evaluated things to see, from battlefields to bird reserves, watermills to playparks. I shall tell you of my favourite villages, churches and coalmines, and of places to make you laugh, gasp or, maybe, weep. At-a-glance symbols (see page 6) indicate length of opening

periods (the symbol for "all year" means a site is open for at least 11 months; many close briefly in December or January). I have indicated attractions where you could spend at least two hours on a wet day and, specially for weekend visitors, places that are open on Sunday mornings.

As well as the regular events in the box above, there is plenty of entertainment at local level.

CARNIVALS OF GIANTS

The north of France is a land of jolly giants—more than 300 of them. Known as *reuze* in Flemish dialect and *gayant* in Picard, the 4- to 8-metre-high figures are borne proudly in carnivals, painted and clothed to represent local heroes.

Their origins are medieval. Mentioned in 13th-century Portugal, they were first recorded in Flanders in 1398 and based on Biblical figures.

They became ever more numerous—but increasingly disrespectful—during the 16th to 18th centuries, and fell from favour after the French Revolution. In the 19th century giants were gradually revived as non-religious subjects. Today, in Flanders, they are a focus for local pride in 100 towns and villages.

Built around a light frame of willow, each *géant* weighs 80kg or so, and is drawn or carried by a team of *porteurs*. They are often based on legendary characters: a Viking at Sailly-sur-la-Lys, a miller at Boeschèpe, a woodcutter at Steenvoorde, a Customs officer for the frontier village of Godewaersvelde. Those of Cassel—the stately Reuze Papa and Reuze Maman, dating from 1827 and 1860 respectively—have been

declared "*monuments historiques*" and accorded World Heritage status.

Twirling and dancing each to its own traditional song, the giants emerge on their town's carnival day, and may also be invited to festivities elsewhere. There have been "marriages", too (which can result in the creation of new giant "children"!).

Outside carnival season, giants often spend quieter times of year in a corner of a museum (the Tisje Tasje family at Hazebrouck, and Totor, pictured left, at Steenwerck), or a town hall (Colas and Jacqueline tower over passers-by at Arras).

Information on the giants' outings is in the *Calendrier des Géants*, available in tourist offices from February, or at www.geants-carnaval.org/

Signs advertise *fêtes* (festivals), *ducasses* (funfairs), *vide-greniers* (car-boot sales), and also *braderies* and *réderies* (street sales of new or second-hand items). Everybody loves brocante (bric-à-brac) fairs; a Sunday crowd is more likely to be heading to one of these than to church!

I have usually given titles of museums and events in French, since this is how you will see them advertised. Many smaller establishments have tours and details only in French, so I have tried to explain enough historical background to give non-French speakers a little understanding of displays or events. Opening details may be varied on public holidays (see page 21). Cut-off point for children's admission rates varies. Many attractions offer family tickets, and a few have rates for senior citizens (*troisième âge*).

Comfortable shoes are vital; bring wellingtons or walking-boots if you intend to visit war cemeteries or ramble through the countryside.

Public conveniences can be hard to find. Try motorway service stations, large supermarkets, or museums (though this may involve an admission charge). Some major war cemeteries have toilets, particularly those with visitor centres. Or take a drink at a café, and use the facilities there.

Though this is essentially a book on what to see, rather than where to stay or eat, I have included a few addresses for mostly mid-range hotels, B&Bs and restaurants. (Some more specialist books are mentioned on page 16.)

You will find hundreds of suggestions for what to do between meals. And if you end up loving the region half as much as I do, you'll soon be back.

Planning Your Trip

WHEN TO GO

The climate of northern France is broadly similar to that of southern England, usually at its most pleasant between late May and late September, with peak French summer-holiday period from 14 July to 15 August. For the British, the area is a popular short-break destination all year. Apart from seaside and purely child-orientated activities, there is still plenty to visit between October and April; many of the main cultural sites are open—at weekends at least—almost all year.

Supermarkets are open six days a week, but town-centre shops may close on Mondays. Restaurants tend to close on Sunday evening and either Monday or Wednesday. Museums are often shut on Tuesdays and for maintenance periods in December or January.

HOW TO GET THERE

The most convenient way to travel is by car, and crossings are rapid by ferry or by tunnel.

By sea

Norfolkline: Dover to Dunkerque. www.norfolkline.com/

P&O: Dover to Calais; Hull to Zeebrugge, Belgium. www.poferries.com/

SeaFrance: Dover to Calais. www.seafrance.com/

Speedferries: Dover to Boulogne-sur-Mer. www.speedferries.com/

Superfast Ferries: Rosyth to Zeebrugge, Belgium. www.superfast.com/

By tunnel

Eurotunnel: Folkestone to Coquelles (Calais). Passengers remain in vehicle during journey, so it is ideal for those with difficulty walking, or who are travelling with pets. www.eurotunnel.com/

By air

EuroExec: Shoreham (East Sussex) to Le Touquet. www.euroexec.com/

Lydd Air: Lydd (Kent) to Le Touquet. www.lyddair.com/

Ryanair: Glasgow, Dublin and Shannon to Beauvais, 60km S of Amiens. www.ryanair.com/

By train

Eurostar: London-St Pancras (London-Waterloo until late 2007) to Calais-Fréthun or Lille-Europe; foot-passengers only. www.eurostar.com/

By coach

Eurolines: London (Victoria Coach Station) to Calais, Lille and Amiens. www.eurolines.com/

WHERE TO STAY

Some guides to hotels, bed-&-breakfasts and restaurants are listed on page 16. Regional tourist boards (see below) produce free booklets listing accommodation in their areas. The Nord/Pas-de-Calais region awards a "Savoir Plaire" badge to attractions and accommodation that offer an especially friendly welcome; free booklet from tourist offices.

Bed-&-breakfast rooms (*chambres d'hôte*) or holiday cottages (*gîtes*) are graded and listed by Gîtes de France (tel: 01 49 70 75 75; fax: 01 42 81 28 53; www.gites-de-france.com), or by Clévacances (tel: 05 61 13 55 66; fax: 05 61 13 55 94; www. clevacances.com).

FURTHER INFORMATION

Nord/Pas-de-Calais Regional Tourist Board 6 Place Mendès-France, BP99, 59028 Lille CEDEX (tel: 03 20 14 57 57; fax: 03 20 14 57 58; www.crt-nordpasdecalais.fr).

Picardy Regional Tourist Board 3 Rue Vincent-Auriol, 80011 Amiens CEDEX 1 (tel: 03 22 22 33 63; fax: 03 22 22 33 67; www.picardie tourisme.com).

Nord Tourist Board 6 Rue Gauthier-de-Châtillon, BP1232, 59013 Lille CEDEX (tel: 03 20 57 59 59; fax: 03 20 57 52 70; www.cdt-nord.fr).

Pas-de-Calais Tourist Board La Trésorerie, Wimille, BP79, 62930 Wimereux (tel: 03 21 10 34 60; fax: 03 21 30 04 81; www.pas-de-calais.com).

Somme Tourist Board 21 Rue Ernest-Cauvin, 80000 Amiens (tel: 03 22 71 22 71; fax: 03 22 71 22 69; www.somme-tourisme.com).

Useful Information

ACCESSIBILITY

Things in France are slowly improving for people with limited mobility (*à mobilité réduite*, or *handicapé*). Parking spaces for disabled-badgeholders are provided at tourist attractions and at supermarkets. A blue "Tourisme et Handicap" label (see below) indicates hotels, restaurants or attractions accessible to wheelchairs and with arrangements in place to help people with other disabilities.

Most beaches now have ramps leading down to them, and sometimes continuing a little way onto the sand. Some resorts, such as Malo-les-Bains and Gravelines (Petit-Fort-Philippe), make a virtue of their wheelchair-friendliness. During July and August, lifeguard stations at these and several other places, including Berck-Plage, provide free loan of beach-buggy-style wheelchairs (known as "Tiralo" and "Hippocampe") on which a bather can be assisted right into the water.

■ **Helping hand: the sign of a friendly welcome for all.**

Wheelchair-bound fishing enthusiasts are well catered for: many riverbanks and lakesides have specially-designed pontoons jutting out into the water. However, the vogue for prettying up towns with bumpy cobbles can be uncomfortable for wheelchair-users, and means that trips round the old quarters of Arras, Montreuil, Hesdin, Boulogne and St-Valéry-sur-Somme are probably better made by car.

Though new establishments are designed with accessibility in mind, and feature such facilities as toilets for the disabled, older hotels and museums can still have daunting flights of steps. I have indicated wherever a venue specifically claims to have easy access (though absence of a symbol does not necessarily mean entry is impossible). For others, I have tried to mention in the text any obstacles that might pose problems. If in doubt, contact the venue for up-to-date information. "*Est-ce que c'est accessible aux fauteuils roulants?*" or "*Y a-t-il des toilettes pour handicapés?*" are useful phrases if you need to check wheelchair access or provision of toilets for the disabled, and "*Avez-vous des chambres au rez-de-chaussée?*" to ask whether there are ground-floor bedrooms.

BEACHES

From the Belgian border to the Somme, the beaches are vast, sandy and excellent; to find the cleanest ones, check out the French Blue Flag website: www.pavillonbleu.org/ The only drawback is that the sea goes out so far you can have a long hike (up to 20 minutes) to the water's edge at low tide. The locals know to study the tide-tables (obtainable from seaside tourist offices) and to arrive when the water is fairly high. Bathing is forbidden around the mouths of the Somme, Canche and Authie rivers, due to the strong currents.

You won't be doing much surfing along the Opal Coast, though the beaches are ideal for sand-yachting, speed-sailing, and fly-surfing (known here as *kite-surf*). If you are not involved in these sports, it's best to watch from a safe distance: speed-sails and sand-yachts can reach 90km per hour and 130km per hour, respectively. Windsurfers make for Wissant to enjoy the most challenging conditions, while kite-fliers take their pick from any sandy beach.

Some resorts, such as Berck and Stella-Plage, post warnings about "*les bâches*", the hollows that form around sandbanks. These can create friendly paddling areas at low water, but beware of strong currents as a *bâche* begins to empty when the tide falls, or of stepping into a concealed one as the tide is rising.

Always watch out for any wartime remnants of rusty metal, barbed wire or old ammunition

that can occasionally be revealed by the tide, and impress upon children not to touch anything metal protruding from the sand. See Safety (page 22).

BIRD-WATCHING

Ornithologists are spoilt for choice. The coast of northern France is on migratory routes for many species, so large numbers of birds are seen in spring and autumn. Bring binoculars to use: on the breakwater at Loon-Plage, near Dunkerque, for seabirds; in the observatories at Platier d'Oye, near Gravelines, for plovers, avocets and waders; in the Romelaëre marshland, near St-Omer, for warblers and bittern; and in the Marquenterre reserve, north of the Somme estuary, near Rue, for egrets, storks, and spoonbills. Inland, the majestic deciduous forest of Crécy is home to woodland species such as woodpeckers, finches and hawks while, between Crécy and Noyelles-sur-Mer, the marshland site of Sailly-Bray is rich in ducks, wagtails and bluethroat.

■ On the wild side: nature-lovers look for birds and seals in the Somme Bay.

Étaples and St-Valéry-sur-Somme. Those arriving on their own boat will find marinas at Dunkerque, Gravelines, Calais, Boulogne, Étaples and St-Valéry.

CHILDREN

There are free playgrounds for children in town centres. The most family-friendly seaside resorts are those bearing the "Station Kid" label, which have safe bathing, a good beach (usually with giant bananas, boats and birds mounted on poles to help children locate their families) and summer entertainment. Among the "Stations Kid" are: Petit-Fort-Philippe, Calais, Wissant, Wimereux, Hardelot, Le Touquet and Berck. Children would also enjoy Nausicaa aquarium, cycle trips, the Rando-Rail (see Cycling, page 14), and the amusement parks, mini-golf courses or treetop trails (according to age). Younger ones could find war-themed visits scary, so if you plan such a trip it would be as well to prepare children in advance (some book suggestions on page 170). Visits to tunnels or to coal-mine experiences also need careful consideration. In such locations, if anyone feels claustrophobic, or needs a trip to the lavatory it's a major problem for the guide to stop the tour to take someone back to the surface.

BOATING

There are canoes for rent on the river Canche beneath the ramparts of Montreuil and also at Beaurainville, farther upstream. If you prefer rowing, try Salperwick, near St-Omer. On the moat around the fortifications of Gravelines and Calais you can hire rowing or electric boats. Electric boats can also be rented on the river Lys at St-Venant and on the lake at Ardres. Most resorts offer dinghy-sailing, and there are trips out to sea on traditional boats from Gravelines,

CHURCH-GOING

The Fellowship of the Anglican Chaplaincy in Europe has a presence in the area, and a resident vicar takes regular Sunday services in English at Calais, Boulogne, Hesdin and Arras (see entries for individual towns, or http://anglchurch.free.fr). Worshippers are always welcome to attend Mass at French Catholic churches—weekly services are held on Saturday evening or Sunday morning (service information given on http://messesinfo.cef.fr).

■ Blown away: sand-yacht at Wissant.

CYCLING

Every area has its signposted cycle trails known as *itinéraires cyclotouristiques* or *pistes cyclables*. Free maps of routes for the Pas-de-Calais are available at tourist offices, which can also advise on bike hire (*location de vélos*). For the western Somme you can download maps from www.baiedesomme.org/ These take you through Crécy Forest, across marshland full of wild birds, or along a disused railway from Abbeville to St-Riquier and beyond. A more unusual form of cycling is the Rando-Rail, a light, flat wagon pedalled along an old railway line (see page 80).

■ **Freewheeling: pedal along one of the cycle trails or quiet country lanes.**

French-speakers is restricted. The letters "VO" (*version originale*) indicate that a movie will be in its original language, with French subtitles.

ELECTRICITY

The electric current is 220 volts, so British equipment or telephone-chargers should function successfully. Adaptors to convert a UK plug to fit a French socket are widely available in Britain and at ferry ports, but not usually in France.

ENTERTAINMENT

Probably the most accessible form of entertainment for non-French speakers is music. There are international festivals of classical music at St-Riquier in July, and at Hardelot, Le Touquet and the Abbaye de Valloires in August.

Son-et-lumière performances are another summer treat. You might not understand every word of these colourful, night-time, open-air shows, but the spectacle is such that it hardly matters. The best-known are at Lillers (June), Montreuil (July and August) and Anzin-St-Aubin, near Arras (September). Book in advance via websites (see individual entries) or tourist office.

Theatre performances in France tend to rely heavily on words, and anyone with limited command of French may find them difficult to follow. There are traditional theatres at Dunkerque Calais, Boulogne, Montreuil, Amiens and Arras.

Most towns have cinemas, including modern multiplexes; listings appear in the local press. With a few exceptions, films will be in French (English-language ones being dubbed rather than subtitled), so entertainment value for non-

FISHING

There are many fishing opportunities, from Flanders canals to the river Somme. Tourist offices can advise on the type that interests you, and also on where to buy permits if necessary. Tackle and bait are on sale in sports and water-sports shops, and hypermarkets.

Freshwater fishing

A variety of rivers and lakes offer a wide choice, from trout and perch to black-bass and carp. Day permits (*permis journée*, or *carte journalière*), from selected cafés and tackle shops for around 7€, allow fishing in all non-private waters of a particular *département*. A holiday licence (*carte pêche-vacances*), for about 30€, is valid on 15 consecutive days between 1 June and 30 September. The Somme *département* is particularly fisherman-friendly. A free bilingual booklet, *Fishing in the Somme,* is available from the Somme Tourist Board (see page 11), and more information on www.unpf.fr/80/

Private fisheries

There are at plenty of establishments in the Pas-de-Calais for what is advertised as "*pêche à la ligne*" or "*pêche à la journée*". Between March and September, you can fish in specially-stocked lakes for around 12€ for a half-day.

Sea fishing

Sea-angling (known as "*surf-casting*") is free from jetties and beaches. Some seaside ports offer boat trips to fish for sea-bass and mackerel.

Shrimping and shellfish-collecting

At low water, you can push a shrimping-net through the shallows or dig for cockles, clams and other shellfish. Best days are those with extra-low tides: look in the tide-tables for days with a figure of more than 90 in the *coefficients* column. Rarely-uncovered sandbanks are popular sites, but stay away from dubious outflow pipes as well as from commercial oyster- or mussel-beds, and always keep an eye on the time. You should not collect anything too tiny, nor harvest more than you can eat at a sitting.

GARDENS

With a climate similar to that of Kent and Sussex, garden-owners and designers in northern France are beginning to create plots to rival those they have admired across the Channel. Several have earned an official status of "*jardin remarquable*". Among magnificent gardens in the region are those of Valloires, Maizicourt and Séricourt. Smaller, private gardens welcome visitors, too—particularly during the "Semaine des Jardins" around the first weekend of June; details in the annual publications *Parcs et Jardins du Nord/Pas-de-Calais* and *Picardie: Parcs et Jardins*, both free from tourist offices. From early May, information can also be found on www.rendezvousauxjardins.culture.fr/

Individual owners are full of enthusiastic commentary. (Luckily, Latin names of plants make for a sort of horticultural Esperanto.) The greatest compliment they seek is your assurance that they have created an "English" garden!

■ **Casting about: fishermen are spoilt for choice along the river Somme.**

GOLF

The north of France is well endowed with golf courses. Dunkerque, St-Omer, Wimereux, Hardelot (two courses), Le Touquet (three), Nampont-St-Martin (two), Belle-Dune, Abbeville and Arras are among favourites with British visitors. Between May and September it is best to book a tee-time in advance. Golf clubs may usually be hired on the spot. Third-party insurance is required, in case you injure somebody while playing. If you intend to enter competitions, you will need to produce a current handicap certificate and may also be asked for a doctor's certificate of fitness. Most of the clubhouses have independently-run bars and restaurants open to all, so even non-golfers are welcome to drop in for lunch. Green fees start at around 45€ (midweek in low season). A "Golf-Pass Côte d'Opale" covering six green fees over 15 days costs 200€ (information from 03 21 10 34 60, or www.golfencotedopale.com).

HOTELS, B&Bs AND RESTAURANTS

Northern France is a popular destination for short breaks, and it is wise to book accommodation ahead, rather than to plan on finding a place at the last minute—particularly during the school-holiday times, at weekends, and near the coast. Bed-&-breakfasts sometimes offer slight reductions from the second or third consecutive night; some city hotels offer cheaper room rates at weekends; and during winter, rural hotels may propose a third night free if you stay for two.

When you plan arrival time, don't forget to take into account that you lose an hour when travelling from the UK. (French time is one hour ahead of UK time throughout the year, changing to and from summer time on the same date.) Always call to let the hotel or B&B host know if you will arrive later than planned or if you decide to cancel, to give them a chance to re-let the room. If you're staying in a fairly basic establishment, pack your own shampoo and soap, as sometimes these items are not provided. Those who have

mobility problems should enquire about ground-floor accommodation (see page 12), as B&B rooms are often in converted roof spaces. Breakfast costs extra at a hotel, but is included at a B&B. Hotels accept credit-card payment, but bed-&-breakfasts usually don't, so make sure you have adequate cash. Secure parking can be an issue if you have a heavily-laden car. You may need to book a garage in advance at a town-centre hotel; however more rural locations usually have private parking.

■ **Café culture: bowls of mussels served at pavement tables.**

Hotels

There are two types of hotels: those that you roost in for a night to break a journey, and those that provide a more leisurely and, occasionally, slightly idiosyncratic taste of real France. The former include the reliable Mercure, Ibis, and Campanile establishments, as well as budget chains such as Formule 1, Nuit d'Hôtel and 1ère Classe. These last may be a little anonymous but offer clean, good-value family accommodation. At the more luxurious end of the scale, you can choose elegant four- and five-star places, with sumptuous décor and Michelin-starred chefs. In between, there are hundreds of two- and three-star hotels that provide plenty of character. The Logis de France umbrella covers a variety of family-run hotel-restaurants that are graded from one to three "*cheminées*", or fireplaces, and often serve good food (www.logisdefrance.com). Useful reference books include the Michelin red guide for both hotels and restaurants.

Bed-&-breakfasts

If you have a spirit of adventure and eclectic tastes, try *chambres d'hôte* (bed-&-breakfasts), which may be anything from working farm to family château. Some serve a *table d'hôte* evening meal (which usually includes mainstream regional specialities, and wine with the meal); you need to book this with your hosts in advance. Such evenings often make for convivial occasions, giving an opportunity to practise your language skills as well as to enjoy French home cooking. Michelin's *1000 Maisons d'Hôte et Hôtels de Charme* picks out some

delightful places, as does Alastair Sawday's *Special Places to Stay: French Bed and Breakfast*. The Gîtes de France brochure and website (see page 11) lists *chambres d'hôte*, graded from one to five *épis* (ears of wheat); Clévacances grades are from one to five *clés* (keys). Three-star/ear/key grade for hotels or B&Bs usually ensures a comfortable room, with bath/shower.

Restaurants

One of the main reasons for making a trip to France has to be for the food. French restaurant "bibles" include the Michelin red guide—which awards up to three rosettes for gastronomic excellence—and the upmarket *GaultMillau*, which accords marks out of 20. From Monday to Friday, most restaurants offer a good-value fixed-price lunchtime menu—an opportunity to sample gastronomic output at affordable rates. Try and reserve a table ahead by phone when possible. Restaurants often close on Sunday evenings and Mondays, or on Wednesdays. If you don't have a booking, it's worth turning up on the dot of noon, or 7.30pm, just in case there's still a table available. Most hypermarkets have brasseries or self-service cafeterias.

For true local flavour, it's worth considering a *ferme-auberge*. These are restaurants that usually adjoin a family farm, and at least half the produce served has to be home-produced. So you're guaranteed fresh duck, lamb, foie gras, pork, or whatever is the farm's speciality. It's essential to book in advance, as owners need to have an idea of numbers.

Another typical place to eat—particularly in Flanders—is at an *estaminet*. A combination of pub, café and restaurant, these are atmospheric places, often with old-fashioned décor, serving a huge range of beers, snacks such as *planches*, and traditional dishes such as *potjevleesch* (both described on page 27). *Estaminets* are often closed in the early part of the week.

Vegetarian eating

In spite of the fantastic vegetable displays in markets, vegetarians are poorly catered for in rural France, especially if they don't eat fish. Restaurants are often a little stunned to be asked for vegetarian dishes, and too often fall back on offering an omelette—though some may be willing to concoct a suitable dish if given 24 hours' notice. Local specialities to consider include *flamiches* (open tarts)—either *aux poireaux* (leek) or *au Maroilles* (strong cheese).

INTERNET

Keeping up with email while on holiday is becoming easier. Those with laptops will find wi-fi arrangements in some hotels, and even in occasional B&Bs, or can use a dialup number from a hotel room to call their usual service provider. (Check before travelling that you know the international number for your dialup). In a town, the tourist office can direct you to a cybercafé; these charge around 2€ an hour to use the internet or to pick up emails.

MAPS

You need good maps to get the most out of a holiday and, since new motorways and bypasses open every year, it is a false economy to use out-of-date ones. This is especially true for the north, as many motorway exit numbers have been changed on the A16 around Calais and Boulogne. Moreover, as soon as you land you are swished away from ferry ports or tunnel straight onto the motorway system, and need to know immediately the direction that you want. Pick the name of some major towns on your route—e.g. Lille, Boulogne, Abbeville, St-Omer, Arras—rather than just a road number, as these are what the signposts will indicate.

Michelin map No 301 (Pas-de-Calais/Somme), widely available in UK bookshops, covers the area in this guidebook. Part of the "Local" series (1:150,000/1cm=1.5km), it incorporates a gazetteer, plans of Arras and Amiens, and good marking of military cemeteries for those interested in battlefield tourism.

The slightly more detailed, though more expensive, IGN (Institut Géographique National) "Carte de Promenade" series (1:100,000/1cm=1km) has shaded contours that bring an area to life. They can be bought in France, at bookshops and at hypermarkets; numbers 01, 02 and 04 cover the area of this book. For even more detail if you want to walk, or explore in depth, nothing beats the IGN "Top 25" series (1:25,000/4cm=1km).

In town centres, although the main square may officially be called Place de la République or Place du Général-de-Gaulle, the locals will probably refer to it—like generations before them—simply as the "Grand'Place".

One of the more bizarre features of northern France is the similarities in place-names, with Naours and Daours, Authie and Authuille, and Houlle and Moulle being within a few kilometres of one another. Conversely, some that sound similar are far apart, so it can be annoying to find yourself in Hesdin rather than in Hesdin-l'Abbé; Mametz (Somme) rather than Mametz (Pas-de-Calais); or Avesnes-sur-Helpe instead of Avesnes-le-Comte.

MARKETS

Markets are usually open-air, and normally end around noon. Here is a selection of the most interesting, with the largest shown in bold type.

Monday

Bergues; Béthune; Hazebrouck; **St-Pol-sur-**

Ternoise; Samer; Le Touquet (1 June-15 Sept).

Tuesday

Amiens (all day); **Arques**; Bailleul; Berck-Ville; Calais; Desvres; **Étaples**; Frévent; Wimereux.

Wednesday

Abbeville (last of month); **Amiens** (all day); Arras; **Audruicq**; Beaurainville; Berck-Plage; Boulogne; Bray-sur-Somme (afternoon); Calais; Dunkerque (all day); **Merville**; St-Valéry-sur-Somme ; Wissant.

Thursday

Abbeville (all day; not last Thurs of month); Amiens (all day); Ardres; Calais; Cassel; **Doullens**; Fauquembergues; **Hesdin**; **Marquise**; Quend-Plage-les-Pins (15 June-15 Sept); Le Touquet.

Friday

Aire-sur-la-Lys; Amiens (all day); Berck-Ville; Corbie; Le Crotoy; **Étaples**; Gravelines; Guînes; Hondschoote; Lumbres; Watten; Wimereux.

Saturday

Abbeville; Albert; **Amiens** (all day); **Arras**; Berck-Plage; **Boulogne**; Calais; Dunkerque (all day); Fruges; Laventie; Lillers; **Montreuil**; **Péronne**; **Rue**; **St-Omer**; **Le Touquet**.

Sunday

Amiens (food hall); Hardelot; Petit Fort-Philippe; **St-Valéry-sur-Somme**.

■ **Market forces:** fresh local produce is on sale daily in towns and villages.

MEDICAL TREATMENT

If you hold a European Health Insurance Card you can claim some reimbursement of medical expenses under the reciprocal arrangement between Britain and France. The card is obtainable free to British nationals from www.nhs.uk/, or using a form obtainable from a UK post office. However, the EHIC does not cover 100 per cent of costs, nor repatriation if necessary, so it is best to take out additional travel insurance.

After consulting, and paying, a doctor or dentist, take the *feuille de soins* (medical treatment form) that you are given and hand it to a chemist with your *ordonnance* (prescription) form. The chemist dispenses the drugs (it is vital to keep any sticky labels from the boxes), and adds their details to the form. Gather together the form and sticky labels, your EHIC and your passport. Take these to the nearest Caisse Primaire Assurance Maladie (CPAM), located in larger towns, where a large percentage of your costs should be reimbursed. Main offices can sometimes hand over the cash, or a cheque that you can cash locally; otherwise the system operates by sending a cheque to your home address in around six weeks.

Chemists are often consulted about minor ailments and discuss them with doctor-like gravity, binding up sprained ankles and dishing out reasonably strong medicines. However, you are not reimbursed for this treatment.

For a minor beach injury, seek out the lifeguard post, where personnel are trained in first-aid. For a serious accident or illness, call 15 from a fixed phone for the SAMU (paramedics), or 18 for the *pompiers* (fire brigade). The *pompiers* have ambulances, too, and are trained in medical emergency treatment; they are often likely to be quickest to the scene if you are a long way from a town. From a mobile phone, call 112 to reach any of the emergency services, and the operator will be able to pinpoint your position. Main hospitals are signposted with a red cross logo, either as: CH (*centre hospitalier*); CHD (*centre hospitalier départemental*); CHR (*centre hospitalier régional*); or CHU (*centre hospitalier universitaire*). There are Accident & Emergency departments (*Urgences*) at:

Abbeville (CH) 43 Rue Isle, off Boulevard des Prés, 1km S of centre.

Amiens (CHU Nord) 2 Place Victor-Pauchet, NW of town centre; junction 39 from N1 bypass.

Arras (CH) Avenue Winston-Churchill, on D266 to W of town centre.

Béthune (CH) Rue Delbecque, Beuvry, off N41 on SE corner of ring road; J6 from A26 motorway.
Boulogne (CH Dr Duchenne) Allée Jacques-Monod; J31 from A16.
Calais (CH) 11 Quai du Commerce, SE of Hôtel de Ville; J43 or J46 from A16.
Douai (CH) On D25 Rocade Est, near junction with N43, to SE of town centre.
Dunkerque (CHD) Avenue Louis-Herbeaux, Rosendaël, 1km E of centre; J33 from A16.
Lens (CH Schaffner) 99 Route de La Bassée; J9 from A21.
Lille (CHR) Avenue Oscar-Lombret, on S side of city; J4 from A25.
Rang-du-Fliers (CH) On roundabout at junction of D303 and D140, 7km E of Berck-sur-Mer and 9km SW of Montreuil; J25 from A16.

MONEY

A euro, made up of 100 cents (the locals often call them *centimes*) is worth between 66 and 70 UK pence, depending on currency fluctuations. (For a rough conversion of euros to pounds, subtract one-third: i.e. 30€ is worth a little over £20).

In towns and large villages, banks usually open from Tuesday to Saturday, 9am till noon and 2pm till 6pm. Since the adoption of the euro, foreign-exchange desks have been phased out, so do not count on being able to change British cash, or anything other than euro-denomination travellers' cheques. Banks close for public holidays (see page 21) from lunch-time the previous day. This can catch you unawares, as can the fact that if a holiday falls on a Tuesday or a Thursday there is a tendency to join the day up to the nearest weekend (*faire le pont*) and close for several days. You are often asked for your passport during banking transactions, or when paying in a hypermarket, so it is as well to carry it with you.

A UK cashpoint card will usually work in France, if it bears a logo matching one on the French cashpoint machine (*guichet automatique* or *distributeur*). On-screen instructions are usually in English as well as French. Credit cards (known as *cartes bancaires*) such as MasterCard and Visa are accepted at petrol stations, supermarkets, hotels, restaurants and stores—except B&Bs, cafés, village shops and small restaurants. At the time of writing, UK cards—even with the microchip—will not operate unmanned petrol pumps (see page 20).

MOTORING

You should always have the car's documents—original of registration certificate (plus letter of authorisation from the owner if vehicle is not registered in your name), insurance certificate, and MOT certificate if applicable—as well as your driving licence and passport with you when on the road. You can be stopped for random checks, and it is an offence to be without them. You should also carry a warning triangle in case of breakdown, and a spare set of bulbs. Seat belts must be worn by all occupants. Children under 12 must be in child- or booster-seats; under-10s may not travel in the front seat.

On-the-spot fines are common: penalties for using a mobile phone (even hands-free) or for not wearing a seat belt start at 135€; speeding fines go from around 200€ to more than 800€, plus immediate confiscation of licence in more serious cases. Drink/drive limits, at 50mg/100ml, are actually lower than those operating in Britain, and random breath tests are carried out; your licence can be withdrawn if the result is positive, and penalty points can follow you home. Radar speed-trap detectors are illegal in France. If the police discover one—even disabled—they can issue a fine of more than 1,500€, confiscate the device and impound your vehicle. (This does not include satellite-navigation systems that show positions of *fixed* speed cameras.)

When driving in the countryside, watch out for packs of cyclists on Sunday mornings; for scarily deep roadside ditches; and for large agricultural vehicles, particularly around dusk in winter. Note that if a French driver flashes headlights at you he is not giving you right of way; he is announcing he is taking it for himself.

When visiting the centre of an unfamiliar town for the first time, try to arrive at lunchtime, when streets are quieter and you have more chance of finding a parking space. Towns tend to be busiest around 5pm as people finish shopping, leave offices, or collect children from school.

Priority to the right

Although in many parts of France the old *priorité à droite* tradition (by which any vehicle arriving from your right-hand side had the right of way) has faded a bit, this rule of the road is still very prevalent in northern France, in towns, villages and on the open road. It might not have been so bad when traffic moved at the pace of the horse and cart, but today it's a different story. Unless you are on a motorway or on one of the main, N-numbered roads be extremely careful when approaching a junction to check whether there's a broad white solid, or dotted, line to halt emerging traffic. If there is none, and a driver approaching from the right looks as if he believes he has priority, be prepared to brake; he will not be expecting to slow down or stop. By the same rule, people coming from your left may stop to let you out at a junction. If you are sure of your right-of-way, you may proceed, but don't forget to check for vehicles coming from your own right, that will have priority over you!

Information about priority is communicated rather subtly by road signs. Here is a reminder:

 You are on a main road with priority over those joining it. (An oblique band through it means this is no longer the case.)

 The road you are on has priority at the junction you are approaching, though not necessarily at subsequent junctions.

 You are approaching a junction with priority to the right. This really ought to be encircled with flashing lights and bells!

Motorways

Being a virtual crossroads of Europe, the north of France is criss-crossed with *autoroutes* (motorways). They include the A1 (Lille-Paris), A16 (Dunkerque-Abbeville-Amiens-Paris), A25 (Dunkerque-Lille) and A26 (Calais-Arras-Rheims). In the pipeline is the A24 which, by 2015, will link Amiens with Courtrai, in Belgium.

Traditionally, French motorways are subject to *péages* (tolls), though some sections, particularly around a large town, are free. Usually you pay the operator in the tollbooth. However, some smaller exit points have entirely automatic *péage* systems, so you have either to use a credit card, or to get out of the car and look for a special machine nearby that accepts coins and notes (up to 20€) and then issues a ticket to insert at the toll barrier. UK credit cards (Visa or MasterCard) can be used at both manned and automatic motorway toll booths; it's very quick, there's no minimum amount (it can be for the equivalent of a few pence, if that's what the toll comes to), and you don't have to sign or punch in your PIN.

At larger *péage* stations you will see lanes marked "*t réservé*" in orange. These are only for drivers with a *télépéage* (automatic payment) box fixed to their windscreens. (If you want to join this élite band, you can enquire about a "Liber-t badge" from the Herquelingues office of the Sanef motorway company, on the northbound carriageway of the A16, south of Boulogne.)

To relieve driver boredom, brown roadside panels have been positioned to alert travellers to the delights of the next town (with pictures of its famous buildings, agricultural produce, etc); to point out distant features such as Vimy Ridge and Notre-Dame-de-Lorette war memorials; or to indicate the "*méridienne verte*", the "green meridian" that runs 1,000km along the Paris longitude (see page 166). Sometimes there are added attractions such as, on the A16: wittily-sculpted white figures of sportsmen on the bridges between Calais and Boulogne; an opportunity to eyeball giant wind turbines at the Aire de Widehem pull-off area, near Camiers; or a chance to learn about wildlife at the Aire de la Baie de Somme service station, near Abbeville.

Fuel

Petrol and diesel are cheapest at supermarkets. However, at the time of writing, a UK credit card

will not operate automatic pumps (marked "24/24") in France, so you can use these outlets only during the hours they are manned—which means not on Sundays, public holidays, after about 7pm or at lunch-times. Be particularly careful not to run low on fuel at these times. Petrol stations on main roads are open longer hours; those on motorways are staffed 24 hours a day.

■ **Traffic calming: driving is still a pleasure on France's empty roads.**

Speed limits

130kph/81mph on motorways (110kph/68mph in bad weather conditions).

110kph/68mph on dual carriageways (100kph/62mph in bad weather conditions).

90kph/56mph on other roads (80kph/50mph in bad weather conditions).

50kph/31mph in towns and villages, unless marked otherwise, from the moment you pass the village's name-board until you pass the crossed-out name on the way out—even if no speed limit is marked.

30kph/19mph in some town centres.

Where visibility is reduced to 50 metres, limits on all open roads are 50kph/31mph.

Parking

In villages and small towns, at non-resort beaches, and for major events, parking is usually ample and free. If there does not appear to be street parking, then you must pull right off the road onto a verge, a wide pavement, or a layby—even just to read the map.

Where parking meters are installed (such as in Arras, Amiens and Calais), look closely at the times and days before inserting money. A free period often covers protracted French lunch-times in inland towns, while at seaside resorts even Sundays and public holidays require payment (though out of season there may be no charge at all). In streets and car parks the system is often one of pay-and-display (*horodateur* or *distributeur*)—again, check exactly what hours and days require payment. The third method of regulation is by cardboard parking disc. Central areas of towns such as Montreuil, Lens and Péronne are designated "*zones bleues*" by street signs or by painted blue marks on the road. Display the disc, showing your arrival time, and you can park free for about 90 minutes. If you do not own a *disque de contrôle de stationnement*, ask at the nearest tourist office, *hôtel de ville*, police station, or *tabac*; they cost about 2€.

PETS

It's a relatively new concept for the British to be able to take pets abroad on holiday, and it still needs a good deal of planning, as animals must be microchipped and vaccinated against rabies six months before the first trip. It is imperative to understand the rules of the Pet Travel Scheme (PETS) and to follow them to the letter, as any error could mean delaying a return crossing while the required tick and flea treatments take effect. Contact the Department for Environment, Food and Rural Affairs on UK number 0870 241 1710 for up-to-date information, or www.defra.gov.uk/ Another important consideration is to check with the place you intend staying that pets are welcome. Once you arrive in the area, contact a local veterinary surgery in advance to make sure they will be able to do the necessary scanning and paperwork for you on the day before you return home.

PUBLIC HOLIDAYS

Public holidays (*jours fériés*) are: 1 January, Easter Monday (*lundi de Pâques*), 1 May, 8 May (Armistice 1945, or VE Day), Ascension Day, Whit Monday (*lundi de Pentecôte*), 14 July (*Fête Nationale*), 15 August (*Assomption*), 1 November (*Toussaint*), 11 November (Armistice 1918), and 25 December.

PUBLIC TRANSPORT

There is little public road transport in the countryside; most secondary towns are served by train.

Foot-passengers arriving at Calais-Fréthun or Lille-Europe by Eurostar from London can pick up TGV (high-speed) or TER (local) trains to the rest of France. Ferry passengers need to take bus or taxi from the port to town stations at Dunkerque or Calais-Ville. Before boarding, rail travellers must validate tickets—a process called *compostage*—at a machine by the platform entrance. Train information is on www.sncf.fr/

RIDING

Anything *hippique* or *équestre* is to do with horses: horse show (*concours hippique*), race track (*hippodrome*). There are many riding centres (*centres équestres*) in the region; tourist offices have details. Style can be a bit more casual and "wild western" than in Britain, and not all establishments seem to provide hard hats (*bombes*), so it is as well to check this point first if you have not brought your own. Equestrian tourism is popular in France, and if you have a horse it is possible to bring it, too, across the Channel for a change of scene. The British Horse Society publication *Kent/Nord et Pas-de-Calais* in the "On Horseback" series (from www.bhs.org.uk) gives 20 trails in the area. Regularly updated practical information (in French) can be found on the website of the Comité de Tourisme Équestre for the Pas-de-Calais, www.cdte62.com/

■ Splashing out: riding on the Somme coast.

SAFETY

Safety standards are improving, yet not always as stringently adhered to as they are in Britain. You are usually issued with lifejackets or protective headwear before canoeing, riding or karting, but safety arrangements at zoos, wildlife parks,

viewpoints and some amusement parks often seem more casual than one is accustomed to.

The remains of billions of tonnes of ordnance that rained on France throughout both world wars will work their way to the surface through the action of rain, ploughing or tidal movement for centuries to come. If you are visiting coastal areas or sites connected with World Wars I or II, bear in mind that shards of metal, contaminated barbed-wire, live ammunition and even unexploded gas-filled shells could still be lying on or just beneath the surface, and that it is strictly forbidden to pick up such objects. Roadside heaps of shells piled up by farmers are awaiting collection by bomb-disposal teams. Any other suspect object should be reported to a lifeguard post, police station or *gendarmerie*. The use of metal-detectors in battlefield areas is totally banned, as is collection of war "souvenirs". You can buy genuine, deactivated items from some museum shops; always obtain a receipt as proof of purchase, in case you are challenged by police or Customs on your return journey.

SECURITY

It is easy to forget, in the euphoria of being on holiday, that one must be as aware of personal and vehicle security as one would be back home. Be careful with money and expensive photographic or electronic equipment and leave nothing of value visible in a car. If you are on a shopping visit to northern France, it is a good idea to postpone your major purchases until the last day, en route to the port, so you won't have to carry them all into a hotel room each night. Sad to relate, thefts do occasionally occur from vehicles parked at war cemeteries, memorials and museums, so choose a space in as unsecluded an area as possible.

SHOPPING

Many British visitors cross the Channel with shopping uppermost in their minds. This needs some careful planning though before deciding on your days of travel. Sunday, for example, is not an ideal day. Supermarkets near the coast

may be open on Sunday mornings in July and August, but those inland will be shut. Small local food shops are usually open on Sunday mornings, as are a few larger shops in Calais and Amiens in the run-up to Christmas. Just about every shop is closed on Sunday afternoons and, with the exception of supermarkets, most are closed on Mondays. It therefore makes sense to extend a weekend buying spree to a Monday or Tuesday, so you can do your major shopping on the last day, before travelling back.

The lunch hour is sacrosanct in France; most town-centre shops close between noon and 2pm. The mornings may appear short if you are not an early riser, but the afternoons seem deliciously long, as shops generally stay open until at least 7pm.

For the most atmospheric shopping experience try a traditional street market, usually mornings only (see page 17). Another popular form of shopping is at factory outlets, or *magasins d'usine*; some of the best are included in entries for the relevant towns and villages.

Supermarkets/hypermarkets

Large supermarket chains in the area include E Leclerc, Auchan, Carrefour, Champion, Géant, Cora, Intermarché, SuperU/HyperU and Lidl. They are usually open through lunchtime (except inland, away from tourist areas), so this can be a good time to avoid the queues. Many have good cafeterias or restaurants, as well as public toilets, and cashpoint machines. All take UK credit cards, though the cashier may ask to see the cardholder's passport as extra ID.

Take a coolbox to keep meat, cheese and other dairy items fresher until you get home. Bring a good supply of carrier bags for transporting your shopping, as the major French supermarkets no longer provide them.

Rather than use the more frenetic, crowded retail centres near the ports (particularly in the run-up to Christmas), consider doing your supermarket shopping half-an-hour or so inland. You will find a large Leclerc store near Lumbres (on south side of N42, 1km north-west of the village), and major Auchan stores at Longuenesse

■ **Growing ideas: flower shops have tempting displays.**

(near J3 of the A26, 3km south-west of St-Omer), and near Béthune (just north of J6 of the A26, 3km south-west of Béthune centre). Parking will be easier, the atmosphere less stressful, and items on sale often more interestingly French.

Beer, wine and spirits purchases

There are plenty of beer and wine stores in the Calais area, many listed on www.day-tripper.net/ Among British retail establishments with specialist outlets around Calais are Tesco (in Cité Europe, J41 of the A16) and, across the motorway near the Coquelles Auchan complex, branches of Majestic (called Wine & Beer World), Sainsbury's and Oddbins. For each, you can check prices and place an order from home, and pick it up just before your return to the UK.

If you are importing a large amount of alcohol, even within HM Revenue & Customs limits, you may be asked to justify that your purchases are for personal consumption (i.e. by producing estimates or a printed invitation connected with a wedding or large family party). To know the limits for personal importation of tobacco and alcohol consult HMRC on UK number 0845 010 9000 (00 44 20 8929 0152 if ringing from outside the UK), or website www.hmrc.gov.uk/ Before you load up the trolley, check your vehicle's handbook to see the weight it can safely carry. One bottle of wine weighs around 1.3kg; don't forget to add the weight of the passengers—especially if they have all eaten a hearty French lunch!

Brocante

Antiques and bric-a-brac fairs (*foires aux antiquités* or *foires à la brocante*) are held regularly, as are car-boot sales (*vide-greniers*). For dates, consult monthly magazines *Le Chineur* or *Aladin*, or websites www.pointsdechine.com/, www. aladinmag.com/ and http:// vide-greniers.org/ Brocante fairs are sometimes called *braderies* in the Nord/Pas-de-Calais, or *réderies* in the Somme. From mid March each year you can buy from bookshops and newsagents *L'Officiel des Braderies*, which lists antiques fairs and Christmas markets for the Nord/Pas-de-Calais and part of Belgium.

■ **Aladdin's cave: bargains can be found in French brocante shops.**

The Emmaüs organisation—part of a charity set up in 1949 by the late Abbé Pierre to gather donated junk which the homeless could sort, mend and sell in aid of the association—has several shops in the area. Details of some appear in the following pages under relevant towns. Another type of junk shop is the *dépôt-vente*, which sells items deposited by owners on sale or return.

SWIMMING-POOLS

Most towns have leisure centres, sometimes under fanciful names such as Sportica at Gravelines, Hélicéa at Boulogne, Aqualud at Le Touquet, and Agora at Berck. Male bathers must wear proper swimming-trunks; there is a total ban on the "shorts" style in public pools—including those at campsites. Swimming-caps are sometimes compulsory, too.

TELEPHONING

Telephone cabins no longer take cash. If you need to use one, you can buy a *télécarte* from post offices and tobacconists (*tabacs*).

To call within France, simply dial the 10 figures of the number. To call a number in Britain, dial 00 44, followed by the British number but omitting its initial zero. Cheap-rate time for calls to England from a landline is Monday to Friday from 7pm to 8am, Saturdays from 2pm, Sundays and French public holidays all day.

To look up a name in a French telephone directory, you need to know in which town or village a person lives, as entries are listed under localities. If you don't know your correspondents' *commune* (the village under which their hamlet falls administratively), it can be difficult to locate them.

Mobile phones

If you are intending to use your UK mobile phone in France, check with your service-provider to see if you need to make special arrangements and, if you use a pay-as-you-go phone, find out how to top it up from abroad. Once in France, to call a French number just dial the 10 figures. To dial a UK number (including a UK-based mobile—even if it, too, is in France), dial 00 44 followed by the UK number without the initial zero. Anyone ringing you from within France must do the same, though a person calling your mobile from the UK just dials your normal mobile number as if you were in the UK. At the time of writing, you are charged to *receive* calls while using your UK mobile abroad, as well as to make them, so you may prefer friends to text rather than to telephone. French mobiles are known as *portables*; all their numbers start with 06.

Emergency numbers

EC-wide number for all emergency
services, when calling from a mobile   112
From a landline, the individual ones are:
Fire, and medical emergencies (*pompiers*)   18
Police (or *gendarmerie* in rural areas)   17
Ambulance (paramedics, or SAMU)   15

TENNIS

The grandest hotels may offer guests use of their own court. All resorts, such as Wissant, Wimereux, Hardelot and Le Touquet, have friendly tennis clubs that welcome visitors, though it can be advisable to book a court in advance at popular times. Most villages have a municipal court, which can usually be booked by the hour, for a modest fee, a day or so in advance. For information on the nearest place to play, ask the tourist office or the village *mairie*.

TIPPING

Strictly speaking, service is now included in the bill for bars, hotels and restaurants, and indicated by the words "*prix nets*". However, people do sometimes leave a little extra—even if it is just the bits of loose change on the plate—if service was particularly good or if they are likely to return. It is still customary to tip hairdressers and taxi-drivers about 10 per cent of the bill; and to slip a coin to a guide after an interesting tour.

WALKING

Almost every village has signposted footpaths (*sentiers de randonnée*, or *sentiers pédestres*) guiding visitors to local beauty spots and places of interest. Maps are usually shown on large panels located near church, tourist office or *mairie*. It's also worth visiting tourism websites before leaving home. You can download maps and descriptions of routes from the sites for the Nord, Pas-de-Calais and Somme (see page 11).

Long-distance walks

The IGN map 903 shows all the "Grande-Randonnée" (long-distance footpath) routes in France; special large-scale maps (*topo-guides*) describing individual walks in detail are obtainable from good bookshops in the area. The GR du Littoral, stretching from Dunkerque to Berck, is part of the E9 European Coastal Path. "GR Pays" walks, marked in red-and-yellow, are laid out as circuits through picturesque areas such as the Boulonnais, and take several days to complete. Shorter ones are called "PR" (*Sentiers de Promenade et de Randonnée*). You can, of course, walk shorter sections of any route.

The Via Francigena—a 1,800km route from Canterbury to Rome—has been popular with pilgrims since Archbishop Sigeric walked it in the 10th century. Largely following a Roman way—the Voie Leulène—it passes through Wissant, Guînes, Thérouanne, Bruay and Arras en route for Italy, via Rheims, Besançon and the St Bernard Pass. Information on www.francigena.ch/

Refreshments

Distances between points of refreshment can be long, so take drinks and snacks as well as sunhat, sweater, waterproofs, sticking-plaster, mobile phone and sun block. In the regional park of the Caps et Marais d'Opale, inland from Calais and Boulogne, a network of more than 20 friendly *estaminets de randonnée* provide drinks and snacks for walkers and cyclists, plus tourist information—and often a chance to play some of the traditional pub games. Addresses in the *Estaminet Randonnée* or *Guides Rando* brochures, both free from tourist offices.

WEATHER

Northern France enjoys a climate and rainfall similar to that of south-east England. You will find green, leafy springs; summers that are not excessively hot; golden autumns; and winters that can be cold, wet and even snowy. If the temperature climbs, the coolest places are air-conditioned museums, hypermarkets or shopping malls. These can be good in rainy weather, too, though it's best to head inland to avoid the crowds. (You won't be the only ones to have thought of indoor seaside attractions such as Maréis, at Étaples, and Nausicaa, at Boulogne.)

WILDLIFE

If insects are troublesome, you can buy plug-in insect repellants from supermarkets or citronelle oil from chemists, to rub on skin.

Among bird-life, storks and buzzards are not uncommon (see page 13). As in Britain, the only poisonous snake is the *vipère* or adder, a shy creature that might bask on sunny heathland but will beat a rapid retreat if it senses your approach. Largest wildlife are the members of the seal colony that reside off the mouth of the river Somme. They can be seen in the harbours of Le Crotoy and St-Valéry-sur-Somme, or basking on sandbanks off Le Hourdel and La Maye.

Food and Drink of the North

In northern France the watchword for food tends to be "hearty". Away from the most sophisticated restaurants, you are likely to feast on traditional *potjevleesch*, rabbit, *andouille*, beef carbonnade, and *waterzooï*.

■ Shelling out: succulent local mussels.

HEALTHY SHOPPING

Buying organic foods is starting to take off in France. Look for the words *bio* or *agriculture biologique*, sometimes showing a special green-and-white "AB" logo. The "Label Rouge" (Red Label) designation confirms that produce —from beef to beans—has been farmed in accordance with stringent rules governing natural conditions and feeding. The phrase "*sans OGM*" means a product contains no genetically-modified organisms.

For people with allergies, the French have begun to mark products that might contain peanuts (*arachides*) though you have to read the small print carefully. "*Traces éventuelles d'arachide et autres noix*" means "may contain traces of peanuts and other nuts"; biscuits and other items containg *huile végétale* or *matière grasse végétale* may also contain peanut oil. Some manufacturers specify whether oil used is the more acceptable *tournesol* (sunflower seed), *palme* (palm), *colza* (oilseed rape) or *olive*.

VEGETABLES

Northern France is big vegetable country. The market gardens around St-Omer, Arras and Amiens grow carrots, leeks (a popular filling for the local *flamiches*, or open tarts), summer cauliflowers, turnips, garlic, shallots and watercress. Potatoes are another favourite—often on sale at roadside farm shops. (Look for the abbreviation "*PDT*" for *pommes de terre*.) The sandy soil near Le Touquet produces the delectable *ratte* variety.

A big crop from October to April is chicory (northern France produces 190,000 tonnes of it a year). Confusingly, it is known in French as *endive*, and in patois as *witloof*. The roots of the parent plant, *chicorée* (curly endive in English!), are lifted and replanted indoors, where they are grown on in the dark to produce the tight, white shoots, used either as a winter salad or served, braised, with meat. The root of the versatile *chicorée* plant can be roasted and ground to make a coffee substitute; its seeds also impart a subtle coffee flavour to aperitifs, ice-cream and desserts.

Lingots du Nord are small, firm-fleshed, white haricot beans grown in the clay soil around Merville, and dried on tall wigwam-frames in autumn. Another important crop is sugar-beet, encouraged by Napoleon when his blockade of English ships (see page 37) had cut off supplies of cane sugar. France produces 4.6 million tonnes of white sugar per year, with processing factories at Abbeville, Attin, Lillers and Pont-d'Ardres.

FISH AND SHELLFISH

Since Boulogne is France's largest fishing port, you will find plenty of fresh fish, from traditional herring—smoked, marinated or kippered—to luxury catches of sole and turbot. Shrimps and prawns are usually sold cooked (the little brown *crevettes grises* have the most flavour). Popular dishes include *waterzooï de poisson*, a light fish stew. Mussels are a favourite, served in black casseroles and at their best from October to March. You see them growing on wooden stakes in the sands of Wissant Bay and Quend-Plage.

■ **White gold: farm shops sell the freshest of local cauliflowers.**

MEAT AND POULTRY

Lamb raised on the 1,200 hectares of salt-meadows around the Somme estuary is known as *agneau de pré-salé*. The best, on menus from July to February, has the "Estran" label, telling you it has nibbled the grass of the *mollières* for a minimum of 100 days and earned a coveted *appellation d'origine contrôlée*.

Turkeys and other poultry are the speciality of Licques; early December sees a parade of *dindes* through the little town, before they are despatched to Christmas tables. Chicken, like fish, is sometimes poached with vegetables as a *waterzooï*. Rabbit (*lapin* or, when young, *lapereau*) is another tasty dish, often served with prunes, or *à la bière* (in beer). Also simmered in beer is *carbonnade de boeuf*, a rich Flemish beef stew. *Hochepot* is another meat dish, usually a combination of oxtail, mutton, veal and pork stewed slowly with vegetables.

Unusually for France, the combination of sweet and sour is popular in the north. Carbonnade is always flavoured with *cassonade*, or brown sugar; *boudin à la flamande* (black pudding) contains raisins and cinnamon; and duck is often accompanied by spiced gingerbread. Every restaurant in the region seems to have its own version of *potjevleesch* (spelt variously, but pronounced "potch-yer-fly-sh"). A delicious combination of white meats—usually rabbit, chicken, veal, pork—simmered in white wine and then allowed to cool, this is eaten cold in its flavoursome jelly, accompanied, a trifle bizarrely, by piping-hot chips. *Andouille* and *andouillette* are chitterling sausages, specialities of Aire-sur-la-Lys and Arras. They often crop up on menus, and as a filling for crêpes.

There is still a taste for horsemeat here, sold in specialist butchers' (*boucheries chevalines*) and also in supermarkets as *viande chevaline*. As it is just as expensive as beef, you don't need to worry about being fobbed off with it as a cheap alternative.

The copious snacks served in bars and *estaminets* correspond to British "pub grub". The unexpectedly-named "*Welsh*" is a local version of welsh rarebit—cheese melted in beer, spread on toast and then grilled. You are certain to come across *planche* ("plank"), a kind of "ploughman's". Traditionally served on a wooden board, it consists of salad, bread and, occasionally, hot potatoes served alongside ham, cheese, pâté or *andouille*. Down in the Somme area, expect to be offered *ficelle picarde*, a pancake stuffed with ham, mushrooms and cheese and served hot in a creamy sauce. Another Picardy dish is *bisteux*, a pasty filled with potato, onion and diced meat that is popular around the town of Rue. The word "*lard*" on a snack menu means bacon or ham. For a really heart-stopping appetiser, however, you are sometimes offered little pots of real lard (*saindoux*) to spread on a slice of bread and sprinkle with salt.

CHEESE

Many of the local cheeses, being washed in either beer or brine, are extremely strong-smelling—though their taste is often milder than you would expect—and are at their peak in summer and autumn. Most famous is the pungent Maroilles, made from cow's milk, and often encountered in a baked tart called *flamiche au Maroilles*. Its powerful bouquet is outclassed, however, by that of Vieux-Boulogne—ranked officially as France's smelliest cheese. Running it pretty close are the grey-rinded Vieux-Lille and the distinctive cone-shaped, paprika-encrusted Boulette d'Avesnes. Tome de Cambrai is a creamy cheese made from unpasteurised milk, washed in beer and ripened in cellars. Other local delights include the ball-shaped Mimolette du Nord, the slab-sided Wissant, beer-washed Bergues, and the flat, round Sire de Créquy.

The light, white Mont des Cats is manufactured by monks at a hilltop abbey near Godewaersvelde, while Abbaye de Belval cheeses, are made by nuns near St-Pol-sur-Ternoise.

BREADS, DESSERTS AND SWEETS

Among speciality breads are *faluche*, a flat loaf from Flanders, and *fouace*, a heavier version of brioche. Slightly more cake-like is *gâteau battu*, a tall, brioche-style sweet bread from Picardy that is beaten four times during its making. *Galette au beurre* is a plain cake, made with butter. Other tea-time treats include *gaufres*—slim wafers, sometimes sandwiched together around fillings of butter or vanilla.

Strong links with overseas trade have added some surprisingly exotic ingredients to "local" specialities, including *cannelle* (cinnamon) and the flavourings for a spicy gingerbread called *pain d'épice*. Similarly aromatic are the crunchy *speculoos* biscuits, with a taste and texture between ginger-nuts and digestives. Another hint of the long connection with the West Indies is the popularity of brown sugar (*cassonade* or *sucre roux*). If you have a sweet tooth, try *tarte au sucre*—a dessert usually made of pastry, with a sugar topping . Thoroughly home-grown is the coffee flavouring imparted to crème brûlée and ices by the ubiquitous *chicorée*.

Almost every town has a speciality sweet, linked to a local product or tradition. Among the best-known are: *bêtises de Cambrai*, mint-flavoured toffees; *succès Berckois*, colourful boiled sweets; the rich, almondy *macarons d'Amiens*; and the irresistible *chocolats de Beussent*, manufactured in the Course valley and sold through boutiques in Montreuil, Wimereux and elsewhere.

BEER, AND OTHER DRINKS

Forget sampling the local wines. The area may claim to have a couple of small vineyards, but you will not come across any of their output in the shops. The north of

France is beer country, and any self-respecting *estaminet* will offer 40-plus different ones, at alcohol content of between 5.5 and 12 per cent.

The thirst of hard-labouring miners, factory-hands and agricultural workers created huge demand, and in the 19th century an *estaminet* stood on every street corner. Since the demise of heavy industry, brewers have turned to speciality beers. Supermarkets stock a wide range of local beers. Many microbreweries produce *bières de garde*—long-matured, with their corks harnessed by champagne-style twists of metal. Beer-lovers wait eagerly for *bières de printemps* in spring and *bières de Noël* in December. Look for Hommelpap beer, brewed near Bailleul; Esquelbecq, in the village of the same name; and Ch'ti from north of Lens. The Cistercian monastery on the Mont des Cats sells several Trappist beers made at other religious establishments. Hops can still be seen growing around Bailleul and Hazebrouck.

Picardy's orchards produce the raw material for *cidres du pays*, ciders made around Naours and Bray-sur-Somme. Delicious fruit juices are concocted from rhubarb, strawberries, apples and other locally-grown fruits; old-fashioned fizzy lemonades, under the name La Gosse, are flavoured with rose, violet and poppy.

People have traditionally created apéritifs by soaking fruit, seeds or leaves in a blend of wine, sugar and alcohol. Look for Perlé de Groseille, a sparkling apéritif flavoured with redcurrants from Loison-sur-Créquoise, or for the coffee-flavoured Chicorette, made near Dunkerque.

■ **Unbeatable: the light, fluffy gâteau battu is a Picardy speciality.**

Among stronger local specialities, *genièvre* (pronounced "shurn-ee-air-vr") is distilled from grain and perfumed with junipers in the village of Houlle, near St-Omer. If anybody suggests a *bistouille*, expect a tiny cup of black coffee with a healthy slug of *genièvre* tipped in and twirled twice (*bis*) with a spoon. Accept—but only if you're not driving!

Architecture

There is such a variety of styles and materials in northern France that it's impossible to generalise about the architecture—apart from the ubiquitous pantiled roofs. In Flanders, crow-stepped gables predominate; ancient brick houses are sometimes decorated with codified designs called *runes*; and isolated farmhouses share the countryside with picturesque cottages that often have gaily-painted shutters.

Towards Boulogne, Montreuil and the "Sept Vallées" area, farmhouses are usually single-storey, whitewashed, with outbuildings made of wattle-and-daub (*torchis*). Farther south, half-timbering (*colombage*) is still apparent in the walls of Picardy houses. Along the Somme river, 18th-century châteaux are often in a warm combination of stone and brick, while flint (*silex*) is widely used for walls of castles and churches.

The ancient villages and fortified farmsteads of southern Artois are characterised by *rouge-barre*, a dramatic banding of brick and stone. Some Artois towns hold an astonishing range of Art Deco buildings, a legacy of the large-scale reconstruction that followed World War I.

Seaside architecture has its own diversity, whether it's the decayed elegance of Berck; colourful early 20th-century villas of Wimereux (see page 69); or luxurious 1930s hideaways at Le Touquet (page 106) and Hardelot (page 100).

Certain architects have left their marks: military engineer Sébastien Le Prestre de Vauban, through his 17th-century military fortifications; Louis Marie Cordonnier, whose new "regional" style of the 1920s helped restore civic pride to war-devastated towns; Edwin Lutyens and Reginald Blomfield, responsible for many memorials in Allied war cemeteries; and, more regrettably, Fritz Todt, the German civil engineer who created the indestructible bunkers and pillboxes of Hitler's Atlantic Wall.

Typical of northern towns are the idiosyncratic belfries, 23 of which are now on the Unesco World Heritage list. Originally wheeled towers for use during sieges, these evolved during the Middle Ages into symbols of a town's freedom. Their bells warned of attacks from without and fires within, or called up an instant army. Today they often have beautiful carillons, or chimes, so it's worth listening out for their merry tunes.

Religious pride has shaped the architecture, too, leaving a heritage of great Gothic churches near the Somme, and of wide *hallekerke* (or hall-churches) farther north. Devout countryfolk built wayside shrines, to seek divine protection or to give thanks for prayers answered.

Among other structures that catch the eye are windmills, in brick, stone or wood, which produced flour or oil, or drained waterlogged land. Almost as tall are water-towers, which are often elegant, wittily shaped or fancifully painted.

■ Architectural variety: the "rouge-barre" style at Bertangles, top; crow-stepped gables in Bailleul, far left; and the traditional town hall of Péronne, left.

A Little French History

Frontier zones are always settings for skirmishes and battles, as neighbours seek to annexe extra territory. Northern France has changed hands more often than most, and every village, however small, has vivid memories of times of war. Invaded first by Romans and then by Vikings, and on the edge of land controlled by the Spanish Netherlands, the Dukes of Burgundy and the Austro-Hungarian Empire, this part of France has seen countless battles and occupations. It has provided a springboard for invasions of England by Julius Caesar and William the

DATE	FRENCH HISTORY	BRITISH PERIOD
EARLY TIMES		
200,000-9,500 BC	Paleolithic period (*flint tools*).	Paleolithic period.
7,500-2,000 BC	Neolithic settlements (*dolmens, menhirs*).	Neolithic period.
1,800-700 BC	Bronze Age *(tools, weapons, objects)*.	Stonehenge built.
850 BC	Start of Iron Age *(Gaulish farms and oppida)*.	Iron Age.
57BC	Julius Caesar becomes governor of Gaul.	
55BC	Julius Caesar sails for England.	Roman Conquest.
MIDDLE AGES		
481-751	Merovingian period.	Anglo-Saxons.
751-987	Carolingian period (dynasty of Charlemagne).	Saxon kingdoms.
800-1100	Flanders a flourishing centre of commerce.	
886-911	Viking raids.	
1066	William of Normandy sails for England.	Norman Conquest.
1220	Foundation stone of Amiens cathedral laid.	Henry III (Plantagenet).
1337-1453	**HUNDRED YEARS WAR between France and England.**	
1346	Battle of Crécy: English victory.	Edward III (Plantagenet).
1347	Seige of Calais: English take Calais.	Edward III.
1415	Battle of Agincourt: English victory.	Henry V (Lancaster).
1430	Joan of Arc captured (died 1431).	Henry VI (Lancaster).
MODERN TIMES		
1515	Accession of François I of France (d 1547).	Henry VIII (Tudor).
1519	Accession of Charles V (Charles Quint) to Holy Roman Empire (abdicates 1556).	Henry VIII.
1520	Field of the Cloth of Gold.	Henry VIII.
1556	Accession of Philip II of Spain (d 1598).	Mary I (Tudor).
1558	French retake Calais and Guînes.	Mary I.
1562-98	Wars of Religion: destruction of churches.	Elizabeth I (Tudor).
1588	Spanish Armada: English victory at Gravelines.	Elizabeth I.
1598	Edict of Nantes: Protestants free to worship.	Elizabeth I.
1618-48	Thirty Years War between France and Spain.	James I (Stuart).

Conqueror, as well as for less successful attempts by Philip II of Spain, Napoleon Bonaparte, Kaiser Wilhelm and Adolf Hitler.

Prehistoric man left a few vestiges in the north in the shape of menhirs and other stones. His descendants developed an expertise in flint-sharpening that led to a whole civilisation being named "Acheulean" after the suburb of modern Amiens where such tools were first documented in 1854. Remains of Bronze- and Iron-Age settlements near the banks of the Somme, and signs of hill-forts above, are testimony to the local tribes that dwelt here before the Romans. The Belges and Morins lived

■ **Norman Conquest: William set out from St-Valéry-sur-Somme.**

DATE	FRENCH HISTORY	BRITISH PERIOD
1624-42	Cardinal Richelieu chief minister to Louis XIII.	Charles I (Stuart).
1643	Accession of Louis XIV (d 1715).	Charles I.
1648-53	"La Fronde": rising against French monarchy.	Oliver Cromwell.
1659	Treaty of the Pyrenees: Gravelines and the Artois handed to France.	Oliver Cromwell.
1668	Treaty of Aix-la-Chapelle: St-Omer and some of Flanders handed to France.	Charles II (Stuart).
1678	Treaty of Nijmegen with Holland & Spain: the rest of French Flanders handed to France.	Charles II.
1680s	Vauban builds many fortifications.	
1685	Revocation of Edict of Nantes: 400,000 Huguenots (French Protestants) flee France.	James II (Stuart).
1785	First crossing of Channel by hot-air balloon.	George III (Hanover).
1789	**FRENCH REVOLUTION.**	George III.
1793	War between France and England.	George III.
1802	Treaty of Amiens: temporary end to hostilities between France, England, Spain and Holland.	George III.
1803-05	Camp de Boulogne (Napoleon prepares army to invade England).	George III.
1804-14	First Empire: Napoleon I (Bonaparte).	George III.
1804-15	Napoleonic Wars between England & France.	George III.
1805	Battle of Trafalgar: British victory over French.	George III.
1814-15	First Restoration: Louis XVIII.	George III.
1852-70	Second Empire: Napoleon III (Louis-Napoléon).	Victoria (Hanover).
1870-71	Franco-Prussian War between France and Germany.	Victoria.
1909	Louis Blériot crosses Channel by plane.	Edward VII (Saxe-Coburg-Gotha).
1914-18	**WORLD WAR I.** Northern France is part of the Western Front.	George V (Windsor).
1939-45	**WORLD WAR II.**	George VI (Windsor).
1940-45	Northern France is under German occupation.	
1994	Channel Tunnel opens.	Elizabeth II (Windsor).

inland from today's Boulogne; the Ménapiens, south of modern Calais and Dunkerque; and the Atrébates, around the town that later became Arras.

■ **Taking aim: English archers cut down French knights at Crécy.**

The occupying Romans built a network of roads radiating from Cassel (Castellum), Thérouanne (Tarvenna), Arras (Nemetacum) and Amiens (Samarobriva). Still marked *"ancienne voie romaine"* on maps, they are sometimes also called "Chaussée Brunehaut", an allusion to a Frankish warrior queen who was put to death by being dragged by her hair behind a galloping horse. Artois and Picardy folklore later transformed Brunehaut into "the mother of Caesar", and ascribed the building of the roads to her supernatural powers.

Vestiges of the early Merovingian age are seen in funerary material unearthed in the area. Frankish power developed with Clovis I, who received a Christian baptism in 496. The acceptance of Christianity brought a blossoming of creativity, though as monasteries grew wealthier they became targets for raids by Vikings sailing up the rivers in their shallow-draught ships.

After Caesar, the next leader to use northern France as a jumping-off point for an invasion of England was William, Duke of Normandy. In October 1066 the Conqueror finally found a favourable wind at St-Valéry-sur-Somme.

The intertwining of royal families of both countries led to dispute over inheritance of the throne of France, giving rise to the Hundred Years War from 1337. The battlefields of Crécy and Agincourt here recall English victories, though overall the honours were fairly even. Captured by the Burgundians and sold to the English for £10,000, Joan of Arc was taken to her trial and execution at Rouen; her passage through this region is commemorated at Lucheux, Le Crotoy and St-Valéry. After 1431, the English lost ground until, by 1453, the French had succeeded in winning back everything but the town of Calais—which remained in English hands until 1558.

Shifting alliances between the great powers of England, France, Austria and Spain gave rise to many battles during the 16th century. The Anglo-French summit meeting at the Field of the Cloth of Gold in 1520 was an attempt by François I to ensure support from Henry VIII against Austro-Hungary and Spain.

There are surprisingly strong Spanish links with the history of northern France. The French province of Artois had passed from the Duchy of Burgundy to the Hapsburgs in 1477. The Holy Roman Emperor Charles V—known to the French as "Charles Quint"—inherited the Hapsburg empire (including Austria and Germany) in 1519, in addition to Spain and the Spanish Netherlands that he already ruled. Having his eye also on the kingdom of France, he waged many battles against François I, which continued into the later 30 Years War with Spain. The territory occupied by the Spanish extended south to the Authie river until 1659 when the Treaty of the Pyrenees restored the Artois province to the French crown. Flanders was handed to France under the treaties of Aix-la-Chapelle (1668) and of Nijmegen (1678).

The French retook Calais, England's last remaining French stronghold, in 1558, to the chagrin of the English queen Mary I. Her husband, Philip II of Spain, made an attempt to conquer England with his "invincible" Armada in 1588 but was defeated by Francis Drake off Gravelines, near Dunkerque.

Continuing persecution of Protestants, and particularly the Revocation of the Edict of Nantes in 1685 by Louis XIV, caused around half a million Huguenots to flee to more tolerant countries such as the Netherlands and England. With them they took their skills of silk-weaving and pottery, and their art of draining marshland to create fertile market-gardens.

The French Revolution of 1789 brought about the end of great monasteries. The huge social upheaval saw aristocrats banished or beheaded, lands confiscated, castles and abbeys ruined and their stone ⇘➔ *page 37*

■ Attractive town: Amiens waterside.

Pick of the North

So that you don't miss the best sights, here is a personal hit parade arranged by themes. My 30 favourites are marked with stars; their numbers relate to the map on pages 6 and 7.

ATTRACTIVE TOWNS

Amiens Medieval enclaves, waterside St-Leu district (pictured, above), museums shops, boat trips and cathedral (see page 113).

☆**Arras** Arcaded squares, museums, shops and markets (see page 133).

Auxi-le-Château Quaint town hall and interesting museum (see page 118).

Bergues Walled town, pretty canals and a great Monday market (see page 41).

☆**Cassel** Characterful hilltop Flemish town (see page 42).

Gravelines Fortified town, with museums, marina and nearby beach (see page 53).

Hesdin Huge Thursday market, plus shops, church and museum (see page 102).

☆**Montreuil** Rampart walks, and cobbled medieval streets (see page 104).

SEASIDE RESORTS

☆**Wimereux** Elegant villas of Edwardian era (see page 85).

Hardelot Beach, golf and dignified seaside mansions of the 1930s (see page 100).

Le Touquet Golf, luxurious houses, sea-water spa and smart shops (see page 106).

Le Crotoy Fishing village, with seal-watching, and the only south-facing beach on the Opal Coast (see page 121).

St-Valéry-sur-Somme Chic seaside town on the Somme estuary (see page 128).

PLACES FOR CHILDREN

☆**Nausicaa** Huge sea-life centre (pictured, below) in Boulogne (see page 67).

☆**Cité souterraine, Naours**

5 Children: in the swim at Nausicaa.

Underground passages near Doullens (see page 124).

☆ **Dennlys Parc** Fairground rides for younger children, near Fruges (see page 98).

☆ **Rando-Rail** Wagons to pedal along an old railway line, near Lumbres (see page 80).

Aqualud Watery fun near Le Touquet beach (see page 108).

MUSEUMS & ART GALLERIES

Musée des Beaux-Arts, Arras Fine art and religious pieces (see page 133).

Musée municipal, Berck Seaside views by early 20th-century artists (see page 91).

☆ **LAAC, Dunkerque** Great modern art (see page 45).

Louvre-Lens (from 2009) New branch of the Louvre to open in Lens (see page 158).

☆ **Hôtel Sandelin, St-Omer** Wonderful displays of fine art, and local history (see page 82).

LOCAL ATMOSPHERE

☆ **Arc International factory tour** Glass-making at Arques, and factory-shop bargains (see page 66).

't Kasteelhof Picturesque *estaminet* at top of Cassel hill (see page 43).

■ Entertainment: son-et-lumière in the Artois.

Ferme de Bommelaers Wall Room-settings show vanished rural life near Dunkerque (see page 49).

☆ **Maréis** Brilliant evocation of the work of today's fishermen, at Étaples (see page 95).

☆ **Centre Historique Minier, Lewarde** Coal-face tours with retired miners (see page 161).

Musée de la Vie Rurale, Steenwerck Souvenirs of rural skills (see page 41).

Musée Jeanne Devos Pretty cottage, and photographs of 1950s rural life in and around Wormhout (see page 51).

CHATEAUX

Bagatelle Lovely town house and garden (pictured, left) in Abbeville (see page 112).

Boulogne 13th-century walls and ramparts (see page 68).

Olhain Time-warped, moated farmhouse near the mining town of Bruay-la-Buissière (see page 157).

Long Summer-time tour of stately home (see page 124).

Créminil Restored gardens around fairy-tale castle, near Lillers (see page 152).

ENTERTAINMENT

☆ *Cathédrale en couleurs* Amiens cathedral is "painted" with light (see page 114).

Histoires et Rêves d'Artois Son-et-lumiere show (pictured, above), near Arras, with locals re-enacting their history (see page 136).

Flanders carnivals Parades of giants, with music and fancy-dress (see page 10).

Les Misérables Victor Hugo's epic tale, performed in the open at Montreuil (see page 105).

Festival de St-Riquier Chamber orchestras and classical soloists (see page 128).

■ Château: a bagatelle.

■ Wild places: between les Deux Caps.

■ Villages: Long on charm.

Festival de Valloires Hear top international classical soloists near Montreuil (see page 118).

GARDENS

☆ **Les Hortillonages** Boat trip through Amiens' former market gardens (see page 117).

☆ **Maizicourt** Superb colours, near Auxi (see page 119).

☆ **Séricourt** Witty design with a palette of greens, near Frévent (see page 122).

☆ **Valloires** Breath-taking displays of roses alongside ancient abbey, near Montreuil (see page 118).

Herbarium des Remparts Flowering medicinal plants, above St-Valéry (see page 129).

CHARMING VILLAGES

Bertangles Strange brick architecture, and a handsome château (see page 124).

Boubers-sur-Canche Green-fingered residents near Frévent fill their gardens and verges with flowers (see page 122).

Crécy-en-Ponthieu Sleepy Picardy village, site of Battle of Crécy (see page 120).

Esquelbecq Typical Flanders village, with *hallekerque*, and houses decorated with *runes* (see page 50).

Godewaersvelde Frontier village in Flanders Hills, near Belgian border (see page 51).

Long Château, fishing and a mini hydro-electric station in riverside village (pictured, left), on the Somme (see page 123).

St-Riquier Gothic church, ancient houses and cobbled pavements (see page 127).

St-Venant Quirky architecture and riverside walks along the river Lys (see page 152).

WILD PLACES & VIEWPOINTS

Deux Caps Clifftop scenery (pictured, above), off D940 near Boulogne (see page 86).

Forêt de Crécy Listen for birdsong among the ancient trees near Crécy (see page 120).

Les 7 Vallées Seven charming valleys alongside small rivers, near Hesdin (see page 102).

☆ **Parc Ornithlogique de Marquenterre** A paradise for migrating birds, on wetland near Rue (see page 127).

Marais Audomarois Guided boat trips among St-Omer's market-gardens (see page 84).

27 World War I: entrenched at Vimy.

Views of the Somme river

Look out over lakes and woods from Samara, near Amiens; from above Corbie; and from Vaux, near Bray-sur-Somme (see pages 120, 140 & 138).

HISTORICAL MUSEUMS

Musée de Picardie, Amiens Beautiful displays, especially neolithic tools (see page 115).

★ **Château-Musée, Boulogne** State-of-the-art museum in 13th-century fortress (see page 68).

★ **Musée Portuaire, Dunkerque** Everything you want to know about how a

24 Religious: Amiens.

great seaport works, from the time of corsairs and privateers to the present (see page 46).

★ **Centre Historique, Azincourt** Battlefield and visitor centre about Henry V's victory over the French, near Fruges (see page 99).

★ **Tour de l'Horloge** Hands-on activities in Guînes, with a Field of the Cloth of Gold theme (see page 78).

RELIGIOUS BUILDINGS

★ **Amiens cathedral** World Heritage site (pictured, below left), with medieval sculptures inside and out (see page 114).

Arras cathedral Magnificent 18th-century building, restored after World War I with much 1930s detail (see page 134).

Valloires abbey Beautifully preserved buildings and amazing wood-carvings, near Montreuil (see page 118).

St-Omer cathedral Maze, astrological clock, and coffin of St Erkembode (see page 82).

WORLD WAR I SITES

★ **Musée Somme 1916** The Battle of the Somme explained, in tunnels underneath Albert (see page 132).

★ **Lochnagar crater** Staggeringly deep hole, from mine explosion on 1 July 1916, near Albert, (see page 132).

★ **Vimy Ridge** Preserved trenches (pictured, left) at Canadian memorial, near Arras (see page 168).

★ **Historial de la Grande Guerre** Excellent modern presentation of causes and effects of the Great War, at Péronne (see page 146).

★ **Last Post, Ypres** The moving nightly tribute to the fallen, across the border, in Belgium (see page 53).

WORLD WAR II SITES

Musée 39-45, Ambleteuse Presentation of WWII, from invasion of Poland to surrender of Japan (see page 63).

Mémorial du Souvenir, Dunkerque Clearly-told story of Operation Dynamo, the 1940 Evacuation (see page 47).

★ **La Coupole** Modern museum in a bunker near St-Omer covers WWII in Northern France, and the development of space technology with the V2 rocket (see page 71).

Blockhaus d'Éperlecques Massive bunker near St-Omer, built as V2 base (see page 70).

SHOPPING CENTRES

Amiens, Arras, Boulogne, Calais, Dunkerque, St-Omer, Le Touquet.

sold off. The new government had to defend itself against foreign monarchies waging war from almost all sides.

Napoleon Bonaparte, a string of military successes under his belt, overthrew the post-Revolutionary government in 1799 and had himself appointed First Consul of France then, later, Emperor. Determined to invade England, he camped his "Grande Armée" for two years outside Boulogne, with his eyes fixed on the English coast. However, the Emperor never embarked on the much-feared invasion. Trying other methods to bring his adversary to its knees, Napoleon imposed the "Continental System" from 1806 to 1812, a total blockade against the import of goods from Britain to Europe.

Napoléon III engaged the country in the Franco-Prussian War of 1870 to 1871 (some battles of which were fought around Péronne). France lost its north-eastern provinces of Alsace and Lorraine, which were recovered only in 1918.

The event of modern times that has marked northern France the most is World War I. Its Western Front stretched 640km, from the Belgian coast to Switzerland. The northernmost sector, including the areas of Ypres and Armentières, was for logistical reasons manned largely by British and Commonwealth forces. The French army, after heavy fighting early on in the battles of the Artois (notably at Lorette and Loos), was moved south towards the river Somme by 1916, and the British sector was extended south to join up with it there to prepare the jointly-mounted Battle of the Somme.

Although the French, like the British, refer to World War I as "La Guerre de 14/18", or "La Grande Guerre", they often speak of World War II as "La Guerre de 39/40", rather than "39/45". Indeed, for France, 1940 effectively marked the

■ An eye on England: Napoleon kept his army for two years at Boulogne.

end of the fighting. Be prepared for flashes of French bitterness about the evacuation of the British Expeditionary Force at Dunkerque. Far from being viewed as a heroic effort, as it is in Britain, the operation is remembered by some here as a time when the British abandoned them to death or captivity, and as the start of five years' occupation and extreme hardship.

From being mainly devoted to agriculture and to the cloth industry in the Middle Ages, northern France saw industrialisation take off in the first half of the 19th century. The textile industry was revolutionised by the adoption in 1804 of Joseph Marie Jacquard's system of punch-cards that made it possible to weave complicated designs easily. In 1816, lacemakers from Nottingham smuggled machines to Calais and set up a lace industry that flourished for decades. Coal from the mining basin fuelled iron and steel industries, whose output was conveyed along the wide canals and rivers and, from 1850, by rail. Now, mining and metallurgy, once the region's largest employers, have gone. Textiles, too, have succumbed to cheap competition though lace is still made in Calais, and northern France is the headquarters of the nation's main catalogue-shopping businesses.

Today, oil refineries, aluminium-making factories and chemical plants, are concentrated on the coast near Dunkerque, France's third-largest freight port. From its base near St-Omer, famous glass producer Arc International turns out millions of items of glassware a day. Boulogne is the country's top fishing port. On a more pastoral footing, fertile fields from Flanders to Picardy supply beet for the important sugar-refining industry of the Nord/Pas-de-Calais, while the reclaimed marshlands furnish vegetables for canning and for other sectors of today's diverse food industry.

Area 1

France may be unquestionably "abroad" but, with its Norse roots, the northern province of Flanders feels a hundred times more so. Separated from the rest of France by the river Aa and by a chain of fortified towns, the area has a turbulent history, a specific culture and cuisine—and hundreds of beers. Between the North Sea and the Flanders Hills, its villages defy you to pronounce their names. Their inhabitants, often Dutch-speaking, are loyal to the lion of Flanders, proud of their strong regional identity and warmly welcoming to visitors. Flat the landscape may be, but there are plenty of opportunities to look up at cloud-tickling belfries; historic windmills; 6-metre-high carnival giants; the strange sport of vertical archery; and the vast skies filled with never-ending interest in the way of colour and cloud formations. And if the weather turns bad somebody will always reassure you that, here in the north, the sunshine is in people's hearts!

North Sea

Ferry

DUNKERO

COMMERCIAL DOCKS

Grand-Fort-Philippe

Petit-Fort-Philippe

Ferry terminal

Loon-Plage

29

31

28

Gravelines

N 1

N 316

25

A 16

24

18

River Aa

Canal de Bourbourg

23

51

to Calais

D 1

Bourbourg

D 2

D 17

Canal de la Haute Colme

Départem of Nord

D 1

D 600

Bollezeele

D 226

D 928

D 11

Watten

Rubrc

River Aa

Eurostar line

D 213

MARAIS AUDOMAROIS

FORET DE RIHOULT-CLAIRMARAIS

ST-OMER

Arques

North

to Calais

Dunkerque, Cassel and French Flanders

De Panne

Bray-Dunes

o-les-Bains

Veurne
(Furnes)

② N 365

N 35

① Canal de Furnes

1a

BELGIUM

N 1

36

N 8

Diksmuide

N 364

River IJzer

*Écomusée: Ferme de
Bommelaers Wall*

D 947

Canal de la Basse Colme

Bergues

Hondschoote

D 110

Grenier
du Lin

A 25

D 916A

N 364

☉ SUNDAY-MORNING BEST

*In addition to the sites marked with the above
logo in the following pages, here are a
few more suggestions for places to visit on a
Sunday morning in this area:*
Markets: *Petit-Fort-Philippe (Gravelines);
Rosendaël (Dunkerque). Also (May-September)
Sunday markets in a rota of villages near Cassel.*
Belfry tours: *Bailleul, Bergues.*
General: *churches, war cemeteries and
memorials, beaches, walks.*
Ask the local tourist office, *in advance,
for information on Sunday carnivals, festivals and
flea-markets.*

Oost-Cappel

R Yser

elbecq

Wormhout

15

D 17

D 947

N 308

N 321

N 369

ge
usillés

D 916

4

N 38

IEPER
(YPRES) ★

N 375

Steenvoorde

Calicanes

13

Poperinge
(Poperinghe)

N 38

0   6   12km

For explanation of symbols, see page 6.

Cassel ★

D 37

Boeschèpe

N 331

Godewaersvelde

Mont de Boeschèpe

Mont des Cats

D 10

Mont Noir

St-Jans-Cappel

D 23

Conservatoire
Botanique

N 365

D 833

D 916

MONTS
DE FLANDRE
(FLANDERS HILLS)

N 42

D 933

12

11

Bailleul

Hazebrouck

D 916

D 946

D 947

10

D 933

Nieppe

Steenwerck

A 25

9

La Motte-
au-Bois

Armentières

8

FORET
DE NIEPPE

to Lille

D 943

V1 launch site

River Lys

Sailly-
sur-la-Lys

D 945

Estaires

to Béthune

to Béthune

Canal d'Aire

River Lys

D 186

Merville

38

St-Venant

■ Striking: quaint belfry at Bailleul.

BAILLEUL

ⓘ 3 Grand'Place (tel: 03 28 43 81 00 fax: 03 28 43 81 01)
www.montsdeflandre.fr
tourisme@montsdeflandre.fr

Bailleul, 12km east of Hazebrouck, is an attractive small town near the Belgian border. Its 18th-century courthouse, called Le Présidial, is a reminder that from 1713 Bailleul (pronounced "by-erl") was the judicial centre of western Flanders. Although much rebuilt since the devastation of World War I, it has retained its Flemish character.

The tourist office and its website are the focus of information on the "Monts de Flandre", or Flanders Hills, and on the many charming wayside chapels in the area. In summer there are tours of the belfry, town or museum.

❯ **Musée Benoît de Puydt** A 19th-century lawyer left his tall, gabled house, and his collection of paintings, sculpture, furniture, pottery and lace, to the town as the nucleus of this charming museum. Both house and collection have been painstakingly rebuilt since World War I, and a number of late-19th-century paintings by local artist Pharaon de Winter have been added. De Puydt's personal passions included: "cabinets of curiosities" (of which there are several); Flemish paintings (look for the *Adoration of the Kings* by Pieter Brueghel the Younger); carved ivory; and 18th-century pottery, from Lille to Lancashire. Sturdy oak chests and brass household items give a pleasantly domestic feel. A portrait of the benevolent-looking founder by Cassel artist Alexis Bacop hangs on the first floor. The second level, under renovation, will display more of the house's treasures. ● *Mon, Wed-Sat 2-5.30pm. Closed public holidays & two weeks around 24 Dec-1 Jan. 24 Rue du Musée (tel: 03 28 49 12 70). 3.20€, over-60s 2.50€, children free.*

❯ **Maison de la Dentelle** In the front room of a step-gabled house behind the town hall, is a small museum of lace-making—a Bailleul tradition since the 17th century. The hallway has descriptive panels (in French) about the history of the craft, which was revived here after World War I by William Nelson Cromwell, an American commemorated by a bust outside. In the back room, students click bobbins back and forth, creating designs with such names as *l'araignée* (spider) and *la vierge* (virgin). ● *Mon-Sat 2-5pm. Closed public holidays, carnival time & during Christmas holidays. 6 Rue du Collège (tel: 03 28 41 25 72). 2.50€, children free.*

❯ **Conservatoire Botanique National de Bailleul** It's worth persevering along the byways to find this immaculately-presented plant collection (referred to on some signposts as a "centre de phytosociologie"). Sheltered by trees, the neat, wattle-edged beds contain plants related by family or by colour, showing wild varieties that are the ancestors of present-day culinary or decorative plants. Jokey flower sculptures raise their heads above small ponds and winding pathways. Everything is labelled in Latin and English. ◐ *Early Apr-mid Oct, Mon-Thurs 8.30am-noon & 1.30-5pm, Fri 8.30am-noon & 1.30-4.30pm. Haendries, 2km NE of Bailleul. Take D23 Ypres road, turn right by hospital, & then left after 1km (tel: 03 28 49 93 07). 3€, children free.* ♿

BAILLEUL EXTRAS

Market: Tues.

Specialities: Beck beers.

Accommodation: Belle Hotel 3-star hotel on main square. Rooms from 85€. 19 Rue de Lille (tel: 03 28 49 19 00). www.bellehotel.fr/

Restaurant: Ferme-Brasserie Beck Snacks, fruit juices & Hommelpap beer at rural brewery. 1 Mar-30 Nov, Sat from 7pm, Sun from 5pm. Eeckelstraete, 2km E of Bailleul (tel: 03 28 49 03 90).

Brocante: Emmaüs Furniture, objects & clothes. Tues & Thurs 2-5pm; Sat 10am-noon & 2-5pm. 514 Ruelle des Rameaux, off D122, 9km SE of Bailleul & 1km W of J9 of A25, nr water-tower (tel: 03 20 48 78 74).

Factory shop: Texaffaires Jalla, Descamps & other quality household linen. Mon-Sat 9am-noon & 2-6pm. 2 Rue du Rivage, Nieppe, 9km SE of Bailleul; off D933.

Festival: Fête des Crèches 400 Nativity scenes in village church, Steenwerck, 6km SE of Bailleul, early Dec.

> **Musée de la Vie Rurale** It's a surprise to walk through this modern building and emerge in a typically Flemish farmyard. Inside an 18th-century farmhouse are atmospheric recreations of a grocer's, draper's and hatter's shop of the early 1900s. Every room is packed with memorabilia, though with no explanations anywhere it's rather like wandering through a giant brocante shop. You pass a basketmaker's and a clogmaker's workshop; an old hairdressing salon; and a chemist's, with equipment for making pills and suppositories. Schoolroom displays include toys, comics, and chilling classroom posters warning of unexploded bombs—a real hazard for children here in the aftermath of both world wars. Outhouses contain dairy equipment and neatly-arranged woodworking tools; you may even meet "Totor", the village's dapper carnival giant (pictured, page 10). You can try local beers, soft drinks, snacks and some traditional pub games in the museum's old-fashioned *estaminet*. ◗ *1 May-31 Oct, Sun 3-7pm (1 July-31 Aug, Mon-Fri 3-6pm). 49 Rue du Musée, Steenwerck, 6km SE of Bailleul (tel: 03 28 44 20 04). Admission free.* ↰

> **Musée Communal Marguerite Yourcenar** You need to be passionate about the works of this writer to spend more than 15 minutes in the small museum that pays homage to the first woman elected to the prestigious Académie Française. Marguerite Yourcenar (a near-anagram of her real

■ Fun: botanic garden.

family name of Crayencour) spent childhood holidays at her family's country house on the slopes of the nearby Mont Noir and is revered here for her reminiscences of idyllic summers among the woods and bluebells. (To English-readers Yourcenar is probably best known for her historical novel *Memoirs of Hadrian*.) From 1938 until her death in 1987 she lived in America, sharing a house in Maine with her close friend Grace Frick. A 10-minute video shows Yourcenar's life; a sparsely-furnished room replicates her study in America; a third room presents old photographs of the village and the family château. A 6km *Sentier des Jacinthes* (bluebell path) starts from the museum, leading to the grounds of the long-vanished house. ◗ *1 Apr-30 Sept, Sun 3.30-5.30pm. 55 Rue Marguerite-Yourcenar, St-Jans-Cappel, 3km NW of Bailleul (tel: 03 28 43 81 00). 2€.*

BERGUES

ⓘ **Place de la République (tel: 03 28 68 71 06 fax: 03 28 68 71 06)**
www.bergues.fr
tourisme@bergues.fr

Surrounded by water and stout walls, this delightful market town, 9km SE of Dunkerque, is full of winding streets and canals—giving it the air of a mini-Bruges. The houses, which have been crammed in over the centuries, have façades full of architectural detail: dates wrought in metal; holy statues to protect occupants from harm; and strange, sculpted faces known as *mascarons*.

In the 17th century Louis XIV commissioned Vauban (see page 46) to improve its defences. His system of sluices made it possible to divert the river Aa at the first hint of attack and to surround the town with water within a week. (Water from the sea did the job quicker, but when released at the end of hostilities its salt content poisoned low-lying soil for years.)

The town's commercial history is written in the names of its streets: Marché aux Chevaux, aux Fromages, aux Poissons, au Lin, aux Volailles. So, as you would expect, the Monday-morning market is a huge affair spilling from square to square, while two hours of jolly tunes jingle from the magnificent belfry. Bergues

looks like a theatre set, and that's just what it becomes on occasion, notably for a dramatic night-time show *La Nuit du Miroir aux Alouettes*, given only four times a year (in April and October). You have to book at least six months ahead to be sure of a place on this 4km promenade, for which historical tableaux are performed by 100 locals. In late June, you can join in the Feux de la St-Jean, an illuminated procession that ends with a spectacular bonfire in the main square.

❯**Musée du Mont-de-Piété** A 17th-century building behind the church, north-west of the main square, contains the town's historical and art collections. ("*Mont de piété*" translates as "pawnbroker's", but in France these were state-controlled money-lending institutions—hence the building's imposing size.) On the ground floor is a series of local views, a model of Bergues and portraits of town worthies. Climb the stone stairs, past some Renaissance-style paintings to the first floor, where you find a small still-life by Jan Brueghel; a Van Dyck portrait of Ferdinand of Austria; and a masterful canvas by Georges de la Tour of a hurdy-gurdy player (one of these instru-

■ **Bergues belfry: market-day jingles.**

ments—a *vielle*, in French—is on show alongside it). In the attics, is a dusty collection of stuffed birds, reptiles and animals, plus insects, fossils and birds' eggs. ◑ *Mid Apr-mid Oct, Wed-Mon 10am-noon & 2-5pm. 1 Rue du Mont-de-Piété (tel: 03 28 68 13 30). 3.60€, children 1.20€.* ⦿

CASSEL

ⓘ **20 Grand'Place (tel: 03 28 40 52 55 fax: 03 28 40 59 17)**
www.ot-cassel.fr
contact@ot-cassel.fr

❯ ★ Sticking up above the plain, the 176-metre Mont Cassel ("the Everest of Flanders") is the highest point for miles around. Cobbled roads lead up the steep slopes to the picturesque town centre, its sloping main square surrounded by tall, Flemish-style houses.

Fortified by the Celts around 300BC, it later became a stronghold for the Romans, who called it Castellum Menaporium, and made it the hub of seven highways that still lead off, arrow-straight, in all directions. Its elevated position has made Cassel a focus of fighting over the centuries. It has been besieged, taken or retaken 13 times, demolished, burnt, bombed—and restored. Its three most significant battles were in 1071, when Robert le Frison took the town from the king of France Philippe I; in 1328, when Philippe VI put down a Flemish peasant revolt; and in 1677, when the French, under the brother of Louis XIV, triumphed over the Dutch/English king William of Orange, leading to the Treaty of Nijmegen, which accorded this part of Flanders permanently to France. Cassel is also reputed to be the hill up which, in 1793, the Duke of York marched his "10,000 men".

For the ultimate view, take a short walk from the square to the summit (or drive up, from Place Vandamme). From here you look out, it is said, over five kingdoms: France, Belgium, Holland, England—and the kingdom of heaven. The view makes it clear why the place was so attractive to military commanders, from Julius Caesar to Marshal Foch. Foch had his headquarters in the town from October 1914 to June 1915 (in the building that now houses the tourist office), and is commemorated by a handsome equestrian statue (pictured, right). The tourist office is the departure point for walks within the town, or down towards the surrounding villages, and to a circuit of little shrines that dot the countryside.

❯**Casteel-Meulen** On top of Cassel hill stands a massive wood-built former flax mill—a reminder of the 20-odd windmills that once turned on this breezy spot, grinding wheat (for flour), seeds (for oil) or oak bark (for tanning leather). During an interesting 40-minute tour (in French) you are shown the technique of extracting poppy, sesame, flax or sunflower oil, by mashing the seeds to a pulp and then squeezing in a press.

You need a good head for heights to climb 30 steep outdoor steps to the first level and a further 12 steps inside to see the mighty shaft that is rotated by the sails. Sacks of grain are winched up through one-way hatches, their contents fed to the millstones, and spewed out as flour. This passes through a series of sieves, to emerge with differing degrees of fineness. Like the captain of a ship, the miller pivots the 35-tonne mill according to changes in the wind, heaves on ropes to furl or unfurl the sails, and keeps a constant eye on the weather. ● *Sat, Sun & school holidays 10am-12.30pm & 2-6pm (1 Apr-30 Sept, Tues-Sat 10am-noon & 1.30-6.30pm; Sun 10am-7pm). Jardin Public (tel: 03 28 40 52 55). 2.80€ (includes a bag of flour), children 2.40€; family (2+4) 10€.* ❸

❯**Cassel Horizons** As well as containing the town's tourist office, the 16th-century Hôtel de la Noble Cour houses a sort of "Cassel Experience", which sets out to give visitors an idea of the area's traditions and history.

The 30-minute visit starts well, with buttons to press and light up town gates and important buildings, and to hear brief commentaries on the three major battles of Cassel (see page 42), in English and Dutch, as well as French. Once you get to the less concrete side of history, however, the exhibitions disappoint. The descriptions of Cassel's legends have no translations. The tales of a mysterious well; of the creation of Cassel hill by its giants, Reuze ("giant") Papa and Reuze Maman; and a video telling of a supersititious farmer's encounter with a wraith-like maiden as he prepares his birds for a cock-fight; can be puzzling even for French-speakers. On the plus side, there is a jolly video of Reuze Papa and Reuze Maman dancing at the Easter carnival and, in the brick-vaulted cellars, some romantic images of the countryside and architecture. Flemish sports are explained, including vertical archery (see page 50), darts and cock-fighting, and examples of popular wooden pub games are on show (though, sadly, not playable). ● *Mon-Sat 10am-noon & 2-5pm (1 Apr-31 Oct, Mon-Sat 10am-noon & 2-5pm; Sun 2-5pm). 20 Grand' Place (tel: 03 28 40 52 55). 2.80€, children 2.40€; under 13s free; family (2+3) 10€.* ♿

■ **Commanding: Foch at Cassel.**

❯**Estaminet 't Kasteelhof** Reeking with atmosphere, and with wonderful views from windows or from outdoor terrace, this bar/restaurant near Cassel windmill serves delicious Flemish tarts, *planches*, salads, *potjevleesch* and other dishes. Its two dining-rooms are crammed with kitchen paraphernalia: enamel pots and wicker baskets dangle from every beam. Main dishes cost around 10€, desserts such as rose-petal ice-cream or three-beer sorbet 4€, plus 50 beers, unusual aperitifs and a

CASSEL EXTRAS

Market: Thurs, Grand' Place. Sun (May-Sept) in outlying villages, on rotation.

Specialities: Boulet de Cassel cheese. Zannekin beers.

Accommodation:

Châtellerie du Schoebeque Smart new 4-star hotel off main square. Rooms from 155€. 32 Rue Foch (tel: 03 28 42 42 67). www.schoebeque.com/

Hotel Foch Small, 2-star Logis; pretty rooms from 72€; menus from 16€. 41 Grand'Place (tel: 03 28 42 47 73). www.hotel-foch.net/

Restaurants:

't Kasteelhof Great estaminet, at highest point of town (see main entry).

Het Kerelshof Typical estaminet, dating from 1724, with traditional dishes, & dozens of beers. Closed Wed. 31 Grand' Place (tel: 03 28 42 43 02).

La Taverne Flamande Terrace at back, with panoramic views. Ham, ox tongue, waterzooi & other regional dishes. Menus 11-16€. Closed Tues evg & Wed. 34 Grand'Place (tel 03 28 42 42 59).

Brocante: Salon des Antiquaires Three-day antiques fair, early Sept.

Festivals:

Carnaval d'Hiver Procession with appearance by Cassel's ancient giant, Reuze Papa, Sun before Shrove Tues.

Carnaval d'Été Carnival, parade with Reuze Papa & Reuze Maman, bands, hobby-horse & a hobby-cockerel, Easter Mon.

range of local fruit juices. On Saturday evening and Sunday lunchtime the owner often tells jokey traditional stories, encouraging his customers to back him up with sound effects ("The wolves howled…" "Whoo-ooo-ooo"). There's also a shop selling the best of local produce. ● *Thurs-Sun 11am-10pm (Sat until midnight). Booking advisable. Closed late Jan & early Oct. 8 Rue St-Nicolas (tel: 03 28 40 59 29).* Ⓢ

■ **Crazy décor: Cassel's 't Kasteelhof estaminet.**

❯**Maison Guillaume de Rubrouck** Beside the church in a neighbouring village, a curious, low-key museum retraces the epic journey to Mongolia of a Franciscan monk, born in Rubrouck around 1220. On behalf of the king of France, he set out in 1252 (two years before Marco Polo was born) on a 16,000km round trip to seek out leaders among the war-mongering Tartars who might be converted to Christianity and join the Crusades. Brother Guillaume's descriptions of his two-year journey to the Mongolian capital, via the steppes of Central Asia, make up the first-ever travel literature. Wall-panels (in French) tell of riding recalcitrant ponies, of being received in yurts, and of suffering cold so intense that he was obliged to go against his monastic vows and put boots on his feet. He made notes on his hosts' rites and their idols, and described paper money and Chinese writing. The original journal is held in Corpus Christi College, Cambridge. Photographs from a 1990 French expedition that recreated his voyage illustrate scenes that seem almost unchanged since the 13th century. Alongside some excellent maps are present-day Mongolian textiles. Afterwards, between June and September you can visit a yurt in the garden behind the nearby Café de la Mairie (if you book ahead, you can even eat lunch inside it). ❶ *1 Apr-30 Sept, Sat, Sun 2.30-5.30pm. La Place, Rubrouck, 10km NW of Cassel (tel: 06 84 68 09 81). 3€, children free.*

DUNKERQUE

ⓘ Rue de l'Amiral-Ronarc'h (tel: 03 28 66 79 21 fax: 03 28 63 38 34)
www.ot-dunkerque.fr/ www.lesdunesdeflandre.fr
accueil.dunesdeflandre@ot-dunkerque.fr

Those whose only experience of Dunkerque is the bleak wasteland that surrounds today's ferry port, 18km west of the centre, should make time to visit the town itself. It has much more going for it than you would imagine. Almost totally reconstructed since 1949, its main streets are lined with pleasant, low-rise, brick buildings and offer good shopping, museums and art collections.

Since passing into history books for the evacuation of the British Expeditionary Force in 1940, the name of Dunkerque (or Dunkirk) has evoked mixed emotions of pride in the "Dunkirk spirit", and sadness at the death toll. A visit to the excellent memorial museum, and to the vast beaches east of town, will lead to greater understanding of the operation.

The city's destiny has always been closely linked with the sea. Founded in 1180 on land that once lay beneath the waves, Dunkerque (pronounced here "derng-kairrk") was at first a herring-fishing village. Its strategic position at the entrance to the North Sea caused English, Dutch, French and Spanish to compete for ownership. Carve-ups, treaties and changes of alliance included its being allocated to the English in 1659 and bought back by Louis XIV in 1662. The king commissioned Vauban (see page 46) to make Dunkerque impregnable, gave it the status of a free port (through which goods could pass without incurring Customs duty), and encouraged privateers to prowl the seas and capture foreign warships and cargoes. Foremost of these was Jean Bart, and you won't be in Dunkerque long before you come across *his* name. Born in 1650, Bart earned near-mythic status with his maritime exploits, which included the capture of 130 Dutch grain ships at a time when famine was rife back home. The statue of the swashbuckling superhero, by the church, was one of the few things left standing after World War II bombing.

When the 1713 Treaty of Utrecht obliged Dunkerque to destroy its military port, the locals turned to fishing for cod off Iceland and to trade with distant colonies. The 19th century saw a large increase in commerce and wealth, and rich industrialists began to build Art Nouveau villas in the seaside suburb of Malo-les-Bains (see page 48).

Damaged during World War I, Dunkerque was practically wiped out during World War II. A pocket of German resistance, the city was not liberated until 9 May 1945, one day after the Armistice. Docks and factories were destroyed, and surrounding farmland rendered useless by flooding with sea water (see page 41). Heroic rebuilding efforts reopened the port to its first ship in 1946. However, the shipbuilding yards shut in 1987, and the closure of the steel, textile and coal-mining industries inland had their effect on the port's traffic.

Today, however, an optimism seems to reign. The commercial docks are the third largest in France; the perimeter bristles with steel-making and petro-chemical plants; the town possesses a thriving student population; and it has visionary urban-regeneration plans, drawn up by British architect Richard Rogers. You can get some idea of the docks' awesome size by driving along the Chaussée des Darses that loops north, towards Fort-Mardyck.

Shoppers should visit Rue Clemenceau, Rue Poincaré and, a few blocks south, Rue Nationale and Rue du Sud, and the Centre Marine—a modern mall behind the tourist office. The tourist office has information on summer outings that include boat rides around the port installations, and sea-fishing trips.

> ★ **LAAC** Puzzlement over its uninformative acronym (standing for Lieu d'Art et Action Contemporaine) could cause you to miss Dunkerque's marvellous modern-art museum and sculpture garden. It is located in a park backing onto the Mémorial du Souvenir museum (see page 47); from the car park, coloured dots lead along a path past some interesting modern sculptures to the white-tiled building. Inside is a collection of art and textiles from 1950 to 1970, presented to the town by a local connoisseur. They range from vividly-coloured works by Alexander Calder, Karen Appel and Niki de Saint-Phalle to sculptural pieces by French-born artist Arman (creator of the column of welded anchors outside) and by César (showing a

DUNKERQUE EXTRAS

Market: *Wed & Sat (9am-4pm), Place de Gaulle area.*

Restaurants: Au Petit Pierre *Small, popular town-centre restaurant off Bd Alexandre III. Menus from 15.50€. Closed Sat lunch & Sun evg. Booking advisable. 4 Rue Dampierre (tel: 03 28 66 28 36).*

Brocante:

Emmaüs *Huge place full of furniture & bric-à-brac. Tues-Sat 2-5pm (Wed, Sat 10am-noon & 2-5pm). 62 Rue de la Gare, Grande-Synthe, 5km SW of Dunkerque; J25 of A16 & follow signs for 3km (tel: 03 28 21 24 88).*

Antique market *First Sat of month, Place de la Gare.*

Festivals:

Carnaval *Most famous of all Flanders carnivals, Sun before Shrove Tues.*

Marché de Noël *Christmas market, Place Jean-Bart, mid Dec.*

Golf: Golf de Dunkerque *(see page 41).*

Ferry port: *Loon-Plage, 18km W of Dunkerque. Follow signs "Port Rapide/Car Ferry/Loon-Plage" from J24 of A16.*

■ Art house: Dunkerque's LAAC presents colourful modern works.

penchant for crushed car parts). It's bright and welcoming, with a few hands-on activities for children. ● *Tues-Fri 2-5.30pm; Thurs until 8.30pm; Sat, Sun 10am-12.30pm & 2-5.30pm (15 May-15 Sept, Tues-Fri 2-6.30pm; Thurs until 8.30pm; Sat, Sun 10am-12.30pm & 2-6.30pm). Closed 1 Jan, Sun before Shrove Tues, 1 May, 1 Nov & 25 Dec. Avenue des Bains; parking on Rue des Chantiers-de-France (tel: 03 28 29 56 00). 4.50€ for first ticket, 3€ for others in party; students 1.50€, children free; also admits to Beaux-Arts museum (see page 47) within 48 hours.*

› ★ **Musée Portuaire** Looking across the inner harbour, you can't fail to spot an elegant three-masted sailing vessel, a tug and a scarlet lightship alongside the far quay. They mark the town's Port Museum, established in a 19th-century former tobacco warehouse. Inside, every aspect of the sea and fishing is covered: pirates, dockers, fishermen, shipowners, shipbuilders, and the workings of a great industrial and commercial port. Most of its panels (though not the films) are in English, and it's so full of interesting features that a visit could take a couple of hours.

The ground floor looks at the development of the port, starting with a timeline showing how many times Dunkerque was in the hands of different countries (eight, from 862 to 1662). You learn about the dashing privateerJean Bart (see page 44), and about another great man of the 17th century—military engineer Sébastien Le Prestre de Vauban. Vauban was responsible for 33 fortresses across France, and for improvements to more than 300 others. His Dunkerque plans show six forts at sea, plus citadel, arsenal, jetties and workshops, ensuring that the town could be defended by 8,000 men—but that more than 100,000 would be needed to capture it.

Information on herring-fishing and on the 19th-century cod-fishing campaigns is followed by displays of handling equipment. Hooks and lifting gear give an idea of the tough work of dockers, shovelling loose cargoes, hauling 100kg sacks, and carrying hot residue from tar distilleries. Photographs and short films tell you about the 19th-century family shipping companies and about the rapid evolution of the port. Some good short films show the work of harbour pilots and of the local (British-run) seamen's mission. Up on the second floor is a wonderful collection of model ships: liners, tankers, schooners, frigates, cutters, brigs and troop-carriers. Outside, during summer, you can visit the real ships alongside the quay. ● *Museum: Wed-Mon 10am-12.45pm & 1.30-6pm (1 July-31 Aug, daily 10am-6pm); closed 1 Jan, Mon before Shrove Tues, 1 May & 25 Dec. 4€, students, disabled & children 3€, under-7s free; family (2+ all children) 10€.*

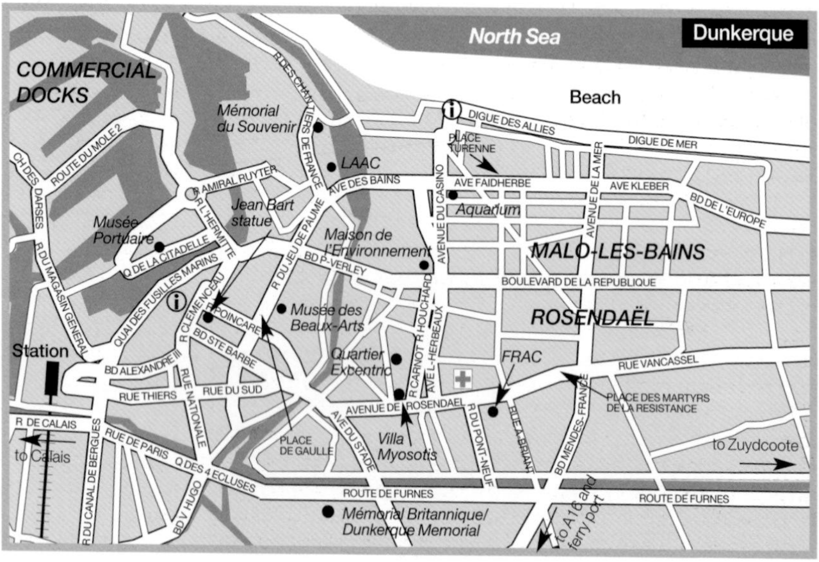

■ **Maritime heritage: ships lie alongside old warehouses at the Musée Portuaire.**

O *Ships: 1 Apr-30 June, Sun & public holidays 1.30-6pm; 1 July-31 Aug, daily 10am-6pm; 1 Sept-30 Nov, Sun, times vary. 7.50€, students, disabled & children 6€; under-7s free; family 18€. Joint ticket for museum & ships 9€, 7.50€ & 22€. 9 Quai de la Citadelle (tel: 03 28 63 33 39).* **S**

>Musée des Beaux-Arts Dunkerque's fine-arts museum on the market square presents European art from the 16th to 21st centuries. Changing exhibitions are held on the ground floor; above is the permanent collection of works from France, Flanders, Holland and Italy. Bright and spacious, the upstairs gallery shows some charming late-19th-century works: views of local towns, and a heart-wrenching procession of orphan girls by Henri le Sidaner (1862-1939); a painting by Camille Corot (1796-1875) of the towers of Dunkerque; and a depiction of the beach at Trouville, by Eugène Boudin (1824-98). Among the most striking works is a richly-textured portrait of a young black boy, painted by Hyacinth Rigaud (1659-1743). There are religious subjects by Dutch and Flemish artists; depictions of battles, massacres, decapitations and martyrdoms; and pottery from Arras, Lille, Chantilly, Tournai, Nevers and Desvres. Curiously, there's a death mask of the English king James II—who died in 1701, having lived in exile in France since 1688—wearing a lace bonnet made by nuns from an English convent that once stood near this site. In the basement, a small natural-history collection features rocks and fossils, plus stuffed birds, snakes, an alligator and a lioness. **●** *Wed-Mon 10am-12.15pm & 1.45-6pm. Closed 1 Jan, Sun before Shrove Tues, 1 May, Ascension Day, 15 Aug, 1 Nov & 25 Dec. Place du Général-de-Gaulle (tel: 03 28 59 21 65). 4.50€ for first ticket, 3€ for others in party; students 1.50€, children free; also admits to LAAC modern art museum (see page 45) within 48 hours.* **S**

>Mémorial du Souvenir Housed inside fortifications that were part of French World War II defences, this museum looks at the 1940 Battle of Dunkerque and at Operation Dynamo, the nine-day evacuation of British and Allied troops from the 15km of beaches east of Dunkerque.

You could easily spend two hours here, so morning visitors need to arrive as the doors open. Start by viewing the 10-minute documentary to the left of the admission desk, screened alternately in English and French. Throughout, the excellent descriptions on the walls are almost all in English. You can ask for an extra English document at the entrance that gives a helpful overview.

After the outbreak of World War II, in 1939, a British Expeditionary Force of 13 divisions had been deployed across the Channel. Having invaded the Low Countries on 10 May 1940, German troops advanced rapidly into France. The British fought on at Arras, Boulogne and Calais, but eventually had to withdraw, as did part of the French 1st Army, which had been defending the city of Lille. Destroying their abandoned vehicles and equipment, all made their way by whatever means possible towards Dunkerque via a 16km-wide "corridor" that French and British tried to keep open. The German land advance inexplicably paused for several days, though the Luftwaffe launched strafing and bombing raids on the exhausted troops awaiting embarkation.

Exhibits include French, German and British guns, uniforms and equipment, and images of Dunkerque before it was bombed on 21 May. In contrast, photographs and models show the devastated town that the Germans took over. Apart from its two belfries, and the Jean Bart statue, the city is hardly recognisable. Almost 1,000 ships took part in Operation Dynamo, including British fishing boats, paddle-steamers and small private craft. Even the soldiers who managed to board a vessel were not safe, however, as many ships were sunk. The scenes, on film or in photographs, leave you speechless at the unimaginable scale of the operation. A series of panels carries the increasing totals rescued each day, from 4,817 on 26 May to 67,141 at its peak, on 31 May. In all, 338,226 men were saved, with a further 61,111 killed, wounded or taken prisoner. Many of the dead are commemorated at the Dunkerque Memorial, on Route de Furnes.

Here, too, the delicate matter is touched on about French resentment over the allegedly small number of their troops taken onto British ships—a feeling fostered by the pro-German Vichy government. Even today you meet these sentiments about the operation. To many French, it is not seen as a glorious triumph, but rather as an abandonment by the British to five years' occupation and its attendant deprivations, incarceration in prisoner-of-war camps, or deportation to even greater suffering. The museum stresses that, by June, Churchill ordered British and French soldiers to be evacuated in the same proportion, and that an extra day's operation was added, rescuing 35,000 remaining French troops. ❶ *1 May-30 Sept, daily 10am-noon & 2-5.30pm. Courtines du Bastion, 32 Rue des Chantiers-de-France (tel: 03 28 66 79 21). 3.50€, children free.* ❧ ❸

❯**Carnaval de Dunkerque** To the French, the name of Dunkerque is synonymous with the craziest carnival in the calendar, involving a day of posing and parading by thousands of locals in outlandish costumes and garish make-up. Accompanying the giants Reuze and Reuzinne (*reuze* being the local word for "giant"), plus their three giant children and five giant bodyguards, the revellers brandish artificial flowers, lurid feather-dusters and gaily-decorated umbrellas, and clamour for the plastic lobsters and shrink-wrapped kippers that are thrown from the town-hall balcony. *Sun before Shrove Tues. Town centre.*

MALO-LES-BAINS & ROSENDAËL (DUNKERQUE)

ⓘ (Apr-Oct) Pl du Centenaire, Malo (tel: 03 28 58 10 10) or see Dunkerque (page 44)

■ Deliciously Art Deco: a house in Rosendaël's Quartier Excentric.

Dunkerque's once-fashionable seaside suburb of Malo-les-Bains, 3km to the east, contains some picturesque Art Nouveau villas, nicknamed "*folies de l'époque*". The seafront, with its pretty, painted beach-huts, is particularly welcoming to children (with colourful giant objects perched on poles, to help little ones remember where they left their parents).

Towards the Belgian border, along the beaches that saw the evacuation of May 1940, run some 15km of wild dunes, past Zuydcoote and today's seaside resort of Bray-Dunes. Under the global name of Les Dunes de Flandre, they offer sand-yachting, kite-sailing and other spectacular, wind-driven sports.

Immediately south of Malo lies the Rosendaël district. Near the large hospital complex, you can set off in search of its architectural curiosities: the *maisons en bois*, and the "Quartier Excentric" (see page 49).

❯**Aquarium/Musée Aquariophile** A brick building within a leafy little park just back from the seafront contains a series of small aquariums that conjure up lakes and coral seas. In the crystal-clear waters you can admire the diamond-shaped surgeon fish, golden koi carp, and striped clownfish in their piscine motley. There's also a tank with some amazingly-camouflaged turbot—only by watching the gravel carefully can you see the fish breathing. The labels are mostly in French; visiting fish-lovers are encouraged to provide the owner with any English translations that are lacking. ● *Wed-Mon 10am-noon & 2-6pm. Closed 1 Jan, 1 May & 25 Dec. 45 Avenue du Casino, Malo (tel: 03 28 59 19 18). 2€, students 1€, children free.* ❸

> **Maisons en bois** The streets north and west of Rosendaël's modern hospital contain several houses built in wood. The concept dates back to a time when constructions within a certain perimeter of a fortified town had to be of a material that could be destroyed instantly by burning if an attack looked imminent. The prettiest is Villa Myosotis, on the corner of Rue Carnot and Avenue de Rosendaël. Built in 1894 by a wealthy wood trader, the elegant structure won awards for Dunkerque architect Arthur Gontier. You can view its blue-and-cream façade and lacy fretwork from the pavement, though there is no admission to the property. The adjoining streets hold one or two more. Another delightful example is on the edge of the Jardin Ziegler: continue north along Rue Carnot and Rue Houchard and you will see it on Boulevard de la République—it is now the Maison de l'Environnement. ● *Various locations, Rosendaël district.* ◐

> **Quartier Excentric** One block west of Rue Carnot is another unusual architectural gem, a small, horseshoe-shaped enclave of streets lined with around 30 small houses—all in Art Deco style but each with its own decorative eccentricities. It is the work of Rosendaël builder and designer François Reynaert, who received the commission in 1927. A descriptive panel on the corner of Rue Martin Luther King draws attention to all the different features that make each unique. Look for the concrete rings on "Les Anneaux", and the wood-shavings effect at the top of "Les Copeaux". Some houses are gaily painted; others a bit less cherished, but the ensemble is a delightful treat. ● *Rue Martin Luther King & Rue André-Chénier, off Rue Eugène-Dumez, Rosendaël.* ◐

> **FRAC/Fonds Régional d'Art Contemporain** The FRAC organisation has been investing in modern art on behalf of the region of Nord/Pas-de-Calais since 1983, and lends works to exhibitions in France and abroad. At its Dunkerque base, it puts on small shows of sometimes challenging works and installations by the new generation of artists. The building is part of an old hospital complex, and approached through a brick archway. Signposting fails once you arrive; only a discreet sign on the gates of the old hospital on the *north* side of the road points south, across to where the collection is based. An orange line painted on the drive leads through the grounds to the door of the FRAC building. ● *During exhibitions: Tues-Sat 2-6pm (free guided tour Sat 4pm). 930 Avenue de Rosendaël (tel: 03 28 65 84 20). Admission free. (The FRAC may be moving to the Dunkerque port area in around 2010.)*

> **Écomusée: Ferme de Bommelaers Wall** At this arable farm, set in windswept surroundings up the coast from Dunkerque, the owners have diversified from the traditional wheat, peas and sugarbeet. The 18th-century barns are now an extensive museum of life in rural Flanders. You see a Flemish farm kitchen; a doctor's surgery; wooden toys—from hoops to catapults; stuffed stoats, curlews and snakes; and a reconstructed schoolroom, complete with dunce's cap, and a cardboard tongue to be hung on talkative children. One area contains items related to witchcraft: between the 15th and 17th centuries some 350 suspected witches were burned in this region. To be accused of being one, it was enough to be a healer, a herbalist or just a loner.

The stables hold dairy equipment, old photographs of the farm, and a film about the cultivation and myriad uses of chicory—employed as everything from a salad and a cooked vegetable to an aperitif (on sale in the shop) and coffee. To finish, you can play with the large selection of traditional "pub games", such as giant jenga ("*badaboum*"), tiny table-tennis, bagatelle and blow-billiards. Though there's little concession to non-French-speakers, the lively guided tours are such fun that it's worth joining one. (Allow an extra hour if you do; gales of laughter have to subside before the guide can move on.) ❶ *1 Apr-31 Oct, Mon-Sat 10am-6pm, Sun & public holidays 2-6pm (guided tour first Sun of month, 4pm). 20 Route de Furnes (N1), Ghyvelde, 12km E of Dunkerque, near J34 & J35 of A16 (tel: 03 28 20 11 03). 4€, children 2.50€.* ♿ 🐾

ESQUELBECQ

ⓘ Place Alphonse-Bergerot (tel: 03 28 62 88 57 fax: 03 28 62 49 57)
www.esquelbecq.com
maison.westhoek@wanadoo.fr

The attractive main square of this typically Flemish village, 20km south of Dunkerque, is dominated by a tall, 16th-century hall-church (built with three wide aisles). Its mellow brick walls are covered with contrasting lozenge patterns, and its bells ring out a merry tune on the quarters. A plaque outside recalls a 1793 battle between 3,000 French soldiers and Anglo/Austrian troops commanded by the Duke of York, second son of King George III.

Round behind the tourist office, look out for a spindly, 26-metre-high mast with short cross-pieces near the top. This is part of the bizarre Flemish form of archery called *tir à la perche* or *tir à l'arc vertical* (vertical archery), played in many Flanders towns and villages. At competitions, held here and elsewhere between June and October, contestants shoot rubber-tipped arrows straight upwards at brightly-coloured clusters of feathers on the cross-pieces, gaining points for each *papagay* they dislodge.

❯**Maison du Westhoek** Doubling as the village's tourist office, this house on the main square holds interesting exhibitions, from June to October, on aspects of local culture. On changing permanent display are wall panels full of information (in French and Dutch) on the Westhoek region, which straddles the Franco-Belgian border and shares a common culture. You might read about "*runes*", the strange script descended from Old Norse/Scandinavian whose shapes decorate so many of the village's buildings. Invested with quasi-magical significance (hearts stand for faith and motherly love; lozenges for fertility and abundance), they were used to seek protection from the gods or to plead for divine intervention. Other panels may show local architecture, recount the strife-torn history of the area, or explain the meanings of some of the strange-looking Flemish place-names. ● *Tues-Sat 10am-noon & 2-6pm, Sun 3-6pm (1 Apr-30 Sept, Tues-Sun & public holidays 10am-noon & 2-6pm). 9 Place Alphonse-Bergerot (tel: 03 28 62 88 57). Exhibitions 2€-4€.* 🅢

❯**Grange des Fusillés** In the heart of the countryside a Union Jack flies above a memorial to the Wormhout Massacre, a bloody incident that took place at the time of Operation Dynamo (the Dunkerque evacuation, see page 47). On 28 May 1940, 80 soldiers of English regiments were ordered to hold German forces at bay in this area for 24 hours. Taken prisoner by members of the SS, they were shut in a barn into which—in total contravention of the

ESQUELBECQ EXTRAS

Specialities: Beer.
Accommodation/food:
Hostellerie St Louis
Friendly 3-star Logis hotel, popular with the British. Rooms from 55€; menus from 23€. Restaurant closed lunchtimes, except Sun. 47 Rue de l'Église, Bollezeele, 9km W of Esquelbecq (tel: 03 28 68 81 83). www.hostelleriestlouis.com/
Le Pantgathof *Welcoming, comfortable 3-épi B&B. Rooms from 48€; evening meal (on reservation) 21€. 27 Rue de Metz (small road 2km NW of Bollezeele), 9km W of Esquelbecq, signposted Gite No 1104 (tel: 03 28 68 00 87). http://pantgat.free.fr/*
Restaurant: La Table des Géants *Local dishes with a sophisticated twist, in stylish place beside tourist office. Main courses from 14€. Closed Mon, & Tues-Thurs evg. 9 bis Place Bergerot (tel: 03 28 62 95 84).*
Festival: Patate Feest *Potato festival, with scarecrow competition, games & old crafts, late Aug.*
Shop: Brasserie Thiriez *Microbrewery selling Blonde d'Esquelbecq & other strong brews. Mon-Sat 10am-1pm & 2-7pm (tours by appointment). 22 Rue de Wormhout (tel: 03 28 62 88 44).*

■ Chequered past: the decorative brick front of Esquelbecq's ancient church.

rules of war—their captors tossed grenades. A handful of the captives survived to tell the story. Here, at the site, beeches and oaks have been planted in memory of the victims; an older tree, maybe a witness to the events, bristles with memorial crosses placed by modern-day pilgrims. Panels around the site spell out different parts of the story; a replica of the little thatched barn (financed by readers of *The News of the World*) holds dozens of poppy wreaths brought by visitors; and a brick-built monument pays tribute to a further 300 locals who died at the hands of the Nazis. ● *Site de Mémoire, La Plaine-au-Bois, Rue des Dunkerque Veterans (off the Wormhout road, just past Au Bon Coin café), 1km SW of Esquelbecq.* 🅂

❯Musée Communal Jeanne Devos An enchanting, creeper-covered cottage stands at the end of a cul-de-sac in the village of Wormhout. Once past the garden gate you step into another world. In the early 20th century the house was the home of a local priest, Abbé Lamps, a talented photographer who passed on this passion to his devoted housekeeper, Jeanne Devos. After the death of Lamps she continued to take pictures to earn a living. As well as weddings, first communions and baptisms, Devos turned her lens on local people and customs, leaving some 100,000 images of Flanders life. Since her death in 1989 the house has remained as she left it. Guided tours (in French) show the kitchen, dining-room, *salon*, and a garden room displaying some of her huge collection of photographs. Upstairs are a reconstructed schoolroom, and a bedroom. Your guide is usually Yvonne, companion to Jeanne Devos in the latter's declining years. Her ceaseless flow of reminiscences includes the revelation that the spirited old lady once said she had enjoyed "all the advantages of marriage and none of the inconveniences". This is perhaps borne out by the fact that Devos and the *abbé* are buried side by side under the trees at the end of the pretty garden. ● *Mon, Tues, Thurs-Sat 2-5pm; first & second Sun of month 3-6pm. 17 Rue de l'Église, Wormhout, 2.5km E of Esquelbecq (tel: 03 28 62 81 23). 2€, children 1€.*

GODEWAERSVELDE
ⓘ see Bailleul (page 40)

The tongue-defying name of this attractive village (pronounced "god-vars-veld"), 12km south-east of Cassel, simply means "Godfrey's field". It has several *estaminets*—some still dual-purpose (*café-boucherie*), as so many originally were.

Godewaersvelde lies at the foot of the 158-metre Mont des Cats. Like most of the Flanders Hills, this is a favourite spot for Sunday-afternoon walks, with marked trails through woods and fields. (The hill's name has nothing to do with felines, of course; it is said to come from the "Cattes", a Germanic tribe who lived in the area around 460AD.) Mont de Boeschèpe (pronounced "boss-kep"), 4km north-east of here, is another popular walking area, with signposted paths from the large, beautifully-restored windmill known as Ondankmeulen ("mill of ingratitude").

❯Musée de la Vie Frontalière Local giant Henri, the Customs officer—3.8 metres tall and weighing 70kg—with his giant companions, Dick (a Customs dog) and Tom (a smuggler's dog), greets visitors to this small modern museum devoted, appropriately for a village just 2km from the Belgian border, to frontier life. Displays on the first floor focus on common traditions (bowls, vertical archery, singing, superstitions, pigeon-racing, parades of giants) shared by villages either side of a border whose present position was fixed only in 1820.

Downstairs, imaginatively-designed cardboard cut-outs illustrate some of the clandestine activities that went on along the frontier. (According to a local saying: "Out of every 10 Flemish people, eight are smugglers and two are liars!") Much of the information has, apparently, been provided by a reformed smuggler of tobacco—until the 1960s one of the most lucrative items of contraband,

■ **Living dolls: the characterful "gigottos".**

which was often transported in sacks carried by swift-running dogs. In the wider battle against trafficking of all sorts, you see gauges used to measure alcohol content, and methods of scanning lorries to reveal illegal stowaways. All material is in French, but you can ask for an English leaflet that gives an overview. ◑ *1 Mar-31 Oct, Wed-Sat, & first & third Sun of month 2-5pm. 98 Rue de Calicanes (tel: 03 28 42 08 52). 2.50€, children under 12 free.* ♿ *(ground floor).*

❯ **Abbaye du Mont des Cats** Below the tall pinnacles of the Cistercian-Trappist monastery above Godewaersvelde, a community of 60 monks makes the well-known Monts des Cats cheese, on sale—along with cheeses and Trappist beers from other monasteries of France and Belgium—in the modern shop near the abbey gates. Also on sale are religious books and objects, plus candles and gift items. In the abbey's visitor centre you can watch several excellent 25-minute documentaries (one available in an English version, the rest in French) about different aspects of monastic life. (Entrance to the screenings is on the left as you go into the courtyard.) ● *Sun, Mon 2.30-6pm; Wed-Sat 10am-noon & 2.30-6pm. Visitor centre Charles Grimminck, Mont des Cats, 2.5km SE of Godewaersvelde (tel: 03 28 43 83 70). Admission free.*

❯ **Steenmeulen/Musée Rural Flamand** Descendent of five generations of millers, retired engineer Joseph Markey gives wonderfully animated tours (in faultless English, if requested) of his beautiful, brick-built working windmill. You climb ladder-like stairs, and hear about the oak that furnished the main shaft, the elm that provides the mighty vertical support, and the applewood used for the cogs. It has three sets of millstones, each capable of producing 100kg of flour an hour. (You can buy some in the café alongside; it makes delicious bread.)

■ **Sailing by: the wooden windmill at Boeschèpe.**

A room off the café contains a museum of rural life, with many vintage agricultural machines—from a 1916 steam-engine to a 1920s McCormick tractor—all expertly restored. Alongside old TV sets are sewing-machines, washboards, lace-making cushions and smoking paraphernalia. A small reproduction of a hop field explains the cultivation of this plant that imparts its distinctive flavour to beer (only the pistil of the flower is used). Don't miss the rack of brightly-coloured feathers near the ceiling. These are the targets used in the local sport of vertical archery (see page 50), and usually positioned so high up that you would never get a close look at them. In the yard at the back are an old reaper and binder, a flax-crusher and a potato-lifter. ◑ *1 Apr-early Oct, Mon-Thurs, Sat & most Sun 9am-noon & 2-6pm; closed last Sun of month. 550 Route d'Eecke (D947), Steenvoorde, 4.5 km NW of Godewaersvelde (tel: 03 28 48 16 10). Museum 2€, mill 2€, combined ticket 3.50€; children 1€ & 1.75€; under 6s free.* ♿ *(museum only; a video link is planned from the windmill).* ⑤

➤ **Gigottos Automates** On one of the main roads into Belgium, passers-by do a double-take at the sight of the hard-working lady endlessly cleaning the window of Bruno Dehondt's workshop. There is even more to laugh at once you step inside and meet his gloriously eccentric creator, who introduces you to his all-but-human automated creations. Made from recycled materials, the life-sized mechanical figures sing, polish shoes, dish out leaflets, knit, chatter, play music or juggle—all on spoken commands. Children (and adults, too) are mesmerised, particularly by the old lady (pictured, left), who is galvanised into activity whenever anybody says: *"Il y a du monde, mémé!"* ("We've got company, Gran!"). ● *Wed 2-6pm (but check before making a special journey). 237 Route de Poperinghe (D948), Calicanes, 2km N of Godewaersvelde (tel: 03 28 48 15 95 or 06 74 30 43 08). 3€, children 2.50€.*

➤ ★ **"Last Post" ceremony at Ypres** Although across the border, in Belgium, this supremely moving daily ceremony takes place so near this corner of French Flanders that it would be a pity to miss it. Every evening buglers from the Ypres fire brigade sound a "Last Post" for members of the British Empire who fell in the Ypres area during World War I. It was first played here on 1 July 1928, and has been a nightly tradition (apart from the years of occupation during World War II) since 11 November 1929.

Forget those grim, war-time images of the town. Ypres today has been reconstructed in its original medieval style, and is a ravishing city. Follow signs to Poperinge, then towards Ieper (local spelling of Ypres), and finally to *Zentrum* (town centre). The beautiful main square, Grote Markt, is lined with shops and restaurants, and dominated by the magnificent Cloth Hall, or *Lakenhallen*, which houses the tourist office and the "In Flanders Fields" visitor centre. Parking meters take euro coins, and local people speak English more readily than French.

The remembrance ceremony starts on the dot of 8pm, just 150 metres from the south-east corner of the square. Beneath the Menin Gate, an archway designed by Reginald Blomfield to bear the names of 54,896 missing soldiers, traffic is halted and the first notes on the bugle ring out. Sometimes special wreath-laying ceremonies follow, for which someone will recite the lines from Laurence Binyon's "For the Fallen"; everyone present joins in repeating the last one: "We will remember them".

On the way back towards France, remember that names on signposts will be given in Dutch (the language of this part of Belgium). Place-names to look out for that might help to find your route include Frankrijk (France), Rijsel (Lille) or Duinkerke (Dunkerque). ● *Daily 8pm. Meensestraat, Ypres/Ieper, 20km NE of Godewaersvelde (tel: +35 57 239 220).*

GODEWAERSVELDE EXTRAS

Specialities: Mont des Cats cheeses.

Restaurants:

Het Blauwershof Well-known estaminet, popular with walkers, serving 45 beers, carbonnade & coq à la bière, with pub games & occasional live music. Closed Mon in Aug. Booking advisable. 9 Rue d'Eecke (tel: 03 28 49 45 11).

De Vierpot Convivial estaminet at the foot of Boeschèpe windmill, serving planches, sausages, pancakes & 50 local beers. A "vierpot" is a pot of hot embers for lighting pipes; dozens hang here from the rafters. Closed Mon-Fri (1 Apr-30 Sept, closed Mon & Tues; 1 July-31 Aug, closed Mon). 125 Rue du Moulin, on D139/D10, Boeschèpe, 4km NE of Godewaersvelde (tel: 03 28 49 46 37).

Festivals:

Carnaval de Godewaersvelde Carnival, with local giant, "Henri le Douanier" & friends, Jan.

Fête du Houblon Hop festival & large flea-market, Steenvoorde, 4km NW of Godewaersvelde, Oct.

GRAVELINES

ⓘ **11 Rue de la République (tel: 03 28 51 94 00 fax: 03 28 65 58 19)**
www.ville-gravelines.fr
gravelines.cote.opale@wanadoo.fr

The power lines marching out across Flanders from Gravelines' nuclear power station may seem off-putting, seen from the A16 motorway. However, once you pass from its modern suburbs into the walled heart of this unspoilt fortified town, 16km south-west of Dunkerque, you seem to step back in time. Gravelines (pronounced "grav-leen") was founded in the 12th century on the north bank of the river Aa. Its position on the border between the kingdom of France and the Spanish Netherlands gave it great strategic importance, and caused it to be fought over by combinations of English, Dutch, French and Spanish. In 1588, at a time of Spanish occupation, the English fleet defeated Philip of Spain's "invincible" Spanish Armada off the coast here. After Gravelines was taken by the French in 1658, Louis XIV brought in Vauban (see page 46) to improve the town's Spanish-built defences with his trademark water obstacles, half-round *demi-lunes* and snakeshead-shaped brick projections that make this walled town one of the best examples of bastion architecture in France. The tourist office organises guided tours of the fortifications in July and August.

The central area of the town is quite small, and by the time you have found the museums, the tourist office, and the impressive 17th-century *caserne* (barracks) near the south corner, you will probably have covered most of it. In summer, at the picturesque Porte aux Boules (a town gate on Rue de Dunkerque, topped with stone balls), you can take a spin round the moat in pedaloes, electric-powered boats or rowing boats. There are more activities (swimming, bowling and roller-skating) on offer at the Sportica leisure centre located on the Petit-Fort-Philippe road that is signposted "La Plage".

> **Musée du Dessin et de l'Estampe Originale** Beneath the arched brick roof of the arsenal's 18th-century powder-store, Gravelines' fascinating printmaking museum shows techniques used for woodcuts, linocuts, engraving, etching, lithography, silk-screen printing and other forms of reproduction. All the explanations are in French, but the displays are so good that you seize the idea readily. Prints on show include some by Dürer, Goya, Vlaminck, Hokusai, Utagawa, Picasso and Léger. You can appreciate the fine quality of Gustave Doré's Arthurian scenes, displayed alongside the carefully-cut wood used to make the prints. Down some steep stairs is a magnificent model of 18th-century Gravelines (such as were often made to help plan a town's defence—or its capture). Pressing a button starts a mini sound-and-light show, played as a dialogue between two characters (pretty incomprehensible even if you speak French!). Stored in the wooden bins alongside the model are good explanations in English of the model-making and of the town's history, describing how Vauban created its present star-shaped form. Alongside the model, some computers with touch-screens take you on a "virtual tour" of the town's streets; the next room holds changing exhibitions of printmaking. ● *Mon & Wed-Fri 2-5pm; Sat, Sun 3-6pm (1 July-31 Aug, Mon & Wed-Fri 10am-noon & 2-5pm; Sat, Sun 10am-noon & 3-6pm). Closed 1 May & 1 Dec-1 Jan. Château de l'Arsenal (tel: 03 28 51 81 00). 2.20€ (free on first Sun of month), children free.* ⓑ *(partial)* ⓢ

> **Maison du Patrimoine** Across from the main tourist office is a small permanent exhibition on the town and its history, mostly recounted through drawings and information panels about Gravelines and the six communes that surround it. ● *Tues-Fri 2-5pm; Sat, Sun & public holidays 3-6pm. 2 Rue Léon-Blum (tel: 03 28 51 84 84). Admission free.*

> **Port Royal/Espace Tourville** *Jean Bart* In an atmospherically-vaulted part of Gravelines' arsenal (once the store for the town's firearms) is a museum devoted to the pirates, buccaneers, filibusters and *corsaires* who ploughed the seas in search of prisoners and booty for themselves or for their country. Instead of crossing the main access bridge into

■ Peacetime armada: Fête de la Mer, off Petit-Fort-Philippe.

Gravelines castle, turn left into the gardens and follow the outside of the walls until you see a little door at the bottom of some steps down to your left.

Pirates, such as the English "Blackbeard" (Edward Teach) plundered at sea or on shore for their own ends. Buccaneers, including Henry Morgan, were European pirates active specifically in the Caribbean. The word "filibuster" was used by the English to denote French pirates, such as Jean David Naud, operating in the same area. Privateers, such as France's famous Jean Bart (see page 44) and England's Sir Francis Drake, had official royal or government commission for their actions. The French term *corsaire* has a similar meaning to privateer, but could also denote a person with more piratical tendencies.

A collection of cannons and artefacts is imaginatively laid out; model sheep, pigs and poultry illustrate how animals had to be kept on board, to provide fresh food; and barrels of fruit act as reminders that sailors had to take in extra vitamins to keep scurvy (*le scorbut*) at bay. Small sacks of cloves and cinnamon represent the spices that were brought back from the West Indies and elsewhere by the adventurers, in exchange for the porcelain, pewter and jewellery they took with them to trade. Near the entrance, panels (in French) deal with details of ship construction, particularly with the aggressive decoration on Roman, Phoenician and Viking vessels that was designed to instil fear in the enemy.

An ambitious project is under way to construct a full-size replica of a French warship of the time of Louis XIV. It is to be called—of course—*Jean Bart*. The ticket for the museum also admits to the boatbuilding site (with the same opening hours) on Rue de Calais, between the *port de plaisance* (marina) and the Lidl shop. There, a rather rambling 20-minute video (in French) outlines the plan; you can see a scale model of the 57-metre-long ship and view the work in progress on the real thing. It's early days, so there's not yet much to see. However, there are hopes of eventually making the site a focus for boatbuilding trades such as rope- and sailmaking, as well as woodworking. ● *Both sites: Mon 2-5pm; Tues-Fri 10am-noon & 2-5pm (second weekend of the month, also Sat, Sun 10am-5pm). Espace Tourville, Arsenal (tel: 03 28 21 22 40). 4€, children 2€.* ⓢ

PETIT- & GRAND-FORT-PHILIPPE (GRAVELINES)

ⓘ Front de Mer, Petit-Fort-Philippe (tel: 03 28 65 51 51);
Oct-May, as Gravelines (page 53)

Gravelines' seaside resort of Petit-Fort-Philippe lies 2km north-west of the town at the mouth of the river Aa. During the blockade imposed by Napoleon preventing English ships trading in European ports (the "Continental System", see page 37), the village became a quasi-official smuggling centre. A neutral territory was created, called "Le Camp des Smogglers" (with an o). Until the blockade was lifted in 1812, English traders came to buy and sell at Petit-Fort-Philippe—paying a hefty 40 per cent duty to the French government.

A stroll along the riverside reveals the small marina; some reproductions of works by the *pointilliste* artist Georges Seurat (1859-91), who painted views of this channel in 1890; and a waterside signpost pointing in the direction of Iceland, to which so many of Gravelines' cod-fishermen sailed in the 19th century. Another sign of Petit-Fort-Philippe's fishing heritage is a clutch of streets named after fish: Rues du Cabillaud (cod), Hareng (herring), Merlan (whiting) and Saumon (salmon). The most obvious link with mariners is the eccentrically-striped lighthouse (see front cover). It was painted white when it was built, in 1843, but was changed in 1931 after complaints that it did not stand out sufficiently against a cloudy sky. In July and August you can climb to the top

■ Saving lives: Grand-Fort-Philippe.

(104 steps) for a seagull's-eye view, and also look at displays downstairs about the lighthouse and its keepers; the last one retired in 1985, after 30 years' service.

Petit-Fort-Philippe's glorious beach faces the North Sea, and offers some fun summer activities for children—though the sea goes out for miles, so try not to arrive at low tide. The resort is bounded on the east by sand dunes, behind which lies a nuclear power station. (Claimed to be the largest in western Europe, it produces 10 per cent of France's nuclear-generated electricity supply.)

As well as being a "Station Kid" (see page 13), Petit-Fort-Philippe is also very disabled-friendly, with blue lines painted on pavements to indicate the easiest routes for wheelchairs, and free loan of Tiralos (see page 12) between June and September. The tourist-office kiosk has information on all activities, and also on sea-fishing trips aboard a vintage boat.

To visit Grand-Fort-Philippe on the other side of the Aa can be more complicated than you would imagine. A small open boat operates a free passenger-ferry service at times across the 150-metre-wide channel that separates the two ports. Otherwise, you have to backtrack inland to Gravelines, and out again. Grand Fort-Philippe has no beach but it has two interesting museums. A delicious smell of woodsmoke hanging over the village is a reminder that it also still has a couple of working smokeries (see Extras, page 57).

❯**Maison de la Mer** On the quayside of Grand-Fort-Philippe, facing the blank wall of a modern building, is a small but fascinating museum about the local fishing industry. The permanent collection on the first floor tells of the epic 2,000km voyages to the waters of Iceland in search of cod that took the village's menfolk away each year from February to August. Back home, their families went shellfish-collecting on shore—photographs show old ladies with nets, and men carrying huge baskets—or fished along the coast in small shrimping boats. Everything is in French only, but the displays are practical and evocative. Beautiful model boats on show include sturdy, straight-prowed *dundees*, and elegant *goélettes*, as well as traditional ships in bottles. Old newspaper-cuttings, pulleys, ships' bells, payslips and paintings bring to life this rugged industry. You can see hooks used for squid, sole or turbot, and learn to tell the age of a cod by the hard deposits that build up between its skull-bones. Alongside medical and navigation equipment are tools for splicing, caulking and sail-making. When you compare the waterside activity in the photographs with today's peaceful view outside the window, it's hard to believe it's the same place.

■ Fishing heritage: displays at Grand-Fort-Philippe's Maison de la Mer.

You can enjoy a brief taste of the life, by taking a sea-fishing trip on a tan-sailed *dundee*; booking via Petit-Fort-Philippe

tourist office. ◑ *Early Apr-late Sep, Mon & Wed-Sat 2-5pm, Sun & public holidays 3-6pm. 42 Boulevard Carnot, Grand-Fort-Philippe (tel: 03 28 23 98 39). 2€ (includes Maison du Sauvetage, below), children free.*

❯**Maison du Sauvetage** The quaint, step-gabled brick building (pictured left) jutting out into the channel is a former lifeboat station. Today's modern, rubber lifeboat is based upriver at Gravelines, and this odd structure, still with its concrete launching ramp, has been turned into a small museum of lifesaving. A traditional lifeboat dominates an interior pervaded by the heady smell of tarred rope. Climb a flight of steps to peer into it; to read newspaper-cuttings (in French) about wrecks and heroic exploits; and to admire the impressive figures for the rescues performed by the modest-looking, be-medalled men shown in the photographs. The volunteer crews went out in the worst conditions (shipwrecks never happen in good weather), originally in large rowing boats. All around are bits of vital equipment: grappling-irons, lifejackets, a canvas sea-anchor, and a device used to convey people from a stricken ship to the lifeboat—called in French a *va-et-vient* (come-and-go) and in English a "breeches buoy". Indeed the example here is just that: a pair of breeches attached to a lifebuoy! A video gives a brief history of lifesaving, from old techniques to the modern activities of today's CROSS organisation (see page 87). ◑ *Early Apr-late Sept, Mon & Wed-Sat 2-6pm; Sun & public holidays 3-6pm. Boulevard de la République, Grand-Fort-Philippe (tel: 03 28 23 10 12). 2€ (includes Maison de la Mer, above), children free.*

PETIT- & GRAND-
FORT-PHILIPPE EXTRAS

Market: Mon, Grand-Fort-Philippe. Sun, Petit-Fort-Philippe.

Shops: Two smokeries at Grand-Fort-Philippe, below, sell beechwood-smoked mackerel, salmon, halibut, herring, sprats & other fish: **Saurisserie Nathalie Dutriaux** *29 Rue Félix-Faure;* **Saurisserie Jannin** *1 bis Ave de Dunkerque.*

Festivals: **Fête du Poisson** *Sale of fish & parade of giants La Matelote & L'Islandais, early Apr, Grand-Fort-Philippe.* **Fête de la Mer** *Procession of boats to lay a wreath at sea, 15 Aug, Petit-Fort-Philippe.*

HAZEBROUCK

ⓘ **Hôtel de Ville, Place du Général-de-Gaulle (tel: 03 28 43 44 37 fax: 03 28 40 78 66)**
www.ville-hazebrouck.fr
contact@ville-hazebrouck.fr

Hazebrouck, 11km south-east of Cassel, is the capital of inland Flanders. In the 1550s, King Philip II of Spain aided its expansion as a centre of the cloth trade by building the canal that links it with the river Lys, to the south.

As a major railway junction through which troops and supplies were moved during both world wars, the town was a target for enemy bombardment—particularly in World War I. The main square is surrounded by shops and restaurants, many with colourful Art Deco façades. Inside the tall brick church of St-Éloi, to the south, a series of imposing marble monuments commemorates the *marguilliers*, former members of the parish council. Behind the church lies the *béguinage*, a charming enclave of white-shuttered almshouses. Their building was financed by a priest and former mayor of the town, Abbé Lemire (see page 58), who lived next door; a statue of him stands in the adjoining park.

❯**Musée Municipal** The tallest of Hazebrouck's giants, modelled on a legendary Crusader, towers over the entrance hall of the town's enjoyable museum. The collection, devoted to Flemish arts and traditions, is housed on the ground floor of a former Augustinian monastery, a mellow 17th-century brick building to the south of the main square. You could spend a good hour taking in the works on show in the enclosed, covered cloisters. They incude a gory rendition of a decapitated John the Baptist by Bruges artist Jacob van Oost de Oude; a gruesome 16th-century painting of St Blaise being tortured with woolcombs; a martyrdom of St Sebastian from the studio of Van Dyck; and some meaty still-lifes. Another section contains a marvellous re-creation of a Flemish kitchen, its fireplace festooned with kitchen tools and its walls decorated with Delft-style tiles. Glass-fronted cupboards holding 18th-century Lille and Torhout pottery stand beside polished sideboards and an exquisitely simple wooden cradle, dating from 1850. In an adjoining room you come face-to-face with a whole family of giants: pipe-smoking father, Tisje-Tasje (pronounced "tish-tash"), posy-carrying mother, son Dan and daughter Babe. Peering up inside at their wicker frames, you feel positively Lilliputian. They parade in early July. ● *Wed, Thurs, Sat, 10am-noon & 2-5pm; Sun 10am-noon & 3-6pm. Place Georges-Degroote (tel: 03 28 43 44 46). 2.10€ (free on first Sun of month), children free.* ♿ Ⓢ

❯**Fondation Abbé Lemire** The brick-built house behind the church was the home from 1899 to his death, in 1928, of Abbé Jules Lemire. Born to a local farming family, he left home to train for the priesthood, and returned in 1878 to teach at his old school. Keen to enter political life, Lemire was elected *député* (MP) for the *département* of the Nord in 1893 and led much social reform. He was also mayor of Hazebrouck from 1914 to 1928, steering the town through its wartime difficulties and overseeing its reconstruction. However, Lemire is best-remembered in France for his launching in 1896 of "*jardins ouvriers*", vegetable gardens for the poor to grow food.

■ **Altarpiece: fine example on the Chemins des Rétables.**

The tour of the house's ground floor is led, in French, by Lemire's elderly great-nephew. After talking about some of the displays, he ushers visitors into his uncle's study, which is shaded by shutters, lined with bookcases, and exudes a pleasant aroma of beeswax. At the desk, the priest would write up to 130 letters a day. The room's folding doors are decorated with some unexpectedly frivolous land- and seascapes, by a Finnish artist whom Lemire had baptised during a stay in Algeria. A second room has the priest's mayoral sash and some items from the Paris flat that Lemire used during his 35 years as *député*. In the little private chapel at the back of the house lies a piece of fabric embroidered with Australian names and images, presented to Lemire in memory of the many antipodean troops who passed through Hazebrouck during World War I. The last room is lined with cartoons relating to the *abbé* and to his political career. Finally comes the screening of a 50-minute video on Lemire's life and achievements. ◗ *1 Mar-early Sept, first Sun of month, 2-5pm (video shown at 3pm). 5 ter Square de l'Église (tel: 03 28 41 84 67). Admission free.*

❯**Site de Lancement de V1** Explanatory panels at a parking area in Nieppe forest guide you to the remains of a launch-site for V1 bombs (see page 70). However, during the hunting season (September-February) check the special notices in the car park first; you should not enter the woods on shooting days. ● *Les Huit Rues, on D916, 9km S of Hazebrouck.* Ⓢ

HAZEBROUCK EXTRAS

Market: Mon.

Accommodation/food:

Auberge de la Forêt 2-star Logis, with great food. Rooms from 40€; menus from 25€. Closed Sat lunch, Sun evg & Mon. La Motte-au-Bois, 6km S of Hazebrouck (tel: 03 28 48 08 78). www.auberge-delaforet.com/

Restaurant: La Taverne Popular place, serving typical local dishes. Menus 15-30€; closed Sun evg & Mon. 61 Place de Gaulle (tel: 03 28 41 63 09).

HONDSCHOOTE

ⓘ **2 Rue des Moëres (tel: 03 28 62 53 00 fax: 03 28 68 30 99)**
www.cc-flandre.fr/hondschoote
otpaysdulin@wanadoo.fr

Lying on a Roman road 15km south-east of Dunkerque, at a point that was once the coast, Hondschoote (pronounced "onz-cot") claims to have the most northerly vineyard of France. Its handsome *hallekerque* has three fine altarpieces. Try to hang around in the square to hear the church's 61-bell carillon, which plays a chirpy tune on the quarters.

Across the way, among a collection of 16th-century buildings, is the beautiful stone *hôtel de ville* (town hall). Its entrance hall contains a series of painted panels recounting the dramatic history of the town since 628AD. Hondschoote was renowned for wool-weaving from the 11th century, manufacturing the finest serge (a trade known as *sayetterie*); in 1581 its serge-makers numbered more than 3,000. The town prospered, until hit by a succession of fires, battles and bouts of plague, and—being at the time strongly Calvinist—was burnt down in 1582, during the Wars of Religion. Hondschoote picked up the threads of its weaving business again but, invaded and pillaged alternately by French and Dutch, it saw its cloth industry finally collapse in 1712.

During the wars that followed the 1789 Revolution, the French trounced a combined English/Hanoverian/Austrian alliance at the Battle of Hondschoote on 8 September 1793, forcing the Duke of York to lift his siege of Dunkerque. A memorial near the church commemorates the victory; one of the *commune*'s two windmills—the Spinnewyn, or Moulin de la Victoire—served as a vantage-point during the battle.

Since the 18th century Hondschoote has turned to flax-growing, an industry that continues today in the fields around the village of Killem; look for the drifts of pale blue flowers in June, or visit the Grenier du Lin (see below).

> **Musée Municipal** Up the polished spiral stairs of the *hôtel de ville*, a large room contains changing exhibitions on different aspects of the culture and history of Flanders. On permanent display here are some 17th-century pictures—mostly rather grisly scenes of martydom, plus nine paintings of valiant women, including Joan of Arc. ● *During exhibitions: Mon-Fri 9.30am-noon. Place de Gaulle (tel: 03 28 49 10 97). Admission free.*

> **Chemins des Rétables** Leaflets available from Hondschoote tourist office, and from others throughout Flanders, list around 150 villages on both sides of the Franco-Belgian frontier whose churches are endowed with magnificent altarpieces (see facing page), painted statues and ornately-carved pulpits. Sadly, due to thefts, most churches are now locked, but arriving just before or after Mass on a Sunday may give you a chance of a peep inside. Otherwise, between June and August, you will find a schedule of guided visits pinned to the doors of relevant churches. O *Various villages.*

> **Grenier du Lin** Valérie Van Robaeys' delightfully rural linen showroom is signposted down ever-smaller country lanes, among a landscape in which the family grows and processes 9,000 tonnes of fibre a year.

On the ground floor are interesting explanations (in French) about the growing of flax and its transformation into linen (the plant and the final product have the same name in French: *le lin*). You can handle samples of flax from different stages in the production cycle. Sown in late March, the shiny brown seeds spring up and blossom into delicate, short-lived blue flowers. The stalks are cut after 100 days, and left to lie in the fields until rain has softened the husk enough for the long filamenlts to be teased out of them with mechanical rollers and combs. The hanks of brownish fibre are shipped to China for spinning into usable thread, and then returned to France where they are woven into cloth.

Upstairs are displays of bags, garments, cushions, tablemats, braids, furnishing fabrics, embroidery kits and voiles, plus linen fabric sold by the metre. (It's not cheap, but linen never is.) Bring measurements from home if you might need tablecloths, bedlinen, curtains or dressmaking fabric; you will kick yourself if you don't. ● *Mon-Sat 2-7pm. 1101 Chemin de Roesbrugge, 2.5km SE of Hondschoote, signposted off D947 about 1km from town (tel: 03 28 62 64 61).*

Area 2

Calais, Boulogne, St-Omer, and World War II

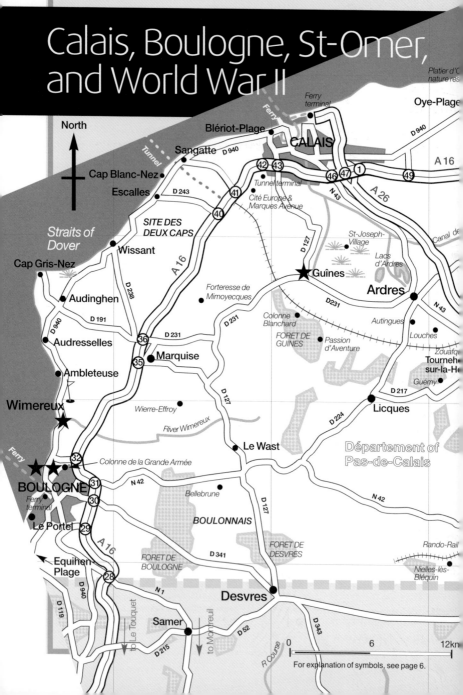

North

Platier d'O
nature res

Oye-Plage

Ferry terminal

Blériot-Plage

CALAIS

Ferry

D 940

Tunnel

Sangatte

D 940

Cap Blanc-Nez

42 43

46 47 1

49

A 16

Escales

D 243

41

Tunnel terminal

Cité Europe & Marques Avenue

N 43

A 26

40

D 127

St-Joseph-Village

Canal de

SITE DES DEUX CAPS

Straits of Dover

Wissant

A 16

Lacs d'Ardres

Guînes

Cap Gris-Nez

Forteresse de Mimoyecques

Ardres

N 43

D 298

Audinghen

Colonne Blanchard

D 231

Autingues

Louches

D 940

D 191

D 231

FORET DE GUINES

Passion d'Aventure

Zouafques

Tourneh sur-la-He

Audresselles

36

D 231

Marquise

Guémy

Ambleteuse

35

D 127

D 217

Licques

Wimereux

Wierre-Effroy

D 224

Ferry

River Wimereux

32

Colonne de la Grande Armée

Le Wast

Département of Pas-de-Calais

BOULOGNE

31

N 42

Bellebrune

30

D 127

Ferry terminal

Le Portel

29

N 42

A 16

BOULONNAIS

Rando-Rail

Equihen Plage

28

FORET DE BOULOGNE

D 341

FORET DE DESVRES

Nielles-lès-Bléquin

D 940

N 1

Desvres

D 119

Samer

D 52

D 343

0   6   12kn

R Course

For explanation of symbols, see page 6.

D 215

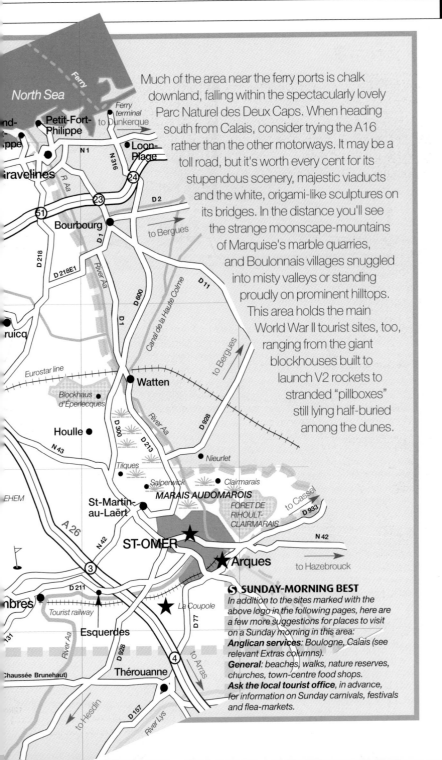

Much of the area near the ferry ports is chalk downland, falling within the spectacularly lovely Parc Naturel des Deux Caps. When heading south from Calais, consider trying the A16 rather than the other motorways. It may be a toll road, but it's worth every cent for its stupendous scenery, majestic viaducts and the white, origami-like sculptures on its bridges. In the distance you'll see the strange moonscape-mountains of Marquise's marble quarries, and Boulonnais villages snuggled into misty valleys or standing proudly on prominent hilltops. This area holds the main World War II tourist sites, too, ranging from the giant blockhouses built to launch V2 rockets to stranded "pillboxes" still lying half-buried among the dunes.

North Sea

Ferry
Ferry terminal
to Dunkerque

Petit-Fort-Philippe

Loon-Plage

Gravelines

Bourbourg

to Bergues

Ruicq

Eurostar line

Watten

Blockhaus d'Éperlecques

Houlle

Nieurlet

Tilques

Salperwick

Clairmarais

EHEM

St-Martin-au-Laërt

MARAIS AUDOMAROIS

FORET DE RIHOULT-CLAIRMARAIS

to Cassel

★ ST-OMER

★ Arques

to Hazebrouck

to Bergues

La Coupole

Tourist railway

Esquerdes

Thérouanne

to Hesdin

Chaussée Brunehaut)

River Aa

River Lys

to Arras

⑤ SUNDAY-MORNING BEST

In addition to the sites marked with the above logo in the following pages, here are a few more suggestions for places to visit on a Sunday morning in this area:

Anglican services: *Boulogne, Calais (see relevant Extras columns).*

General: *beaches, walks, nature reserves, churches, town-centre food shops.*

Ask the local tourist office, *in advance, for information on Sunday carnivals, festivals and flea-markets.*

■ Rock of ages: the
fort at Ambleteuse.

AMBLETEUSE EXTRAS

Market: Mon, Audresselles,
2km NW of Ambleteuse.
Wed, Ambleteuse.

Restaurants:

La Marie-Galante Perfect
for a seafood lunch; menus
from 20€. Closed Sun evg &
Mon. 173 Rue Édouard-
Quenu, Audresselles, 2km
NW of Ambleteuse (tel: 03
21 83 02 32).

Brocante: *L'Étable*
Whitewashed cottage,
selling furniture, tableware &
antique bedlinen. Wed-Sun
3-7pm. 1 Rue du Marais, on
corner of D237 & D237E,
Slack, 2km SE of Ambleteuse
(tel: 06 62 11 16 79).

AMBLETEUSE

ⓘ 1 Place de la Mairie (tel/fax: 03 21 83 50 05)
www.terredes2caps.com
tourisme@terredes2caps.com

Low tide at this unpretentious seaside village, 11km north of Boulogne, sees frenzied activity from a fleet of rubber dinghies and from small open boats known as *flobarts*. Gaily-coloured tractors tow the craft to the water's edge for launching, and retrieve them at the end of their fishing sorties. Direct descendants of broad-beamed Viking ships, the small, clinker-built *flobarts* are used all along the Opal Coast, where their wide shape and flat bottom make them easy to beach in shallow water.

With its dominant view across the approach to Boulogne, Ambleteuse has always been well-placed to protect its larger neighbour. Over the centuries it has been fortified by Romans, English, French and Germans: Henry VIII had a citadel built on the cliff in 1546; later, Louis XIV engaged military engineer Vauban (see page 46) to build a naval base, which was never completed due to excessive silting at the mouth of the river Slack. The river is today part of a nature reserve; alongside it you can follow footpaths through the constantly shifting dunes in search of wild orchids and other rarities.

Audresselles is another sleepy fishing village, 2km north-west of Ambleteuse, with a sea-front fringed by curious flat rocks rather than sand. In the centre, signboards (in French) encourage you to stroll around the *Sentier du Pêcheur*, or fishermen's trail, telling you en route about the typical two-roomed houses, with a large attic above; about the families' diet of fish (no surprise there), supplemented by home-grown vegetables and salt pork; and about the dominant role of the fishwives, who may not have been allowed to set foot on the boats (they were thought to jinx them), but who mended nets, baited lines, sold the catch—and controlled the family's purse-strings.

❯**Fort d'Ambleteuse** Signposted "Fort Vauban" and also known as "Fort Mahon", this strange fortified building in brick and stone (pictured above) dominates the southern end of Ambleteuse's shingle beach. Part of Vauban's abandoned 17th-century plan, it was reinforced in the early 1800s by Napoleon, and served during World War II as a German lookout position. Today, it is in the hands of an association dedicated to protecting the heritage of the Slack estuary.

A challenging route over slippery rocks and uneven stone steps leads to the gate. Inside, there's a slide show (with a ponderously slow French commentary) about coastal erosion, with the message reinforced by relief models showing how the sea has bitten off bits of land over four centuries.

A well-translated English leaflet summarises the history of the site. There are photographs of local architecture and flora; diagrams of land movement; displays of flint, neolithic tools and Gallo-Roman pottery; and a reproduction of the 3rd-century bronze "Ambleteuse vase". (The original is in the British Museum.) Other interesting items include a human skull bearing dents from some long-ago battle, diagrams of 17th-century English invasions of Brittany, Cherbourg and Dieppe—local hero Jean Bart (see page 45) managed to repel them from Dunkerque—and a model of the first hot-air balloon to cross the Channel, amazingly in 1785 (see page 79). World War II photographs show bomb damage near Boulogne in September 1943, and the Germans' flooding of the Flanders marshes to discourage Allied invasion. If you climb the 40-odd steps to a spray-lashed lookout point you realise the Kent coast is so close that Germans posted here could watch their missiles dropping. (Back down in the hallway there's a 380mm shell typical of those fired on Britain at that time.) ◗ *Easter-31 Oct, Sun 3-6.30pm (1 July-31 Aug, Sat, Sun 3-7pm). Ambleteuse (tel: 03 21 32 60 44/03 20 54 61 54). 3€, children 1.50€.*

❯**Musée 39-45: Historique de la Seconde Guerre Mondiale** The Sherman tank and 88mm gun outside lure you into this well-laid-out museum that shows the history of World War II on many fronts, from the Polish campaign to Hiroshima. Glass-fronted showcases display military scenes (mostly captioned in English), in which uniformed figures are arranged against appropriate backgrounds to give an idea of battles in Normandy, Japan and snow-bound Russia. Colourfully-costumed Algerian Spahis stand alongside kilted Scottish Camerons. There are rusty relics from Operation Dynamo (see page 47) and information on Allied and German air aces, the naval Battle of the Atlantic, and Germany's campaign against Russia on the Eastern Front. A comfortable little cinema screens a 30-minute film (in English and French) on the 1944 Allied invasion of Normandy, life on the home front in France, and the building of the Atlantic Wall (see Batterie Todt, below). As a brief interlude, after the cinema you pass through re-creations of Paris streets under the Occupation, with German shops full of luxury goods and French ones selling the most basic of products.

The next chronological period of the war starts with the Allied invasion of Italy in 1943. It continues with the June 1944 Normandy landings and the liberation of Paris the same year. Farther afield, it looks at the continuing jungle warfare and war in the Pacific. There are displays of rifles, bazookas, rockets and grenade-launchers, and tributes to the FFI (*Force Française de l'Intérieur*, or French Resistance). In the museum shop you can buy uniforms, entrenching tools and other military items. Allow a good hour and a half for the visit. ◗ *1 Mar-30 Nov, Sat, Sun & public holidays 10am-6pm (1 Apr-15 Oct, Mon-Fri 9.30am-6pm; Sat, Sun 10am-6pm; 1 July-31 Aug, Mon-Fri 9.30am-7pm; Sat, Sun 10am-7pm). On D940 on N side of Ambleteuse (tel: 03 21 87 33 01). 6€, children 4.30€, under-7s free.* ♿ ✎ ⊘

■ **Ace museum: Musée 39-45, at Ambleteuse.**

❯**Musée du Mur de l'Atlantique: Batterie Todt 1939-45** Hitler's Atlantic Wall was a chain of 15,000 defensive structures that stretched 6,000km from Scandinavia to the Pyrenees. All were built by the Todt organisation, using Jewish, Soviet and other prisoners as slave labour, working 12-hour shifts in the most inhumane conditions. The museum is in a massive concrete blockhouse, near Cap Gris-Nez, part of a complex built to house a 380mm naval gun. The forbidding exterior bristles with field guns and other artillery, including a huge German K5 railway-mounted gun nicknamed "Audinghen Annie", one of 25 manufactured by Krupp in 1941.

Walk down a steep concrete path to enter the building. It is one of four towers originally on the site, and was home to 18 soldiers and one officer on six-month tours of duty. Captions in English describe the museum's immense collection of World War II weapons, equipment, vehicles, guns and uniforms. You see countless shells, incendiary bombs, grenades, mines, bayonets, revolvers and rifles, and read chilling details about their capabilities. Among less deadly exhibits are German crockery, US battlefield cutlery and RAF flying boots (incorporating a razor so

■ Big bang: gun battery at Audinghen.

that a shot-down airman could cut the tops off and transform his distinctive footwear into more normal-looking shoes). There are motorbikes, bits of aircraft, and some anti-British posters issued by Marshal Pétain's pro-German, Vichy-French government that ran, roughly, the southern half of France from 1940 to 44. On a clear day, the sight of England's white cliffs 30km away shows just how close Hitler came to realising his ambitions. Ordnance fanatics could spend a couple of hours here, and can buy bits of military equipment in the museum's shop. ◑ *1 Feb-30 Nov, daily 9am-noon & 2-6pm (1 June-30 Sept, daily 9am-7pm). Batterie Todt, on D940, 2km S of Audinghen & 5km N of Ambleteuse (tel: 03 21 32 97 33). 5.50€, children 2.50€, under-8s free.* 🌂 🕓

ARDRES

ⓘ **Chapelle des Carmes, Place d'Armes (tel/fax: 03 21 35 28 51)**
www.ardres-tourisme.fr
ardres.officedetourisme@wanadoo.fr

Paved with bone-shaking cobbles, the pretty, wedge-shaped main "square" of Ardres (14km south-east of Calais) is lined with small shops. At its lower end, a flamboyant Gothic church contains a beautiful black-and-gold Madonna and child; halfway up, a pink-painted 18th-century chapel holds the town's tourist office.

Just to the north is an area of lakes, where you can fish, sail, follow nature trails, or drive electric boats (swimming is not allowed).

To the south-west lie picturesque villages, including Autingues, Louches, Zouafques and Tournehem-sur-la-Hem. From the old square of Tournehem you can follow a 9km circuit to the hamlet of Guémy and the hilltop chapel of St-Louis. Licques, 10km south-west of Ardres, is famous for turkeys, and for the annual December festival during which a flock of the birds is driven through the village.

ARDRES EXTRAS

Market: Wed, Audruicq, 13km NE of Ardres. Thurs, Ardres.

Accommodation/food:
Moulin d'Audenfort
Simple hotel in a converted watermill. Excellent meals, served beside a roaring fire in winter. Rooms from 52€; menus from 20€. Closed Sun evg & Mon. 16 Impasse du Gué, Audenfort, 10km S of Ardres (tel: 03 21 00 13 16).
Brocante: Salon des Antiquaires *3-day antiques fair. Bois-en-Ardres, 2.5km N of Ardres, early Oct.*

➤**Les "Poires"** The "pears" of Ardres are a series of nine underground grain silos, built in 1530. Located in the town centre, beneath the corn-market building of the time, they were designed to store 1,000 tonnes of grain—enough to feed the garrison of 500 people, plus their animals, for a year. Seven metres deep, they could be filled from the top, and emptied from beneath via arched access tunnels. The silos fell into disuse from the mid 17th century, but have now been opened up for visits. ◑ *1 Apr-30 Nov, on request for groups of five minimum (1 July-31 Aug, for pre-booked individuals, Wed & Fri, times vary). Esplanade du Maréchal-Leclerc. Group or individual visits must be booked with tourist office at least 48 hours in advance (tel: 03 21 35 28 51). Admission free.*

➤**Maison de la Flore** Fences of living willow surround a brick cottage containing a permanent exhibition about the origins of Ardres lakes and their long tradition of peat-cutting. Information panels (in French) show the lakes, ponds, ditches and *watergangs* (waterways) in this liquid landscape. They describe the marshland flowers, trees, animals, fish and birds, and the dwellings around the water's edge (until 100 years ago, regarded as an insalubrious place, inhabited only by the rural poor). There are pictures of boats, from traditional *escutes* and *bacôves* to modern pedaloes and sailing dinghies. Outside, nature trails lead along the water's edge, past marginal plants and medicinal herbs. If the door of the house is locked, there's usually a volunteer working somewhere in the garden who can let you in. ● *Wed & Fri 2-5pm (1 Apr-mid June, Tues-Fri 2-5pm; mid June-15 Sept, Wed-Sat 2-5pm, Sun 3-5pm). Closed mid-late Sept. Rue des Rainettes, 2km N of Ardres (tel: 03 21 82 89 27). Admission free.*

➤Bal Parc Families with two- to 11-year-olds could spend at least half a day at this rather endearing amusement park. Grassy, with gravel paths, it has trees, picnic-tables and a little land-train to ferry you round the 11-hectare site. Most entertainment is included in the entrance charge: traditional swings, roundabouts, a bouncy "volcano" slide (tough clothes and trainers recommended), a large pedalo circuit (with mini-boats for tinies, on a shallower pond) and an 18-hole mini-golf (2€ deposit required for club and ball). Small quad-bikes for seven-year-olds and over cost 1.50€ for five minutes. Children can see strutting peacocks and turkeys, and stroke goats and the resident donkey. On Sundays and public holidays the adjoining hall holds tea-dances, with live music, from 3pm (included in price). It's good, old-fashioned fun for all. ❶ *1 Apr-1 Oct, Wed & Sat 10.30am-6.30pm, Sun & public holidays 10.30am-7pm; 2 Oct-11 Nov, Wed & Sat 11am-4.30pm, Sun & public holidays 11am-5pm (French school holiday periods Apr-Nov, daily 10.30am-6.30pm). 207 Rue du Vieux-Château (D218), Tournehem-sur-la-Hem, 7km SE of Ardres & 2km SW of J2 of A26 (tel: 03 21 35 97 26). 8€.* ⓢ

➤Eurolac Children love the electric boats and other entertainment at this amusement park halfway along the long, straight Avenue du Lac. Admission is free; you can buy drinks, crêpes and ice-creams at the waterside bar, and you pay for the electric boats, pedaloes, bouncy castles and land-train with tickets purchased singly or in *carnets* of 10 or 20. These remain valid indefinitely, so if you have not used them all you can come back another day to finish them up. The electric boats are easy to drive; competent children of 10 and over are allowed to take one out on the large lake on their own; lifejackets are provided. ❶ *Early Mar-mid Oct, Wed, Sat, Sun & public holidays 10am-5pm (1 July-31 Aug, daily 10am-7pm). 1098 Avenue du Lac, 1.5km NW of Ardres (tel: 03 21 35 13 91). Admission free; charges for activities either by 10- or 20-ticket book (16€ & 26€, respectively), or by paying 10€ per person for unlimited use of boats.* ⓢ

■ **All-electric: boating fun at Eurolac.**

ARQUES

ⓘ **Place Roger-Salengro (tel: 03 21 88 59 00 fax: 03 21 98 07 69)**
www.ville-arques.fr
arques@nordnet.fr

ARQUES EXTRAS

Market: Tues.

Factory shop: Arc International Glassware bargains. Mon-Sat 10am-6.30pm. ZI (zone industrielle), Rue du Général-de-Gaulle (N43), 1.5km SE of Arques (tel: 03 21 95 46 96).

Fire and water are the elements that have most marked this town, 4km south of St-Omer. Visitor attractions focus on Arques' industrial past and present: its 19th-century boat lift, quaint 20th-century train trips, and the visits to the well-known Arc International glassworks.

The position of Arques on the 20km-long Neuffossé canal made it an important inland port from the 1750s. Linking the river Lys with the river Aa, the canal was part of a network conveying coal, industrial goods and raw materials to and from production centres and inland markets. Five locks at Arques raised and lowered boats between two levels, a time-consuming operation replaced in 1887 by the hydraulic lift (see page 66).

> **Ascenseur à Bateaux des Fontinettes** The boat lift at the north end of the wide Canal de Neuffossé is a brilliant example of Victorian ingenuity. Built to raise and lower boats at a point where the canal level changes by 13 metres, it was designed by an Englishman, Edwin Clark (1814-94), who had created a similar system at Anderton, in Cheshire. It operated as two water-filled tanks, one kept at the bottom level and one at the top, like a pair of scales. A boat would enter each; the solid gates would be closed; a little more water added to make the top one heavier; and a valve opened that transferred the hydraulic pressure created by the descent of the top one across to the lower one—which would then rise. The two passed and arrived at their new positions, where each could exit on the other level. However, by the 1960s increased canal traffic and larger boats required a new solution.

The visit takes about 45 minutes, and is fairly low-key. It starts with a room containing a model and diagrams, plus photographs of similar structures throughout the world. (A good leaflet in English explains the system.) You can peek into the cathedral-like interior of the lift, and marvel at the simplicity of its mechanism. Another building houses the machine room and workshop, and screens a video made in 1967 before the lift gave way to a modern single lock. ◖ *1 Apr-30 Sept, Mon-Fri 10am-noon & 2-6pm; Sat, Sun & public holidays 2-6pm. 21 Rue Denis-Papin (tel: 03 21 12 90 23). 3.50€, children under 10 2.40€.*

> **Chemin de Fer Touristique de la Vallée de l'Aa** The 45-minute journey from Arques to Lumbres can be made by old-fashioned diesel train (see page 80). ◖ *1 May-30 Sept. Rue de la Gare, Arques (tel: 03 21 12 19 19).* ⑤

> ★ **Arc International** The products of the great glassworks, formerly called Cristallerie d'Arques, are known worldwide. On this 250-hectare site (the size of 300 football pitches), 11,000 employees turn out almost 6 million items in glass and crystal each day.

A fascinating 90-minute tour, conducted by usually bilingual guides, includes a brief history, a 12-minute audio-visual presentation (in English, or with English subtitles) and a visit to the factory. From the gallery above the factory floor, you can see the roaring jets of flame that weld stems to glasses (you appreciate the free earplugs you are given). Displays and panels describe techniques of moulding and printing, and the temperatures at which the glass is fired.

The company started in 1825, making demi-johns and other bulk containers. Its canalside position ensured easy delivery of raw materials (sand, coal and cellet, or broken glass) and the

despatch of finished products. In 1897 it diversified into drinking-glasses, bringing skilled glass-blowers from Czechoslovakia, Spain, Poland, Italy and Belgium. Mass production began in the 1930s with the introduction of a blower and a press from America. Today, the factory's daily output matches the company's *annual* production in 1825.

The factory shop (not an ideal place to take lively children!) has a huge range of products, from cheap café glasses to fanciful decorative items, and gives 20 per cent discount for tour ticket-holders. There are also changing exhibitions on glass-related themes. ● *Guided tours Mon-Sat (except public holidays) 9.30am, 11am, 2pm & 3.30pm (pre-booking advisable). Follow "Visites" signs, ZI (zone industrielle), Rue du Général-de-Gaulle (N43), 1.5km SE of Arques (tel: 03 21 12 74 74; visite-usine@arc-intl.com/). 6.50€, students & children 4.20€ (children under 8 not admitted).* ⑤ ♞

■ Glass act: tours of the Arc International factory.

BOULOGNE-SUR-MER

ⓘ 24 Quai Gambetta (tel: 03 21 10 88 10 fax: 03 21 10 88 11)
www.tourisme-boulognesurmer.com
info@tourisme-boulognesurmer.com

At the junction of the English Channel and the North Sea, Boulogne is France's largest fishing port. This attractive seaside town is easily reached by ferry; its good shopping,

■ **Old Boulogne: busy Rue de Lille, and the 19th-century cathedral.**

historic features and compact centre have made it a popular destination for a day-trip. To feel Boulogne's history, walk uphill from the port and pass through one of the narrow gateways into the Ville-Haute, or upper town. Its ancient fortifications stand on the foundations of Roman defences, built when Caesar's troops were preparing their invasion of Britain. Among medieval buildings still visible on the cobbled streets are a stone belfry and the solid 13th-century château, which is now a museum (see pages 68 and 73).

Also preparing to invade Britain, Napoleon Bonaparte based himself in Boulogne from 1803 to 1805, training up a "Grande Armée" of 170,000 men, constructing coastal forts, and assembling a navy of 2,000 ships. The emperor's stay is commemorated by the Colonne de la Grande Armée at Wimille, north of Boulogne. However, Napoleon's planned invasion never took place. In August 1805, he decided to march most of his army east to Austerlitz, where he won a resounding victory over the Austrians and Russians.

A vogue for sea-bathing from 1815, the development of steamships in the 1830s and the arrival of the railway in 1848 had profound effects on Boulogne. The train brought Parisian tourists, and the speedier ferries made acess easier for the British. By 1859 the town had 56 hotels. It had six places of worship for the large British community, who also enjoyed tennis tournaments, race-meetings and sailing regattas. Queen Victoria was received in great pomp on her arrival in the royal yacht in 1855.

The lower part of Boulogne has smart shops on Grande Rue, Rue Victor-Hugo, Rue Faidherbe and Rue Thiers (though most are closed on Sunday and Monday). The market is held off Grande Rue, in Place Dalton, also a focus for eating-places. In the upper town, most restaurants are on the pedestrianised Rue de Lille.

For children needing to let off steam after a long journey, there's a well-groomed sandy beach, and also a leafy quayside park with mini-golf and a free playground beside Nausicaa sealife centre.

> ★ **Nausicaa** You could easily spend half a day in Boulogne's great aquarium/marine centre, ogling everything from ethereal jellyfish to teeth-baring sharks. At the start, check out timings of sea-lion shows and other events; all information is given in English and French throughout.

Descending a dark staircase to the sound of strange electronic music, you arrive in front of displays about plankton and its importance as a primary food source. Picking up telephone handsets, you can listen to commentaries on how cockles and scallops hop, skip or jump to escape predators, and experience a fish's-eye view of fishing, where cunningly-positioned mirrors, some netting and a glass cone full of glittering tuna

BOULOGNE EXTRAS

Market: Wed & Sat, Place Dalton.

Specialities: Vieux-Boulogne cheese. "Welsh" (toasted cheese). "Gainée" (fish stew).

Accommodation:

La Matelote 4-star hotel overlooking beach, with acclaimed restaurant. Rooms from 115€; menus 25-72€; possible garage parking; 70 Bd Sainte-Beuve (tel: 03 21 30 33 33). www.la-matelote.com/

Hotel Métropole 3-star hotel in town centre. Rooms from 81€; possible garage parking. 51 Rue Thiers (tel: 03 21 31 54 30). www.hotel-metropole-boulogne.com/

Enclos de l'Évêché Elegant town-house B&B, by cathedral. Characterful bedrooms; great home-made jams. Rooms from 70€. Free public car park alongside. 6 Rue de Pressy (tel: 03 91 90 05 90). www.enclosdeleveche.com/

Restaurants:

La Poivrière Small place in old town, serving classic French dishes. 15 Rue de Lille (tel: 03 21 80 18 18).

Brasserie de la Mer Excellent fish restaurant, overlooking the market square. Menus from 13€. Closed Sun evg. 31 Grande Rue (tel: 03 21 30 29 29).

Snacks: La Mie Câline Good place for takeaway lunchtime sandwiches & cakes. 2 Grande Rue.

Shops:

Philippe Olivier Expertly-ripened cheeses of all types. Tues-Sat 8am-12.30pm & 2.30-7.30pm. 43 Rue Thiers (tel: 03 21 31 94 74).

combine to make you feel you are in there with the fish. Video booths (some of which provide English commentary) describe the changes in tuna-fishing techniques, from the rods and lines of a century ago to the 1,300-metre-long, *seine* nets used today. Farther on, you can try and spot the turbot and plaice lying camouflaged on a bed of sand, invisible until they move; or shudder at the sight of malevolent-looking moray eels lurking inside barnacle-encrusted, fake wrecks.

The action of the tides is re-created in special tanks. You also learn how modern medicine draws on the sea's resources to develop drugs against herpes, shingles and some types of cancer; how architects take inspiration from the shells of marine creatures when creating reinforcing structures; and how the food industry uses seaweed products as gelling agents and thickeners. Displays on an ecological theme stress the dangers of overfishing, and of pollution resulting from oil spills and rubbish-dumping.

In the tourism section, with its artificial mangroves, youngsters squeal with delight as they reach the coral reef and make out the ghostly forms of sharks in a 6-metre-deep tank. Another area is devoted to a simulated voyage from Iceland to the Cape of Good Hope, featuring live penguins. Everybody loves the "touch tank", in which the friendly rays, turbot and dogfish all seem keen to have their tummies tickled. During the entertaining outdoor sea-lion displays, white-gloved trainers encourage their lively charges to jump with impressive accuracy, and to recognise and pick out different geometric shapes.

There are a couple of snack bars on the way round—a better bet for families than the smart restaurant off the entrance-hall. Another alternative is to go out to have a picnic, first having your hand stamped for re-admission. The best time to visit is first thing in the morning or at the end of the day. If you arrive in the last two hours before closing, you can have free re-admission the next morning to finish your visit. ● *Daily 9.30am-6.30pm (1 July-31 Aug, daily 9.30am-7.30pm). Closed 1 Jan (am), three weeks during Jan, & 25 Dec. Boulevard Sainte-Beuve (tel: 03 21 30 98 98). 11.50€, children 8.30€; family (2+2) 35€ (1 Apr-30 Sept, 13€, 9.30€ & 39€). Disabled visitors 7€; free wheelchair loan. Audioguides in English 3€ (must leave a passport as deposit).* ♿ *(90 per cent).* 🐾 🚫

❯**Cathédrale Notre-Dame** The 101-metre-high domed roof of Boulogne's 19th-century cathedral dominates the old, upper town (see page 67). An earlier, Romanesque building was destroyed during the Revolution, along with a statue of the Virgin that had become a focus of pilgrimages. A priest, Abbé Haffreingue, bought the ruins in 1820 and, with no training in architecture, started building this ambitious edifice. The main altar, installed in 1866, is inlaid with 145 different sorts of marble and with alabaster, jasper, agate and rock crystal. ● *Daily 10am-noon & 2-5pm (1 Apr-31 Aug, daily 9am-noon & 2-6pm). Mass: Sun 11am. Entrance on Rue de Lille.* 🚫

❯**Crypte** Beneath the cathedral lies a crypt—one of the longest in France. Its hollowed-out rooms contain sculptures from the original cathedral and are decorated with a few medieval wall-paintings. Among the fine church plate in the Treasure House rooms, look for an enamelled reliquary that contains a fragment of fabric said to be stained with the blood of Christ. Brought back from the First Crusade, it was given in 1308 as a wedding present by the French king Philippe le Bel to his daughter Isabelle, on her marriage to Edward II of England. ● *Tues-Sun 2-5pm. Entrance on Rue de Lille (tel: 03 21 99 75 98). 2€, children 1€.*

❯ ★ **Château-Musée** Only from aerial pictures can you appreciate the extent of this magnificent 13th-century fortress, built on the highest point of Boulogne's old town. Inside, however, presentation is 21st-century, with items subtly lit and stylishly displayed in air-conditioned splendour, yet in sympathy with the ancient walls. Exhibition themes vary, but you can expect to see a well-preserved mummy and exquisite Egyptian statuettes and charms, mostly donated by Boulogne-born Egyptologist Auguste Mariette (1821-81), instigator of the Cairo Museum. Other highlights are the Greek and Etruscan vases (pictured left), Renaissance sculptures, and a superb collection of masks and tribal art from Africa, Alaska and Polynesia. A prehistory ⫸➜ *page 73*

■ Delights of the Opal
Coast and countryside:
clockwise from above:
Wimereux seafront;
Wissant mussel beds;
Tilques marshes; Cap
Blanc-Nez landscape.

The V-weapons of World War II

Confronted by the RAF's Spitfires and new Allied inventions, such as radar, Hitler sought fresh ways to deliver missiles to British targets. The first *Vergeltungswaffen* ("vengeance weapon"), or "V1", was fired on 13 June 1944, a few days after the Allied landings in Normandy. These droning flying bombs, nicknamed "doodlebugs", were small, pilotless planes launched from ramps set up in French and Belgian countryside. Some 20,000 fell on London and Antwerp, killing an estimated 15,500 people.

The second of the new weapons, the even more innovative "V2", was a rocket that took off vertically, flew faster than sound, and carried 725kg of high explosive. Fuelled by liquid oxygen, it was 100 times heavier than its predecessor, and was to be fired from vast concrete bunkers, such as those at Éperlecques and Helfaut. Between September 1944 and March 1945, 1,100 V2s were launched on the British capital alone.

The lesser-known "V3", at Mimoyecques, was a "supergun" installed inside an underground bunker in the Marquise area in 1944. Codenamed "*Hochdruckpumpe*", or "high-pressure pump", it was intended to fire 350 missiles a day on London.

However, persistent Allied bombing damaged the launch capacities of the V2 blockhouses, and totally incapacitated the V3 before it could be brought into action.

>**Blockhaus d'Éperlecques** Emerging from a woodland path, you come across this jaw-droppingly massive World War II bunker, intended to fire deadly V2 rockets on London and on the Allied port of Antwerp. The 22-metre-high monolith is the largest blockhouse ever built, and incorporated a convex roof designed to throw off bombs and other projectiles. As building progressed, the roof was gradually jacked up, so that work could continue in relative safety beneath.

Panels in French (with occasional English explanations), backed up by press-button commentary-points in English, tell you about the rise of Hitler, the building of the blockhouse, and wartime advances in technology such as asdic (echo-sounding) and radar.

The locals were told that this huge project

was a power station, but—having linked the building with information supplied by the French Resistance, with aerial reconnaissance pictures taken by the RAF, and with intelligence on Peenemünde (see La Coupole)—the Allies tumbled to its intended function. Bombing of the site began in August 1943, and continued for almost 12 months, culminating in the use of 5-ton "Tallboy" bombs specially developed by Barnes Wallis to pierce concrete 5 metres thick. (One is on display inside the bunker.) A memorial commemorates French flying ace René Mouchotte, who was killed leading an escorting squadron of RAF Spitfires during a raid. These attacks halted the building work (the bunker is only one-third of its planned size), and the place was given over to producing liquid oxygen to fuel the V2s rather than to launching them.

Within the dank interior, the dimensions are even more awe-inspiring. There's a map of V1, V2 and V3 sites, and a short audio-visual show about the building and the weapons. Outside, you can see a V1 flying bomb on its 45-metre-long launch ramp. Allow at least 75 minutes for the visit; if a tour is about to start, you can join it for no extra charge (but leave a tip for the guide in the American helmet near the exit). ◑ *1 Mar-30 Nov, daily 2.15-5pm (1-30 Apr, daily 10am-noon & 2.15-6pm; 1 May-30 Sept, daily 10am-7pm; 1-31 Oct, daily 10am-noon & 2.15-6pm). Rue des Sarts, Éperlecques, 12km NW of St-Omer (tel: 03 21 88 44 22). 7€, students 5.50€, children 4.50€.* ⑆ ❺

■ Deadly innovations: domed roof and V1 flying bomb, opposite, at La Coupole; model V2 rocket, opposite, and a V1 ramp, below, at Éperlecques bunker.

❯ ★ La Coupole Eat a big breakfast and go early in the day to this vast underground complex, because you are bound to remain mesmerised for hours. Created inside one of Hitler's giant bunkers, this modern museum offers a mass of audio-visual material, and informative displays on two distinct aspects of World War II: the events of 1940-45 in the north of France, and the development of the V2s. An additional exhibition treats a different, associated theme each year.

At reception, staff issue free headsets providing English commentary for film shows; display panels all have English translations. Armed with a descriptive leaflet and a plan, you walk down a tunnel into the hill, and are whisked up in a reassuringly 21st-century lift.

You emerge in a display area beneath the dome, where examples of the redoubtable V1s and V2s hang from the ceiling. Like Éperlecques, La Coupole was intended to be a launch site for the 14-metre-long V2 rockets. An excellent animated model on this level shows them arriving by train, being conveyed inside the hill, and made ready for firing. (Damage from Allied bombing meant the missiles were eventually launched from mobile units set up in nearby countryside.)

From this hall, you have a choice of two circuits, each starting with a 20-minute film. It doesn't matter which you select first: after each you exit to a lower level to find videos and information panels on the same theme, before following "continuation of tour" signs back up to the hall. From here you set out again, starting with the second film show and its associated, different circuit.

The film in the Rex cinema describes Germany's research station at Peenemünde, on the Baltic coast. Here the Luftwaffe developed the engine-powered V1 flying bomb, while brilliant young scientist Wernher von Braun masterminded the design of the V2—the world's first liquid-fuelled rocket. (After the war, the US took Braun to work on its space project, including the Apollo missions; other members of his team joined the Russian, French and British space programmes.) On the lower floor, displays give more detail, including horrific footage of Dora concentration camp, whose inmates were forced to work on building the Peenemünde base and its weapons. Panels, photographs and models show French launch sites for V1s and V2s, and the location of the V3 gun.

In both downstairs sections, be sure to follow the descriptive panels in chronological order (indicated by a number at the top left). Labelling of the short videos can be confusing: one number is shown on your leaflet, a different one by the screen itself and a third on an explanatory panel alongside. There are sometimes two films, one after the other, too. It helps if you tick off each one on your leaflet, as you view it.

The Cinéac cinema shows a film on World War II covering the German invasion of Poland, the fall of Holland, Belgium and Luxembourg, and the Allied withdrawal to Dunkerque. It portrays life in occupied France, when the *départements* of the Nord and Pas-de-Calais were "forbidden zones" and cut off from the rest of the country. The occupiers seized industrial output, banned access to the coast, and requisitioned supplies, leaving the population enduring near-famine. In early 1944, the north suffered bombardment from Britain, designed to suggest that it was the likely site for an Allied invasion. Subsequent displays on the lower level emphasise that at the end of the war the north was among the most devastated regions of France, with ruined ports, paralysed railways, flooded farmland, and wrecked factories and mines.

Still in numbered, chronological order, these panels are grouped under the headings: Invasion, Occupation and Liberation. Some harrowing films show the discovery of the Nazi death camps. Many of the video and sound clips are intensely moving, particularly a letter written by a Resistance worker before his execution, and Churchill's stirring speech of October 1940 assuring the French people that "dawn will come".

Allow at least three hours, for your visit, though you may decide to stay twice as

■ **Tunnel vision: V3 gun site at Mimoyecques.**

long. Take a sweater with you, as the efficient air-conditioning makes it cool inside. If you plan a trip here with children, think carefully about whether they are of an age to take it in. It might suit older ones with an interest in World War II, but there is so much to read, view and reflect upon that younger children could be either bored or traumatised, according to age. ● *Daily 9am-6pm (1 July-31 Aug, daily 10am-7pm). Closed late Dec-early Jan. On D210, 2km N of Helfaut, 5km S of St-Omer; 4km N of J4 of A26 (tel: 03 21 12 27 27). 9€, students 7.50€, children 6€; family (2+5) 19.50€.* ♿ ⚲ ⬤

❯**Forteresse de Mimoyecques** Also called the "Canon de Londres", this sinister site contained the V3, a series of five giant guns designed to unleash 350 shells a day on London, 150km away. Missiles were to be fired through long barrels, with explosions in side-barrels providing the extra thrust to expel the shells at 1,500 metres per second.

After a brief introduction from the site's owner, you head into the hill down a chilly, 600-metre-long tunnel, guided by explanatory panels and occasional buttons to press for a commentary (in English) describing the construction and its armament. Side tunnels lead to the emplacements for the guns; some of their rail mountings can still be seen.

Beneath 100 feet of chalk, slave workers laboured to build installations on several levels. Thanks to local information and aerial reconnaissance, however, the activity was noticed, and Allied Tallboy bombs (see page 71) eventually put the site out of action before a shot was fired. Memorials to aviators who perished in the attacks include one to Joseph Kennedy, brother of John F Kennedy; others commemorate thousands of Soviet, Polish and Jewish labourers of the Todt organisation (see page 63) who died of starvation, ill-treatment and overwork, or were buried alive during raids. ◑ *1 Apr-11 Nov, daily 11am-6pm (1 July-31 Aug, daily 10am-7pm). Landrethun-le-Nord, 7km NE of Marquise (tel: 03 21 87 10 34). 5.50€, children 4€.* ⬤

◀─◀◀◀ section presents flint tools, Bronze Age axeheads and Gallo-Roman glass, all found in the area. The medieval period is evoked with church sculpture, a funeral slab of a former Count of Boulogne and beautifully-carved ivory sconces. Down at lower levels, artful illumination highlights the Roman foundations and the remains of Romanesque carvings. At the end you reach the Barbière, an elegantly-vaulted room that was once a gunpowder store.

For 2€ you can rent a headset at the museum for an hour-long outdoor tour (in English) of the ramparts, from which there are panoramic views over town and port. (Leave passport or other ID as deposit.) ● *21 Jan-22 Dec, Mon & Wed-Sat 10am-12.30pm & 2-5pm; Sun 10am-12.30pm & 2.30-5.30pm. Rue de Bernet (tel: 03 21 10 02 22). 1€ (2€ to include temporary exhibitions), children free; free to all on first Sun of month.* 📞 📎

>Maison de la Beurière There can be no steeper street anywhere than Rue du Mâchicoulis. It is, in fact, a flight of 120 stone steps on the side of a cliff opposite Nausicaa, in Boulogne's old fishermen's quarter of La Beurière. Its little houses, built around 1870, are typical of those once lived in by the closely-knit, 10,000-strong fishing community. Charles Dickens, who spent three summers on holiday near Boulogne, found the locals "the most picturesque people we have ever encountered", and described the women of La Beurière as having "the finest legs ever carved by Nature in the brightest mahogany".

One house, about halfway up, has been turned into a charming museum of the way of life of fishermen and their families. The ground floor, living quarters of around eight people, is furnished in the style of 1900. It has a pristine front parlour; a kitchen (where children would be put to bed in the cupboard, on bunks slotted in one above the other); and a tiny back yard for storing fishing equipment and fuel. Upstairs, in what would have been the apartment of another family, wall panels and photographs describe life in this district—a female domain, since the men spent 300 days a year at sea, fishing herring off Scotland and cod off Iceland; boys would join the fleet at 11. (A few sheets of description in English lie on the window ledge; the information panels contain some of Dickens' rapturous prose.) In the back room are some of the radiant lace head-dresses, aptly called *soleil*, or sunburst (the deeper their band of lace, the more wealthy the wearer), and the showy, gold earrings that every fisherman's wife aspired to own. On the top floor are a library and study centre. ● *Wed, Sat, Sun 10am-noon & 2-5pm (15 June-15 Sept, Tues-Sun 10am-1pm & 3-6pm). 16 Rue du Mâchicoulis (tel: 03 21 30 14 52). 2€, children 1€.* 📎

■ **Gateway to history: Château of Boulogne.**

BOULOGNE EXTRAS

Atelier du Bois An amazing shop, in a renovated farm, sells thousands of modern wooden toys. Tues-Sat 10am-noon & 3-7pm, Sun 3-7pm. La Libourdière, off Route de Crémarest (D238), Bellebrune, 12km E of Boulogne (tel: 03 21 83 83 77).

Anglican services: Eucharist, 1st, 3rd & 4th Sun of month, 10.30am. St Anne's Chapel, 9 Rue Traversière, St-Martin-lès-Boulogne; 1.5km NE of old town.

Ferry port: 1km W of Boulogne, on S side of river Liane. Signposted "Boulogne-Port" & "Car Ferry" from J29 of A16.

>Musée Libertador San Martin/Casa San Martin A dignified town house on Boulogne's main street seems an unlikely place to commemorate a military genius who delivered several South American countries from three centuries of Spanish occupation. General José de San Martin (1778-1850) moved from his native Argentina to Spain at the age of six. After studying at Spain's military academy he returned to his homeland in 1816 and drove the Spanish from it. Next, after a 25-day trek west across the Andes with 6,000 troops (chewing onions and garlic to counteract the lack of oxygen), he succeeded in liberating Chile. He then built a navy and sailed up the Pacific coast towards Peru; the occupying Spanish, hearing that he had set out and that Simon Bolivar was also advancing from the north, fled.

A military man rather than a politician, San Martin declined governmental roles in any of these newly independent countries, and instead took voluntary exile in Europe. In 1848, the "Father of Argentina" and his daughter rented rooms in this house where, after two years, the general died. Some rooms are furnished in the style of San Martin's day; others are filled with maps, uniforms, portraits of steely-eyed military leaders, and large paintings of the general's exploits. Captions are in French and Spanish, but the English-speaking curator is happy to explain all to British visitors. ● *1 Feb-31 Dec, Tues-Sat 10am-noon & 2-6pm. Closed public holidays. 113 Grande Rue (tel: 03 21 31 54 65). Admission free.*

■ **Argentina in Boulogne: home of the Liberator, General José de San Martin.**

LE PORTEL-PLAGE (BOULOGNE)

ⓘ 13 Place Poincaré (tel: 03 21 31 45 93)
www.ot-leportel-plage.com
info@ot-leportel-plage.com

LE PORTEL-PLAGE

Market: Tues & Fri.
Festivals:
Fête du Welsh Brocante
fair, open-air pop concert, &
toasted cheese served
in local restaurants, Aug.

Just south of Boulogne, between the port's wind turbines and the heights of Cap d'Alprech, lies a small, flower-filled seaside resort that is both child- and handicapped-friendly. Near the top of the beach is a large collection of *flobarts*, the small open fishing boats that are often launched around low tide (see page 62) by a fleet of ancient tractors. Low water is also the time for a close look at the strange Fort de l'Heurt, built by Napoleon to protect Boulogne, and endowed by the Germans in 1940 with a concrete machine-gun platform. When the tide is out, the stone building looks like a beached liner, overhanging its eroded, rocky support.

The curiosity of Equihen-Plage, 3km farther south, is "*les quilles en l'air*". In the past, poor families would live under upturned boats ("keels in the air"). Though nobody does so today, you can see that the village's clifftop campsite has adopted the design for its holiday chalets.

❯**Maison du Patrimoine** A surprisingly good presentation of the traditional life of Le Portel-Plage is laid out on the first floor of a mundane-looking building, through a gateway signposted "*radio maritime*". Created on a minuscule budget, but with wit and style, the displays use cardboard figures and good explanatory panels (in French) to describe local customs, the social hierarchy, the life of Le Portel's fishermen, and the village's heyday as a seaside resort from 1825, when the smart set began to flock here for the sandy beach and high-wheeled "bathing machines". You read about the legendary "Route du Poisson" or "fish route", by which (until overtaken by the railways in 1848) relays of sturdy white Boulonnais horses would deliver the day's catch to Paris within 24 hours. There are several photographs of stalwart fishermen; a mock-up of a typical fisherman's house; and diagrams of the intricate knotting used to create fishing-nets. ○ *1 July-31 Aug, Tues-Sun 3-6pm. Rue du Cap, signposted 1km S of Le Portel (tel: 03 21 87 73 73). Admission free.*

CALAIS

ⓘ 12 Boulevard Clemenceau (tel: 03 21 96 62 40 fax: 03 21 96 01 92)
www.calais-cotedopale.com
ot@ot-calais.fr

With its busy ferry port and tunnel terminal, Calais sees the arrival of around 11 million passengers from Britain each year. Its layout can be confusing for first-time visitors, since there are two parts to the town, each with its own history and distinctive character.

Nearer to the ferry port, the "old" centre (in fact, almost entirely rebuilt since World War II) is effectively an island. When fortifying it in the 17th century, Vauban (see page 46) surrounded the walls with defensive canals, spanned even today by only half a dozen bridges. In the 19th century the town was extended southwards onto the "mainland", which is where you find Calais' railway station, the 75-metre-high belfry, and, farther south, the wider streets and boulevards of the former lace-making district of St-Pierre.

The northern part has just the chunky, 13th-century watch-tower, the Tour de Guet, to remind you it was the heart of the town in the Middle Ages. The 1950s rebuilding is mostly in brick; main sights are the Rue Royale shops, Place d'Armes market and Notre-Dame church, plus the tourist office and the fine-arts museum (where you can see a model of medieval Calais, as it was until 1940). Its reconstructed waterfront may not merit the adjective "picturesque", but it does have the town's best restaurants.

To the south of the station, the 800-metre-long Boulevard Jacquard links the flamboyant brick town hall to an area of more sober, Victorian-style buildings. Here, the attractions are Place Crèvecoeur market, the modern shops (including the 4B shopping mall at the junction of the four main boulevards) and—opening in 2008—a new museum devoted to the town's still-active lace industry. In 1816 Nottingham lacemakers imported tulle machines and set up business in the St-Pierre quarter. The adaptation for lace of Joseph Marie Jacquard's punch-card weaving system, in 1838, enabled machine-made lace to compete with hand-made in appearance, but at a far lower price. Demand rocketed, and Calais enjoyed a period of great prosperity.

The town has endured two periods of English military occupation. The first—during and after the Hundred Years War—lasted 211 years, after Calais was successfully besieged by Edward III in 1346-47. Outside the town hall, Rodin's craggy, 19th-century bronze *Bourgeois de Calais*, commemorates the six emaciated dignitaries who handed the keys to the English king on the town's surrender. Calais was won back for France by the Duc de Guise in 1558, a loss resented bitterly on her deathbed by the Tudor queen Mary I.

The second occupation lasted for three years after the fall of Napoleon, with some 30,000 English soldiers garrisoned in the Pas-de-Calais from 1815. In their wake came many civilian residents. Some were disgraced or destitute. Nelson's bereft Lady Hamilton sought refuge from her debts, and died here in 1815. Financial embarrassment forced the dandy "Beau" Brummel to Calais in 1816, where he led a colourful life for 14 years. (Brummel was subsequently appointed British consul in Caen, where he remained until his death in 1840.) By 1819 a 1,000-strong British population in the Calais area had launched two English-language newspapers, later augmented by schools, a bookshop and Anglican chapels.

> Musée des Beaux-Arts et de la Dentelle In a quiet parkside street near the tourist office is the town's modest, but well-presented museum. Its collection of sculpture includes several small pieces by Auguste Rodin, among them models for his celebrated 1885 work the *Bourgeois de Calais* (pictured left). Sharing the space until 2008 is the lace museum, displaying everything from babies' robes to sexy underwear, from 17th-century collars and cuffs to dresses by Dior and Miyake. In the early 20th century, the lace industry employed 40,000 people in Calais; today it's a tenth of that.

Most captions are in English, though the interesting 15-minute video on lace-making is in French only. A model of the town in 1899 gives a rare glimpse of pre-1940 Calais. Elsewhere are watercolours and oil paintings of local scenes, and a selection of modern photographs. ● *Mon & Wed-Fri 10am-noon & 2-5.30pm; Sat 10am-noon & 2-6.30pm; Sun 2-6pm. Closed public holidays. 25 Rue Richelieu (tel: 03 21 46 48 40). Admission free.* &

■ **High drama: Flemish-style belfry with Rodin's moving "Bourgeois de Calais".**

> ## Musée de la Seconde Guerre Mondiale

Calais' large museum on World War II, located inside a creeper-covered German bunker in a park opposite the Hôtel de Ville, is fascinating to those interested in uniforms, guns, ammunition and aircraft. Inside this former naval command post, the tunnels and side rooms are crammed with photographs, posters and objects concerning different aspects of the war in the Calais area. Captions are mostly in English throughout, but it's worth taking an audioguide

■ **Punch-card genius: Joseph Marie Jacquard was responsible for the prosperity of 19th-century Calais.**

as well, which gives brief extra descriptions in English. As the rooms are arranged by themes, rather than chronologically, it does require a lot of reading to absorb the sequence of events, but it is none the worse for that.

Setting off anti-clockwise, you see photographs of 1940 bomb damage to Calais (apart from its Tour de Guet and its lighthouse, almost nothing was left standing). There are copies of Marshal Pétain's speech exhorting the French to collaborate with the invaders, and of General Charles de Gaulle's call to arms to his countrymen, broadcast from London the following day. Photographs and newspapers recount the declaration of war on Germany by France and Britain in 1939. They describe the fall of the town on 26 May 1940, its liberation by the Canadians on 29 September 1944, and a tragic sequel when the Allies bombed Calais on 27 February 1945, killing 127 people, under the impression they were attacking German-held Dunkerque.

Scores of uniformed dummies are dressed as airmen, tank crews and medics; there are weapons, gas masks, bits of fighter aircraft and models of German and Allied tanks. A section on the German "secret weapons" covers the V1 flying bombs, the V2 rockets, and the mighty V3 gun (see page 70), and a map of Kent shows where V1 missiles fell—making it clear why the county was known as "Bomb Alley".

There are drawings and paintings by some of the 1.5 million French servicemen who spent five years as prisoners of war. Young Frenchmen at home were encouraged to go and work in Germany in exchange for the release of the same number of French POWs (who could not legally be made to work by their captors). This was the forerunner of the *Service du Travail Obligatoire*, a scheme that made it compulsory for young men to work for the Germans. Other rooms deal with the Resistance, and with post-Liberation visits to the town by General de Gaulle. There is plenty to read on the way round, so a visit could take a good couple of hours. The shop sells military souvenirs. ◑ *Mid Feb-31 Mar, Wed-Mon 11am-5pm; 1 Apr-30 Sept, daily 11am-5.30pm (1 May-31 Aug, daily 10am-6pm); 1 Oct-15 Nov, Wed-Mon noon-5pm. Parc St-Pierre, Avenue du Président Wilson (tel: 03 21 34 21 57). 6€, children 5€; family (2+2) 14€.* ♿ 🐾 🚫

> ## Église Notre-Dame

This large church, to the east of Rue Royale, was built largely during the English occupation of the 15th and 16th centuries. (Its interior is, unbelievably, still waiting for restoration after World War II bombing.) A plaque near one of the windows inside records a significant event that took place here in 1921—the marriage on 7 April of Captain Charles de Gaulle to a local girl, Yvonne Vendroux. The bride is recorded as having expressed the fear that: "I shall look ridiculous, because he is 40cm taller than I am." ● *Rue Notre-Dame (500m NE of tourist office).*

CALAIS EXTRAS

Market: Wed & Sat, Place d'Armes; Thurs & Sat, Place Crèvecoeur.

Accommodation:

Holiday Inn Calais-Nord Central waterfront position. Rooms from 96€; possible garage parking. Bd des Alliés (tel: 03 21 34 69 69). www.holidayinn.co.uk/

Hotel Meurice Traditional 3-star establishment in centre. Rooms from 79€; restaurant La Diligence, menus 18-50€; possible garage parking. 5-7 Rue Edmond-Roche (tel: 03 21 34 57 03). www. hotel-meurice.fr/

Restaurants:

Le Channel Delicious food, in chic seafront setting. Menus 19.50-65€. Closed Sun evg & Tues. 3 Bd de la Résistance (tel: 03 21 34 42 30).

La Sole Meunière Smart dining, near harbour. Menus 18-70€. Closed Sun evg & Mon. 1 Bd de la Résistance (tel: 03 21 34 43 01).

Factory shops: Marques Avenue Designer-outlet centre with some 60 stores offering cut-price clothes, knitwear, sportswear & bedlinen. Mon-Sat 10am-8pm. Bd de l'Europe, Coquelles; N of J41 of A16.

❯ Musée Européen de la Dentelle et de la Mode Due to open during 2008 is an ultra-modern museum devoted to Calais' lace industry. Located in a disused canalside factory in the town's former lace-making district, it has a pinhole-patterned façade that echoes the punch-cards devised by Joseph Marie Jacquard (pictured opposite) for creating designs in machine-woven fabrics, and later adapted for use in the manufacture of lace. (It's no surprise to find a statue of Jacquard standing outside the town's 19th-century theatre.) From 1840 to 1914 Calais was the world leader in lace, whether made from cotton, silk or even metallic thread. The noisy, dirty, tough labour was regarded as a job for men, with women doing repairs, finishing, embroidery and folding. Ancillary industries sprung up alongside, manufacturing bobbins and other essentials. ● *Opens 2008. Days, times & admission charge not known at time of writing. Rue Sambor (off Quai du Commerce), 600m SE of the Hôtel de Ville (tel: 03 21 96 62 40).* ♿ 🐾

❯ Réserve Naturelle du Platier-d'Oye Off the rather bleak coast road near Oye-Plage, is a 180-hectare seaside nature reserve. Grazed by hardy ponies and shaggy Highland cattle, this wetland has emerged over the last two centuries as the sea has retreated. It offers coastal habitats attractive to lapwing, avocet and other waders. Beyond the car park, a 4km circuit leads through scrub (past remains of German fortifications) to the sea, along the beach and back, with occasional observation hides en route. (Bring binoculars, and also boots for wet weather.)

The not-very-visible entrance is 200 metres east of the "*Tour Penchée*", a weirdly leaning, concrete, World War II lookout tower, left at a cockeyed angle after attempts by the Germans to blow it up in 1944, as they retreated. ● *Open at all times (guided tours, in French, first Sun of month, 9.30am). Maison dans la Dune, Route des Dunes (parallel to D119), Oye-Plage, 17km NE of Calais (tel: 03 28 51 94 00). Reserve admission free; guided tour 3€, children free.* ♿ *(part).* 🕲

❯ Blériot-Plage There's a wonderful view of arriving and departing ferries from the 8km stretch of silky sand just south of Calais harbour, backed by pleasant little modern houses. The village is, of course, called after the French aviator Louis Blériot (1872-1936), who made the first successful crossing of the Channel by aeroplane in 1909, entering the record books and securing for himself a £1,000 prize that had been offered by the *Daily Mail* to the first person to accomplish this feat. Blériot and his main rivals—a Frenchman of English origin, by the name of Hubert Latham, and an expatriate Russian called the Comte de Lambert—had been drawing crowds for weeks to view their practice flights and their various attempts on the prize. At dawn on 25 July Blériot took off from a field near today's Blériot-Plage, landing 37 minutes later on a grassy clifftop above Dover, 38km away, where he was welcomed by a flag-waving French journalist from *Le Monde*. Louis Blériot's triumph is commemorated by a fairly inconspicuous monument on the main street of the little French resort that bears his name and, more flashily, by a brightly-painted water-tower nearby.

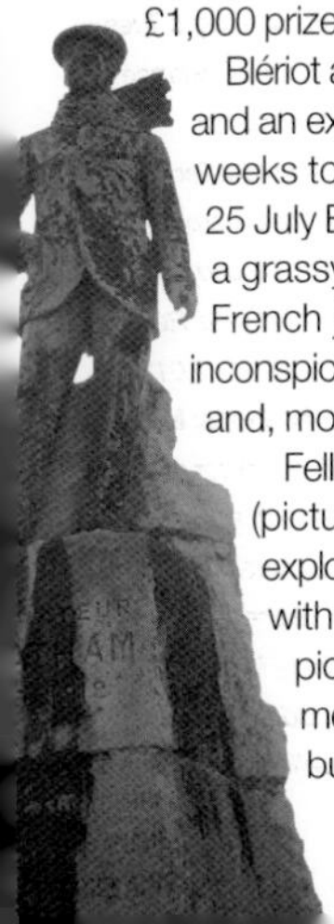

Fellow-aviator Hubert Latham, on the other hand, is the subject of a prominent statue (pictured left), erected by his friends "to commemorate his daring aeronautical exploits". Like a dashing Robert Redford, Blériot's unsuccessful rival stands nonchalantly, with scarf flying, gazing across the Channel from a windswept vantage-point on the picturesque coast road. Latham's interest in aviation reflected his taste for thrills: he met his death in 1912 in Africa, not in a plane crash but in an encounter with an angry buffalo. ● *On D940, near Cap Blanc-Nez, 10km SW of Calais.* 🕲

CALAIS EXTRAS

Shops:

Royal Dentelle Calais lace, from lingerie to table linen. Tues-Sat 10am-noon & 1.30-7pm. 106 Bd Jacquard.

Cité Europe Shopping mall near tunnel, with hypermarkets, restaurants, 130 shops, & Tesco wine-&-beer store. Mon-Thurs 10am-8pm, Fri 10am-9pm, Sat 9am-8pm. Coquelles, 4km W of Calais, J41 or J43 from A16.

Anglican services:

Eucharist, 2nd Sun of month 10.30am, & 4th Sun 5pm. Central Hospital Chapel (through doctors' car park), Calais hospital, 11 Quai du Commerce; 2km SE of town.

Ferry, Tunnel & TGV:

Ferry terminal 3km NE of Calais; follow signs to "Car Ferry" at J47 of A16, & an extension of A26 to the port.

Tunnel terminal 3km SW of Calais; signposted "Tunnel sous la Manche"; J42 of A16.

Calais-Fréthun TGV station 7km SW of Calais; for Eurostar services to & from London, J40 of A16.

GUINES

ⓘ **14 Rue Clemenceau (tel: 03 21 35 73 73 fax : 03 21 85 88 38)**
www.calais-cotedopale.com
ot.troispays@wanadoo.fr

The attractive market town of Guînes, only 15 minutes from Calais, was the setting for a spectacular summit conference between King Henry VIII of England and King François I of France. The Field of the Cloth of Gold, held near here from 7 to 24 June 1520, was a backdrop to negotiations of a possible marriage between the then infant children of the two monarchs, and of a military alliance between their countries against the powerful Emperor Charles V of Austria. Each strove to outshine the other. Henry, at his English-held stronghold of Guînes, dazzled with a 100-metre-long "crystal palace". François, on French ground at nearby Ardres, countered with an equally temporary

■ Top of the town: the Tour de l'Horloge, above Guînes.

structure "as high as the highest known tower". Their meetings took place midway between the two; an unremarkable stone on the D231, 2km SE of Guînes, marks the spot.

The Romans shipped Cornish tin back home through Guînes, which was then a port. Descendants of 10th-century Viking invaders built a motte-and-bailey stronghold, and pilgrims passed through on the Voie Leulène, a Roman road leading from Canterbury to Rome. During the Hundred Years War the town was taken by the English, who held it for two centuries until the Duc de Guise retook it in 1558. With the 1598 Edict of Nantes guaranteeing religious tolerance, numerous Protestants arrived from Flanders, and the town's businesses flourished. However, the effect of the Edict's revocation in 1685 was to halve the population of Guînes, as its non-Catholics fled to more welcoming countries. Economic recovery took almost 100 years. In 1763, town dignitary Pierre le Noir paid for a handsome stone clocktower to mark the return of civic confidence.

➤ ★ **La Tour de l'Horloge** The unprepossessing entrance, and its name that means simply "The Clocktower", do not do justice to this imaginative historical interpretation centre. In about 90 minutes, it recounts the town's past (mostly in English), from the Viking invasion of 928. It covers the meeting of kings François and Henry at the Field of the Cloth of Gold in 1520, ensuing battles with English and Spanish invaders, and the building of the clocktower.

On the ground floor, are miniature recreations of historical events, accompanied by witty questions, and models of foodstuffs of the time. There are opportunities to open flaps and drawers, do brass-rubbing and to finger samples of fabrics and building materials. (You can return to this part later, if your time for the film screening comes up before you have finished.)

For the 15-minute film show, you sit in a re-creation of a *drakkar* (a Norse longship), which rocks gently as you watch the tale of a Viking named Sifrid travelling to this spot, settling here, and building the first fortified place. (Seats near the centre provide the best effect.)

In the next couple of rooms, the continuation of the town's history can be a bit harder to grasp. The first features Sifrid's son Ardolf, seen being dubbed a knight and becoming the first Comte de Guînes. Across the room, a model of Thomas à Becket, chancellor to England's King Henry II, attends a meeting at Guînes in 1169 with Baudouin II, Count of Flanders.

Upstairs, you are plunged into a noisy recreation of the 1558 battle, as the French retake Guînes from the English. Afterwards you emerge into the open, on the mound alongside Pierre le Noir's 18th-century clocktower, for wonderful views over town and countryside.

Back indoors, you enter a multi-media presentation area, where large, swivelling statues represent England's Henry VIII, François I of France and Holy Roman Emperor Charles V (known to the French as Charles Quint). Maps illustrate the inherited territories that made up Charles's empire and explain

■ Moving movie:
watching a film
at Guînes' Tour
de l'Horloge.

diplomatic and family pressures on the three arch-rivals. When you learn of the intricate links between this wife and that monarch (François' wife, queen of France, had once been engaged to Charles V—who was, in turn, the nephew of Henry VIII's wife Catherine of Aragon), you begin to understand the conflicting loyalties involved. Pop on a pair of headphones while you look at a painting depicting the Field of the Cloth of Gold, to hear fascinating details about the conference that almost bankrupted the treasuries of both countries, and failed to create any alliance. On the way out, you can peek behind flaps at sumptuous miniature Renaissance feasts. ❶ *Easter to 1 Nov, daily 2-5pm (1 July-31 Aug, daily 10.30am-5.30pm). Rue du Château (tel: 03 21 19 59 00). 6€, children 3.50€. ♿ (partial)* 🎧 ☊

❯**Saint-Joseph Village** Many signs lead through the marshes to the curious fantasy world of Daniel Baclez. Owner of a successful chain of DIY supermarkets, Baclez felt moved in 1990 to build a small wooden chapel to the memory of his late father, a wheelwright. Later, after adding more buildings, he opened the growing "village" to the public. Some might find it a little twee, but it has been done with passion and dedication, with shops and workshops presenting old trades in slightly smaller-than-life-size buildings of the pre-1950s age. In quite a small, open area are an old-fashioned cycle-shop, garage, grocery store and clockmaker's, all full of genuine old tools. Cutaway displays show the working of a cylinder-block or how a mattress is upholstered, and you can press a button to set a small-scale windmill into action. Its authenticity is confirmed by the coachloads of visiting French pensioners, who stand reminiscing about pulling sugar beet with exactly that type of fork, or how they chopped off a finger on a frosty morning with just that shape of billhook. Visitors can repair to the genuine *estaminet* for drinks and snacks, and to play some of the region's typical pub games. ❶ *Early Feb-15 Nov, daily 10am-7pm (1 July-31 Aug, daily 10am-8pm). 2450 1er Banc, Le Marais, on D248E1, 2km NE of Guînes (tel: 03 21 35 64 05). 10€, over-60s 8.50€, students & disabled 7€, children 5€; family (2+3) 25€. ♿ ☊*

❯**Colonne Blanchard** In a forest outside Guînes, a stone column celebrates the first crossing of the Channel by air—more than a century before Blériot. On 7 January 1785, Frenchman Jean-Pierre Blanchard and Englishman John Jefferies took off in a balloon from Dover Castle, touching down at this spot 2 hours and 25 minutes later. ● *Chemin du Grand-Ballon, 3km S of Guînes; turn off bypass (D231) near cycle-route sign "La Colonne Blanchard".* ☊

❯**Passion d'Aventure** There are treetop trails for the intrepid, aged 10 years and upwards (and at least 1.4 metres in height), on the east side of Guînes forest. Five aerial routes of varying difficulty are strung out among the branches, between 4 and 15 metres above ground, with bridges of netting or of swinging logs, and a 75-metre zip wire. Advance booking is recommended; sessions last about three hours; and you need to wear tough clothes and shoes. Under-16s must be accompanied throughout the activity by a participating adult. ○ *1 July-31 Aug, daily 9am-7pm; last admission 3.30pm. Forêt Domaniale de Guînes, Campagne-lès-Guînes, signposted off D231, 3km SE of Guînes (tel: 06 87 61 32 72). 23€.* ☊

LUMBRES
ⓘ Rue François-Cousin (tel: 03 21 93 45 46 fax: 03 21 12 15 87)
www.pays-de-lumbres.com
otlumbres@pays-de-lumbres.com

The vigorously smoking chimney of a cement works is a clue to one of the main industries of this place 11km south-west of St-Omer. Lumbres is also known for its papermills, still strung out along the valley of the river Aa and formerly powered by its waters. The little town took on increased importance from 1872 as a junction between two railway lines. This industrial heritage is reflected today in Lumbres' tourist attractions: trips on an old-fashioned diesel train; outings on a disused railway track; and visits to a papermill.

Pedal-power: a great family outing on Rando-Rail.

LUMBRES EXTRAS

***Market**: Fri.*

***Golf: Aa-St-Omer Golf Club** On undulating ground, fringed with woodland, are the 9-hole "Haute Drève & 18-hole "Le Val" courses, designed by Dudok Van Heel. Chemin des Bois, Acquin-Westbécourt, 2km NW of Lumbres, & just N of N42 (tel: 03 21 38 59 90). www.aa-st-omer-golfclub.com/*

› ★ Rando-Rail Energetic children (and parents) will love pedalling the blue, flat-bed wagons along a section of old railway line. Strictly people-powered, they have two bicycle-style saddles for those doing the pedalling and a deckchair-type arrangement in between. (Children measuring more than 1.30m in height should be able to reach the pedals.) There are two 5km routes, one through flower-speckled woodland, and the other over a viaduct with views across the Bléquin valley. It's essential to book in advance, as 30 or so vehicles set off together, every two hours. This is not as convoy-like as it sounds, as you have to keep 100 metres of space between each.

Visitors are given a safety talk (in French; a printed English version is coming soon) on maintaining a safe distance, braking in short bursts, and operating the turntable to prepare your wagon for the return run. You are also warned about the possibility of adders (*vipères*) basking on warm days, so not to let children descend and poke about on the ground. Wear trainers or similar shoes, take drinks, and sun protection in hot weather. Special seats are available for babies. As you have to arrive 20 minutes ahead of your booked departure time, allow at least two hours for this enjoyable family outing. ◑ *1 May-30 Sept, daily; departures from 10am. Nielles-lès-Bléquin, 5km SW of Lumbres, on D191 (tel: 03 21 88 33 89). 21€ per wagon (seats four adults, or two adults & three small children; minimum of one adult per wagon).* ♿ Ⓢ

›Chemin de Fer Touristique de la Vallée de l'Aa Climb into a red-and-cream 1950s wagon (a type affectionately known here as a "Picasso") for an old-fashioned diesel train ride along 15km of track through the countryside along the river Aa. During the 45-minute journey between Lumbres and Arques, the train stops at Setques, Esquerdes, Hallines, Wizernes (for La Coupole, see page 71), and Blendecques. The enthusiasts who operate it are planning a railway museum at Blendecques, and hope also to have a steam locomotive hauling the train. ◑ *1 May-30 Sept, Sat, Sun & public holidays. Dep Arques 2pm & 4pm; dep Lumbres 3pm & 5pm (1 July-31 Aug, dep Arques 10.15am, 2.30pm & 4.30pm; dep Lumbres 11.15am, 3.30pm & 5.30pm). Gare de Lumbres, Rue Jean-Baptiste Macaux, Lumbres (tel: 03 21 93 45 46). Day return 6€, children 4€; under-4s free.* Ⓢ

›Maison du Papier Housed in a small factory once powered by the large waterwheel outside, this paper-making centre shows the history of one of the area's most important industries. Informative captions (mostly in English) describe the multifarious uses of paper for making dolls, masks, books and models, and tell you about its vital ingredient, cellulose, which is found only in the plant kingdom.

Probably invented in China, paper reached France in the 14th century. (Before its existence, documents were written on silk, bamboo, tree-bark, leaves, parchment or papyrus.) Demand for it accelerated in the early 15th century, with the popularity of Gutenberg's Bible. The river Aa here furnished energy to almost 100 mills and provided ample water for washing the finished paper, while a ready market existed among the abbeys around St-Omer. Among fascinating paper-related facts, you learn that toilet paper was invented in 1857; corrugated paper in 1871; and brown parcel paper in 1880. Panels explain the work of hammers, shredders and crushers, and a short film gives visitors an overview of a modern paper factory. You may get a chance to make a sheet of your own paper, skimming floating bits of cellulose from water and tipping them onto absorbent fabric to be pressed. Finally, you can see a rather impressionistic 15-minute film (in French) inspired by paper-making. Allow a couple of hours for the visit. ◑ *Early Apr-early Sept, Tues-Sun & public holidays 2-6pm. 15 Rue Bernard-Chochoy, Esquerdes, 6km E of Lumbres (tel: 03 21 95 45 25). 4€, children 2.40€.* ☂

■Papermill: Esquerdes.

MARQUISE

ⓘ Place Louis-le-Sénéchal (tel: 03 21 87 50 52); Sept-June as Wissant (page 86)
www.terredes2caps.com
ot-marquise@pas-de-calais.com

The moonscape-like hills to the east of the A16 between Calais and Boulogne are a legacy of centuries of stone-quarrying. Inside the *mairie* of this pleasant little town 10km north-east of Boulogne are displays of polished Marquise "marble", as used for the steps of the Élysée Palace in Paris, and other prestigious sites. The town has a great Thursday market, a stone museum and, 7km north-east, the site of Hitler's V3 "supergun" (see description, page 72).

❯Maison du Marbre et de la Géologie This interesting geological museum is housed in a brick building with blue shutters, with a forecourt full of large lumps of stone. There is a small car park a few metres uphill.

Marquise "marble" is, in reality, a type of *pierre calcaire*, or limestone, laid down when the whole Boulonnais area was in the tropics. Displays show first the rough stone, and then the cut and polished version that reveals swirling patterns from fossilised vegetation and sea creatures. There are plenty of buttons to press to illuminate insects and plants, and a "please touch" area where you are encouraged to handle different building materials such as flint, stone, chalk and clay. (Ask at reception for the file with English translations of the museum's captions.) An interesting 20-minute film (in French) shows modern quarrying techniques and the huge size of the vehicles that are involved. Anti-pollution measures include constant washing of lorry tyres, watering of roads, and the planting of resinous trees to catch stone dust. Across the entrance hall, you learn that the Channel Tunnel is lined with concrete made from ground-up Marquise stone. An adjacent room contains a model of a sea monster, representing the discovery during motorway excavations near here in 1991 of a 150-million-year-old plesiosaurus.

In July and August, you can also have a 75-minute guided tour (in French) that starts with a steep climb through the woods to view a quarry at the back (sturdy shoes essential). Everyone then takes their own car and follows the guide, in a cavalcade of vehicles, to other nearby sites. At these, you look down on dynamiting and on the endless activity of the gigantic dump trucks taking rocks to be broken and sorted. The largest go to make breakwaters, smaller ones for roadworks, and the finest for the manufacture of toothpaste, make-up and medicines. ◑ *Museum: Early Apr-early Sept, Tues-Sun 2-6pm. 71 bis Rue Henri-Barbusse, Hydrequent, nr Rinxent, 5km E of Marquise (tel: 03 21 83 19 10). 4€, children 3.20€.* ♿ *. Tours to quarry sites: 1 July-31 Aug, Thurs 2pm (must be reserved 48 hours in advance on 08 20 20 76 00). 3.20€, children 1.60€.*

ST-OMER

ⓘ 4 Rue du Lion d'Or (tel: 03 21 98 08 51   fax: 03 21 98 08 07)
www.tourisme-saintomer.com
contact@tourisme-saintomer.com

The massive Gothic cathedral towering above St-Omer, 40km south-east of Calais, and the dignified buildings surrounding the main square, give an idea of the town's former importance. The river Aa was enlarged in the 12th century, opening up St-Omer to more than a century of successful commerce. However, the effects of plague and of the Hundred Years War caused its fortunes to decline from 1300, halving its population. Under Spanish occupation for much of the 16th century, St-Omer became definitively part of France only in 1677. Religious establishments flourished until the Revolution, when many were destroyed. (The stones of the Abbey of St Bertin were taken to build today's 19th-century town hall.)

Though spared by most battles through the ages, the area around St-Omer saw the construction of some of Hitler's most daunting weapons bases during World War II, at Helfaut (La Coupole) and Éperlecques, both subjects of fascinating visits (see page 70).

If you come into St-Omer from the north-west, on the D928, you pass the picturesque district called Faubourg du Haut-Pont, with colourful houses reflected in the river Aa. Another, smaller waterside area lies behind the station, on the Clairmarais road.

Main shopping areas are off Place Foch: Rue de Dunkerque and Rue de Calais, and the narrow medieval streets of Rue Louis-Martel and Rue des Clouteries.

> **Cathédrale Notre-Dame des Miracles** After the destruction of Thérouanne and its cathedral (see page 83), the collegiate church of St-Omer became the focus of a diocese that stretched from Ypres in the north to the river Somme in the south. The magnificent Gothic building contains the tomb of Bishop Audomar (later known as St Omer), who built a chapel on this site in the 7th century. There is an extremely moving painting ascribed to the studio of Rubens, showing the Descent from the Cross, a flagstone maze, and a group of Gothic statues saved from Thérouanne

■ **Angelic: Nativity scene in St-Omer's cathedral.**

cathedral. Beneath the rose window on the north side is an amazing astronomical clock by Pierre Enguerran—a contemporary of Galileo and Copernicus—which has been telling the time, day, month, sunrise, sunset and phases of the moon since 1558. Across from it, small, brightly-coloured shoes are arranged on the stone sarcophagus of St Erkembode (see page 163). Of Irish origin, this fourth bishop of St-Omer regularly travelled his enormous diocese. Pilgrims visiting his tomb in later years took to leaving shoes on his coffin in recognition of his journeys. Today, mothers place on it those of their children who have difficulty walking. An area near the cathedral's south door is devoted to plaques recalling miraculous cures of lameness, dumbness, blindness, and even the restoration to life in 1261 of a child pronounced dead after drowning. You can rent headsets from the tourist office for a detailed cathedral commentary in English. ●
Daily 9am-noon & 2-5pm (1 Apr-31 Oct, daily 9am-noon & 2-6pm). Mass: Sun 10am. Enclos Notre-Dame (tel: 03 21 98 08 51). S

> ★ **Hôtel Sandelin** An elegant courtyard fronts this 18th-century town house, once the winter residence of the Countess of Fruges. (The word "hôtel" has several meanings, including "mansion", as here.) Its basement contains archaeological finds—from 12th-century swords to flintlock pistols, from clubs and daggers to helmets and breastplates. Stone carvings of prophets and exotic animals, a mosaic and other items come from the ruined abbey of St Bertin; fragments of a tomb sculpted by Andrea della

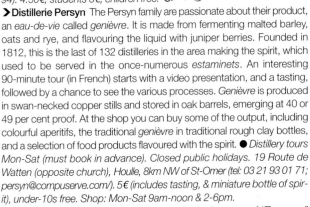

Robbia are from Thérouanne cathedral. The restored ground-floor rooms, with their parquet floors and original panelling, contain ornate silver cutlery, jugs and tankards, cabinets of curiosities and pretty chairs embroidered with scenes from the fables of 17th-century poet La Fontaine (who cribbed many of his stories from Aesop).

Upstairs is a renowned collection of pottery, with pieces from Rouen, Lunéville, Strasbourg, Lille and, of course, St-Omer, plus others from Delft, Spain, Italy and Scandinavia. Don't miss the exquisitely-arranged collection of clay pipes; St-Omer was France's largest manufacturer of these items during the 18th and 19th centuries, when tobacco was an important crop in the area. Patients in the town's hospital provided a cheap source of pipe-making labour. ● *Wed-Sun 10am-noon & 2-6pm (Thurs until 8pm). Closed public holidays. 14 Rue Carnot (tel: 03 21 38 00 94). 4.50€, students 3€, children free.* ♿ 🐾 🛇

■ **Gloriously Gothic: the cathedral of St-Omer.**

❯**Distillerie Persyn** The Persyn family are passionate about their product, an *eau-de-vie* called *genièvre*. It is made from fermenting malted barley, oats and rye, and flavouring the liquid with juniper berries. Founded in 1812, this is the last of 132 distilleries in the area making the spirit, which used to be served in the once-numerous *estaminets*. An interesting 90-minute tour (in French) starts with a video presentation, and a tasting, followed by a chance to see the various processes. *Genièvre* is produced in swan-necked copper stills and stored in oak barrels, emerging at 40 or 49 per cent proof. At the shop you can buy some of the output, including colourful aperitifs, the traditional *genièvre* in traditional rough clay bottles, and a selection of food products flavoured with the spirit. ● *Distillery tours Mon-Sat (must book in advance). Closed public holidays. 19 Route de Watten (opposite church), Houlle, 8km NW of St-Omer (tel: 03 21 93 01 71; persyn@compuserve.com/). 5€ (includes tasting, & miniature bottle of spirit), under-10s free. Shop: Mon-Sat 9am-noon & 2-6pm.*

❯**Musée Archéologique** The Romans made the town of "Tervanna" (today's Thérouanne) the focus of a network of roads leading to Boulogne, Rouen, Paris and elsewhere. By the 12th century it had one of the finest Gothic cathedrals in France; vestiges of it can be seen on a hilltop site to the north of the village. However, in 1533, this French enclave inside Spanish-held territory was totally destroyed on the orders of the Emperor Charles V.

In the *mairie* of the village, on the main street, you can see archaeological discoveries from the area: 2,000-year-old funerary urns, Gallo-Roman glass, medieval objects and sculpted stones from the old cathedral. A fascinating aspect here is the use of large colour photographs to reveal, step by step, the excavation of a 2nd-century tomb, and enable you to share the thrill of discovery. They show exactly how bowls were nested inside each other, one containing a coin so the deceased could pay for crossing the river Styx to the realm of the dead. ● *Mon-Fri 9am-noon & 2-5.30pm. Closed public holidays. Mairie, Grand'Rue (D341), Thérouanne, 11km S of St-Omer (tel: 03 21 93 81 22). Admission free.*

ST-OMER EXTRAS

Market: Sat, Place Foch.

Specialities: St-Omer beer. *Genièvre de Houlle.*

Restaurants:

La Charrette Flemish & vegetarian dishes. Menus 11-22€. Closed Sun evg & Mon. 32 Place Foch (tel: 03 21 98 28 29).

Le Cygne Smart décor & regional dishes. Menus 13-42€. Closed Sun evg & Mon. 8 Rue Caventou (tel: 03 21 98 20 52).

Brocante: Emmaüs Glass, crockery, toys; upstairs section devoted to vintage clothes, bedlinen & bric-à-brac. Tues-Sat 2.30-5pm (upstairs, Wed & Sat only). 54 Rue du Noir-Cornet, St-Martin-au-Laërt; Salperwick road from junction of N43 and N42, 3km NW of St-Omer (tel: 03 21 98 86 34).

Festival: Cortège Nautique Parade of decorated boats on River Aa, Faubourg du Haut-Pont (on NE edge of town), July.

■ Top of the crops: millions of cauliflowers are grown in the Marais Audomarois.

MARAIS AUDOMAROIS
Specialities: Cauliflowers. Chicory. Carrots. Watercress.
Accommodation/food:
Château Tilques 4-star hotel in elegant country house. Rooms from 125€; menus 25-85€. Rue du Château, Tilques, 5km NW of St-Omer (tel: 03 21 88 99 99). www.chateautilques.com/
Relais du Romelaëre 2-star canalside hotel with simple rooms & good local cooking. Rooms from 40€; menus 13-19€. Closed Mon-Thurs evgs. Chemin du Grand-St-Bernard, Clairmarais, 4.5km NE of St-Omer (tel: 03 21 38 95 95). www.relais-romelaere.com/
La Fouace de Tilques Friendly 3-épi B&B, near Château Tilques. Rooms from 32€; evening meal (on reservation) 20€. 29 Rue de la Chapelle, Tilques, 5km NW of St-Omer (tel: 03 21 12 01 65).

MARAIS AUDOMAROIS (ST-OMER)

ⓘ see St-Omer (page 82)

The 3,500 hectares of marshes to the north of St-Omer have been drained by monks and others over the centuries, and the fertile soil now supports a flourishing market-garden industry. Seven million cauliflowers are harvested here from June to October each year, conveyed along the *watergangs* in traditional, black-tarred boats (pictured above) known as *bacôves*. Chicory, carrots and leeks are also important crops, while the sparkling streams around the village of Tilques (pictured page 69) contain beds of bright green watercress (*cresson*). Some 70 families still live along these waterways and work the soil; their canalside letterboxes are served by a postman who makes his rounds by boat.

You can rent boats at Clairmarais, Nieurlet, Salperwick and Tilques, or enjoy guided boat tours from Clairmarais, Salperwick and Arques. Some wilder areas are now nature reserves; the small Romelaëre visitor centre has information on bird-watching and local walks, and on local legends such as that of "Marie Grouette". This spirit is said to live beneath the water and to drag down to her cave any unwary child who strays near the edge. (A mechanical reproduction of Marie-Grouette, complete with her *groët*, or fork, pops out beside the town-hall clock in Arques, 4km to the south-east, as the hour chimes.)

❯ **Isnor boats** The hour-long guided trips into the marshes in large open boats are enlivened with commentary (highly entertaining, if you understand French; otherwise ask for an English leaflet before setting out). During the journey along the reed-fringed waterways the guide steers you across the wide (and busy) river Aa, stops in a small backwater just to let you hear the surrounding silence, and pulls up at a tempting canalside vegetable stall where you can buy field-fresh cauliflowers and other produce to take home. ◑ *1 Apr-30 Sept, Sat, Sun & public holidays from 2pm (1 July-31 Aug, daily from 11am). 3 Rue du Marais, Clairmarais (signposted from church), 5km NE of St-Omer (tel: 03 21 39 15 15). 6.20€, children 5.30€.* Ⓢ

❯ **Le Bon Accueil** Hour-long commentated trips on a different sector of the marshes, with covered boats available in bad weather. ◑ *1 Apr-30 Sept, Sat, Sun & public holidays from 2pm (1 July-31 Aug, daily from 11am). 29 Rue du Rivage, Salperwick (off N43 at St-Martin-au-Laërt), 6km NW of St-Omer (tel: 03 21 38 35 14). 6.30€, children 5€.* Ⓢ

❯ **Maison du Romelaëre** Also referred to as the "Grange Nature", this is the visitor centre for 80 hectares of lakes and marshland that are home to 200 species of bird, and many types of fish, dragonfly and bat. During the 18th century, this huge peat bog was a source of fuel, the extraction of which created the site's 30 hectares of lakes. The small building on the edge of the nature reserve is the departure point for signposted trails ranging from one to four hours in length, across wooden bridges and even using a little hand-operated chain ferry. One 2.5km route, with viewpoints and a hide, is on boardwalks accessible to wheelchairs. Bring binoculars to look at the coal-tits, grebes and migrating birds. ❶ *Early Apr-early Sept, Tues-Sun & public holidays 2-6pm. Rue du Romelaëre, Clairmarais (500m NW of church), 5km NE of St-Omer (tel: 03 21 38 52 95). Admission free.* ♿ *(one route).*

WIMEREUX

ⓘ Quai Alfred-Giard (tel: 03 21 83 27 17 fax: 03 21 32 76 91)
www.wimereux-tourisme.com
officedetourisme.wimereux@orange.fr

★ This delightful seaside resort, 6km north of Boulogne, has a wealth of Edwardian-period seaside houses (pictured above, and page 69) and Art Deco frontages, wide sands, shopping and year-round activity. (Pronounce the name either "wee-merr-err", like the natives, or with a "V" sound at the beginning, which is more typically French.) Stroll round the streets between Rue Carnot and the sea to find colourful façades, pointed turrets, fanciful names, ornate balconies and interesting tilework.

The sea retreats so far along this gently-shelving coast, that most visitors come when the tide is higher, so parking is at a premium then. Children's activities at this "Station Kid" (see page 13) are centred on the north side of the river Wimereux, with games and activities for the under-12s in July and August.

Driving north along the D940 in clear weather, reveals gasp-inducing views of the English coast. The wild dunes around Pointe aux Oies, near the golf course, attract walkers and nature-lovers.

❯Jardins de la Baie St-Jean The sound of trickling water lures you into this ambitious garden project tucked away on the north side of the Wimereux river. More than 40 impeccably-kept plots, each 5 metres square yet very different in style, have been laid out around neatly-paved walkways. Some demonstrate topiary, some major on colour, some are exotic, others wild or formal, and one is laid out in chequerboard design. The adjoining Salle de l'Abbaye St Jean holds short exhibitions of local interest. ● *Daily 9am-5pm (1 Apr-31 Oct, daily 9am-8pm). Rue Ste-Adrienne, 300m NW of tourist office. Admission free.* ♿ ❺

■ Seaside fantasies: the villas of Wimereux.

WIMEREUX EXTRAS

Market: Tues & Fri, Place Albert Ier (1 July-31 Aug, Quai d'Hazebrouck).

Accommodation:

Atlantic Hotel *Seafront 3-star hotel, with acclaimed restaurant, La Liégeoise (menus 35-61€; closed Sun evg & Mon), & brasserie. Rooms from 90€; enclosed parking. Digue de Mer (tel: 03 21 32 41 01). www.hotel-atlantic.fr/*

Hotel du Centre *2-star rooms from 63€; good brasserie menus from 19.50€ (closed Mon). 78 Rue Carnot (tel: 03 21 32 41 08). www.hotelducentre-wimereux.com/*

La Goélette *Atmospheric seafront B&B in 1910 villa. Rooms from 80€. 13 Digue de Mer (tel: 03 21 32 62 44). www.lagoelette.com/*

Shop: Chocolats de Beussent Top-quality locally-made chocolates. Tues-Sun 10am-12.30pm & 2.30-7pm. 9 Rue Carnot.

Golf: Golf de Wimereux *Spectacular views from 18-hole Hutchison & Campbell links course. On D940, 1km N of town (tel: 03 21 32 43 20). www.golf-wimereux.com/*

■ Room for all: low tide on the vast beach at Wimereux.

WISSANT & LES DEUX CAPS

ⓘ Place de la Mairie (tel: 03 21 82 48 00 fax: 03 21 85 39 64)
www.terredes2caps.fr
tourisme@terredes2caps.com

The little seaside resort of Wissant, 20km south-west of Calais, lies exactly between the two points of Gris-Nez and Blanc-Nez. Its 12km stretch of sand, with fabulous views north and south, is beloved of windsurfers, sand-yachtsmen and fly-surfers—and also of families, for the safe bathing and child-friendliness associated with a "Station Kid" (see page 13). There's a lack of seafront bars and restaurants, but make your way uphill towards Wissant's ancient church and you'll find a timeless French village with pretty restaurants, seaside-style shops and simple little hotels. You can see why it appealed to Charles de Gaulle, who enjoyed family holidays in an unremarkable villa opposite the tennis club. Wissant is busy at weekends, so book well in advance if you decide to stay here.

The Site des Deux Caps is the beautiful downland between the two capes, cultivated as vast fields of coloured crops that resemble a patchwork quilt thrown across the landscape (pictured on pages 35 and 69). Even if you have only a few hours in the area, try and drive along the D940 coast road between Boulogne and Calais; in good visibility there are views of England's white cliffs, and of ferries bustling to and fro like clockwork toys. These headlands draw visitors rather in the way that Land's End or John O'Groats do. Geologically, they are very different. The more southerly—Cap Gris-Nez—is composed of grey clay, like the undulating Boulonnais landscape to the east. To the north-east, Cap Blanc-Nez, is made up of the same brilliant white chalk as the cliffs of Kent and Sussex. They have remained relatively uncommercialised, though Blanc-Nez is shortly to be endowed with a visitor centre and improved parking.

There are villages, museums, beaches and lookout points to explore, and signposted footpaths—including a 120km coastal route from Dunkerque to Berck. Fossil-lovers prowl the beaches and base of cliffs from Wissant to Sangatte at low water, especially after storms or spring tides, in search of ammonites, sea-urchins and sharks' teeth. (It is forbidden to use any tools to dislodge these; you may only pick up items from the ground.) Notices around both headlands remind you to stick to footpaths, to keep dogs on leads, not to cycle or play ball games, and not to venture near the edge of the cliffs (the dangers of gusty winds and crumbling rocks are obvious). Down below, you are advised to keep away from the foot of the cliffs in case of rockfalls, and also to avoid being cut off by the incoming tide.

➤ **Église St-Nicolas** A notice outside Wissant's ancient church records that Thomas à Becket returned to England from here on 1 December 1170. (He was murdered at Canterbury just 28 days later.) Inside the church, plaques to drowned fishermen remind you of the perils of the sea. The most curious sight is a small crucifixion sculpture, apparently of a bearded lady. It is said to represent St Wilgeforte who, on being faced with marriage rather than a career as a nun, prayed to be spared. Immediately her face sprouted a beard, making her so ugly that would-be suitors turned away in disgust. ● *Place de Verdun.* Ⓢ

➤ **Musée du Moulin** Adjoining the Hotel de la Plage and the millpond is a tall, 19th-century industrial watermill that until 1968 produced 15 tonnes of flour a day. The ground floor has displays

WISSANT EXTRAS

Market: Wed.
Specialities: Mussels.
"Sablé de Wissant" cheese.
Accommodation/food:
Hotel Normandy *Sea views from simple bedrooms in a dazzlingly half-timbered hotel near church. Dinner & B&B for two people from 116€; menus 19-27.50€. Place de Verdun (tel: 03 21 35 90 11). www. lenormandy-wissant.com/*
Restaurants:
Tie Break *Friendly, modern bar/restaurant at the tennis club. Menu "sympathique" from 12€. Rue du Comte de Lambert (tel: 02 51 68 72 95).*
L'Amiral Benbow *Smart place in a restored stone house opposite the Mairie. Menus from 27€. Closed Mon-Thurs (except July & Aug). 7 Rue Gambetta (tel: 03 21 35 90 07).*
Brocante: Broc'Estival *Annual antiques fair, 15 Aug.*
Festival: Fête du Flobart *Parade of typical local fishing boats, Aug.*

■ **Path to glory: Wissant Bay from clifftop trail linking Les Deux Caps.**

DEUX CAPS EXTRAS

Speciality: Mussels.
Accommodation/food:
L'Escale 2-star Logis hotel. Rooms from 51€; menus 16-38€. Closed Wed lunch. Rue de la Mer (D940), Escalles, 6km NW of Wissant (tel: 03 21 85 25 09). www.hotel-lescale.com/
Restaurants:
La Sirène Seafood & grills at large waterside restaurant overlooking Wissant Bay. Menus 21.50-38€. Closed evgs & Mon. Cap Gris-Nez, near Framzelle, 3km NW of Audinghen (tel: 03 21 32 95 97).
Thomé de Gamond Panoramic views from a hilltop restaurant. Menus 15-34€. Le Mont d'Hubert, 200m S of Cap Blanc-Nez (tel: 03 21 82 32 03).

of baskets and nets relating to the local fishing industry. Up the steep wooden stairs, among motionless belts and machinery, sacks still hang ready to be filled with flour—just as if the workers had gone off for a lunch break and never returned. ● *Daily 2-6pm. Rue Arlette-Davids (tel: 03 21 35 91 87). 3€, children 2€.*

➤**Cap Blanc-Nez** The 151-metre-high white chalk cliffs of "White-Nose Point" are crowned by a monument to the Dover Patrol, celebrating the co-operation between British and French navies in World War I in keeping the straits free of enemy submarines. Wild and windy, the point is a magnet for walkers and model-aeroplane enthusiasts. ● *7km NE of Wissant* 🇸

➤**Cap Gris-Nez** As the closest to England, "Grey-Nose Point" is the arrival place for the 200-odd courageous people who swim the Channel each year. Battling the cold and the jellyfish, they cover the 33km in an average time of 15 hours. A lighthouse stands on the highest spot, surrounded by a compound that is part of the French CROSS organisation (Centres Régionaux Operationaux de Sauvegarde et de Sauvetage). These establishments co-ordinate the handling of rescue operations at sea. As well as having responsibility for this particular maritime area, the "CROSS Gris-Nez" is the French point of contact for other search-and-rescue centres world-wide. ● *6km SW of Wissant.* 🇸

➤**Bouchots de moules** To observe how mussels are grown, head for Châtelet beach, between the two capes. Revealed at low water, but entirely submerged at high tide, are hundreds of large posts called *bouchots* (pictured on page 69). Around them are wound long nets containing the embryo mussels, which are left to fatten at nature's pace. ● *Plage du Châtelet, near Tardinghen, 3km SW of Wissant.* 🇸

➤**Maison du Transmanche** Downstairs beneath the Thomé de Gamond restaurant (called after a 19th-century pioneer of tunnel planning), are illustrations of the often ingenious ways man has dreamt up of crossing the Channel (including one proposal involving a bridge supported by balloons). Until the first steam-powered ships came into service in the 1830s, everyone travelled between Britain and France under sail. Displays show the similarity in geological strata on either side of the Channel, and how Britain and France were first separated when a chunk of land dropped down, creating a rift valley between them and providing a layer of chalk on the sea bed that was ideal for tunnelling. Work first started in 1880 and advanced 1,600 metres on both sides before financial troubles, and Britain's fear of possible invasion, caused the project to be abandoned. A century later the plan was brought to fruition with the seven-year Franco-British project that culminated in the opening of the 50km-long Channel Tunnel in 1994. The last room has a film on this massive undertaking; the moment of the breakthrough, as workers from both sides meet, is surprisingly emotional. ◗ *Mid Apr-mid Nov, Tues-Sun 2-6pm. Closed 1 & 11 Nov. Le Mont d'Hubert, off D940 near Escalles, 7km NE of Wissant (tel: 03 21 85 57 42). 3.80€ (2.50€ for restaurant customers), children 2.30€.*

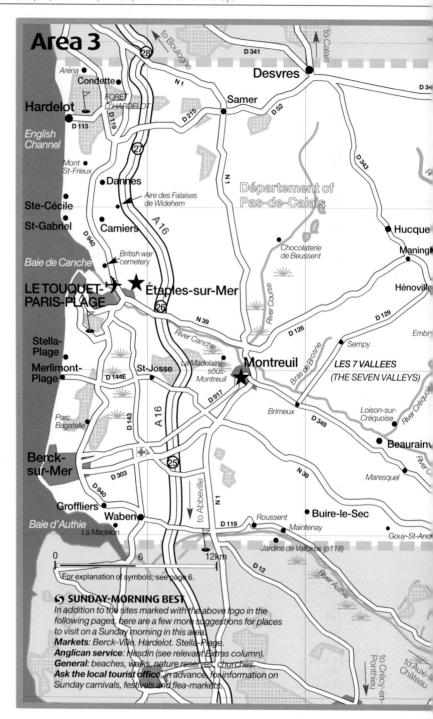

Area 3

to Boulogne

to Calais

D 341

D 34

Aréna

Condette

FORÊT D'HARDELOT

DESVRES

N 1

Samer

D 52

Hardelot

D 113

D 119

D 215

English Channel

27

Mont St-Frieux

Dannes

Aire des Falaises de Widehem

Ste-Cécile

St-Gabriel

D 940

Camiers

A 16

N 1

Département of Pas-de-Calais

D 343

Hucque

Chocolaterie de Beussent

Maning

Baie de Canche

British war cemetery

LE TOUQUET-PARIS-PLAGE

Étaples-sur-Mer

26

N 39

River Course

D 126

Hénovill

D 129

Embr

Stella-Plage

River Canche

La Madelaine-sous-Montreuil

Montreuil

Sempy

Bras de Brosne

LES 7 VALLEES (THE SEVEN VALLEYS)

Merlimont-Plage

D 144E

St-Josse

A 16

D 917

Brimeux

D 349

Loison-sur-Créquoise

River Créquois

Parc Bagatelle

D 143

Beaurainv

River C

Berck-sur-Mer

D 303

N 39

Maresquel

25

D 940

N 1

to Abbeville

Groffliers

Waben

Roussent

Buire-le-Sec

Gouy-St-And

Baie d'Authie

La Madelon

Maintenay

D 119

Jardins de Vallores (p118)

River Authie

to Crécy-en-Ponthieu

to Auxi-Château

0   6   12km

D 12

For explanation of symbols, see page 6.

☉ SUNDAY-MORNING BEST

In addition to the sites marked with the above logo in the following pages, here are a few more suggestions for places to visit on a Sunday morning in this area.

Markets: Berck-Ville. Hardelot. Stella-Plage.
Anglican service: Hesdin (see relevant Extras column).
General: beaches, walks, nature reserves, churches.
Ask the local tourist office, in advance, for information on Sunday carnivals, festivals and flea-markets.

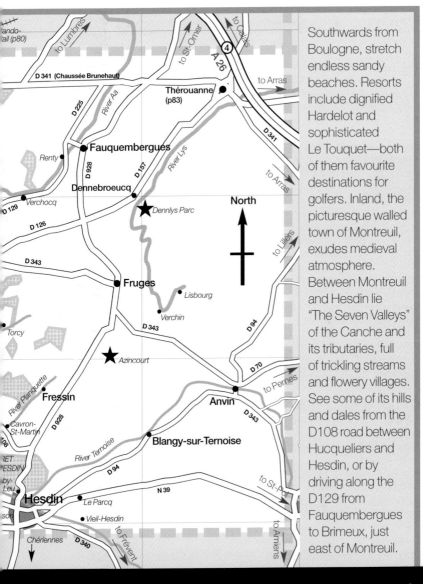

to Lumbres
to St-Omer
to Calais
A 26
(4)
to Arras
D 341 (Chaussée Brunehaut)
D 225
River Aa
Thérouanne
(p83)
D 341
to Arras
Renty
Fauquembergues
D 928
D 157
River Lys
to Lillers
Dennebroeucq
Verchocq
D 129
Dennlys Parc
North
D 126
D 343
Fruges
Lisbourg
Verchin
D 94
Torcy
D 343
Azincourt
D 70
to Pernes
Fressin
Anvin
River Planquette
D 928
D 343
Cavron-St-Martin
Blangy-sur-Ternoise
River Ternoise
D 94
ET ESDIN by-Leu
N 39
to St-Pol
Hesdin
Le Parcq
Vieil-Hesdin
to Amiens
Chériennes
D 340
to Frévent

Southwards from Boulogne, stretch endless sandy beaches. Resorts include dignified Hardelot and sophisticated Le Touquet—both of them favourite destinations for golfers. Inland, the picturesque walled town of Montreuil, exudes medieval atmosphere. Between Montreuil and Hesdin lie "The Seven Valleys" of the Canche and its tributaries, full of trickling streams and flowery villages. See some of its hills and dales from the D108 road between Hucqueliers and Hesdin, or by driving along the D129 from Fauquembergues to Brimeux, just east of Montreuil.

Le Touquet, Montreuil, Hesdin, and The Seven Valleys

BEAURAINVILLE

ⓘ Mairie, 232 Rue de la Canche (tel: 03 2181 03 54)

This village midway between Hesdin and Montreuil, at the junction of the rivers Canche and Créquoise, is on the edge of "Les 7 Vallées" (see page 102). There are opportunities for trout-fishing, as well as for some challenging canoeing and kayaking on the Canche, and for some lovely walks around nearby Loison-sur-Créquoise.

➤**Maison du Perlé** Using a recipe passed down from his grandmother, Hubert Delobel turns out 72,000 bottles a year of "Perlé de Groseille", a sparkling, champagne-style apéritif made from redcurrants. At a shop in the Créquoise valley you can sample this and other fruit drinks, and see a small orchard producing black-, white- and redcurrants. In summer, an outdoor *crêperie* serves savoury and sweet pancakes. ● *Mon-Fri 10am-noon & 2-6pm (1 Apr-30 Sept, Mon-Sat 10am-noon & 2-6pm, Sun 2-6pm; 1 July-31 Aug, daily 10am-7pm). 50 Rue Principale (D130), Loison-sur-Créquoise, 3km NE of Beaurainville (tel: 03 21 81 30 85).* Ⓢ

➤**Jardins d'Evéa** Into their 2.5-hectare garden, behind a suburban house, Sylvie and Alain Dautreppe have crammed more than 20 differently-themed small plots. It takes about an hour to wander round the grassy paths, past azaleas, heathers, passion-flowers and potentillas. (You can pick up a plan in English before setting out.) There are low hedges of box and yew enclosing roses and aromatic herbs, and a Japanese-style bridge to add an exotic flavour to a clutch of oriental plants. Children can look at the pigeons, rabbits, ducks and chickens; crawl through structures made from living willow; or have a shot at the mini-golf. ❶ *1 Mar-15 Nov, Tues-Sun 10am-6pm. 252 Route de Montreuil (D349), Maresquel, 2.5km SE of Beaurainville (tel: 03 21 81 38 88). 5€, children 2.50€; family (2+3) 15€.* Ⓢ

BEAURAINVILLE EXTRAS

Market: Wed.

Specialities: Perlé de Groseille (sparkling redcurrant aperitif).

Brocante fairs Day-long annual events: Beaurainville, mid Aug; Contes, 5km SE of Beaurainville, late Aug.

Festivals:

Fête de la Groseille Celebration of redcurrants & other fruits, with pressings, tastings & sales, mid July. Loison-sur-Créquoise, 3km NE of Beaurainville.

Fête du Cidre Cider & apple-spirit festival, late Oct. Loison-sur-Créquoise.

BERCK-SUR-MER

ⓘ Place de l'Entonnoir (tel 03 21 09 50 00   fax 03 21 09 15 60)
www.berck-sur-mer.com
tourisme@berck-sur-mer.com

In spite of slightly garish first impressions, there is something endearing about Berck (pronounced "baïrk", in case you were wondering). The town is made up of two halves, separated by the north-south Rue du 8 Mai 1945. Berck-Ville is the original fishing village, now stranded 1.5km inland; waterside Berck-Plage grew up later on the encroaching sand dunes, with the 19th-century vogue for sea-bathing. Scattered casually across the sands as if by a giant hand are dozens of substantial beach huts painted in soft opal pinks, blues, greens and yellows—colours appropriate for this major resort of France's Côte d'Opale.

■ **Taking the waters: the healthy sea air of Berck.**

The ozone-laden atmosphere had a positive effect on invalids—particularly children, who in the 1840s were sent to stay with a woman nicknamed "Marianne-Toute-Seule" ("Marianne All-Alone"). Her success in improving the health of her young charges led to the development of sanitoriums, and of hotels to house the families of patients. Grandest of Berck's ailing young visitors was Eugène Louis Jean Joseph, great-nephew of Napoleon Bonaparte. His mother, Empress Eugénie, wife of Napoleon III, brought him here for treatment in 1864, and fell in love with the resort. In her wake came 19th-century aristocracy, who built elegant villas, and enjoyed watching the herring-boats being hauled up the sands.

■ Up, up and away: the spectacular spring kite festival at Berck-sur-Mer.

After World War I, Berck's upper-class image faded as its hospitals filled with maimed war veterans, disabled fishermen and crippled miners. The advent, in the 1930s, of paid holidays for all changed its character again, as industrial workers of northern France decamped here en masse for their annual holidays—rather as the cotton-workers of northern England flocked to Blackpool. Allied bombing during World War II obliterated many fine houses, and an uninspired 1960s style has been favoured for today's seafront.

The town's continuing medical expertise accounts for its vast seaside sanitoriums, and for the slightly surreal sight of people zipping along on the latest crutches or zooming down the promenade in flashy, electrically-propelled wheelchairs. Specialist shops sell state-of-the art equipment, and disabled visitors can borrow beach-going wheelchairs from Agora, on the seafront.

Berck's breezy beach is much prized by kite-fliers (especially for the annual spring kite festival), and by lovers of extreme sports. Kite-buggies and sand-yachts hurtle along the northern end of the 12km-long sands, while fly-surfers perform aerobatic stunts above.

❯**Agora** Indoor leisure complex on the promenade, with covered pool, waterslide, wave-pool, bowling-alley and children's indoor playground. Courses are organised in sand-yachting, kite-flying and other outdoor activities. It's also the place to rent beach-huts or borrow a Hippocampe or Tiralo (see page 12). ● *Swimming-pool: Tues, Fri 5-10pm; Wed 2-6pm; Sat, Sun & public holidays 10am-12.30pm & 2-7pm (school-holiday periods, daily 10am-12.30pm & 2-7pm; Tues & Fri until 10pm). Closed part of Jan/Feb. Esplanade Parmentier (tel: 03 21 89 87 00). Pool: 4.60€, children 3.30€; prices for other activities vary.* ⏳ 🆘

❯**Musée Municipal** Berck's delightful museum has been converted from a former police station. Its bright, air-conditioned interior contains a marvellous collection of works by 19th-century artists—including Eugène Boudin, Jan Lavezzari, Édouard Manet, Charles Roussel and Francis Tattegrain—who were all captivated by the atmosphere of this then-important fishing port. Local industries of herring-fishing and ropemaking are described, and furnished room-settings and traditional head-dresses give a feel for local life. Don't miss the tucked-away collection of 100 mini-portraits of dignified old fishermen and their wives by Roussel and Tattegrain, commissioned by Baroness James de Rothschild. Look out, too, for a shoal of tinkling glass fish by a modern artist, Marcoville.

Upstairs is a beautifully-displayed collection of archaeological discoveries: 2nd-century spoons from the site of the Channel Tunnel; 6th- and 7th-

■ Up the creek: mud berths at La Madelon.

century jewellery that would not look out of place in today's fashion magazines; and some of the region's 17th- and 18th-century pottery. The museum's entrance can be hard to spot; look out for the words "Gendarmerie Nationale" etched into its stone façade. ● *Mon 3-6pm; Wed-Sun 10am-noon & 3-6pm (1 July-31 Aug, Wed-Mon 10am-noon & 3-6pm). 60 Rue de l'Impératrice (tel: 03 21 84 07 80). 3€, children free.* **S**

➤La Madelon An unexpected find is this little harbour in a sheltered creek 5km south-east of Berck, where a few boats sink comfortably into their mud-berths at low tide. Signposted walks lead through reeds, wild mallow and samphire. (It's boggy in places, so good shoes are necessary.) The occasional shacks at the water's edge are the *huttes*, or hides, of wildfowlers. Some are fixed on the bank, others tethered so that they rise and fall with the tide. Always wear brightly-coloured clothing if you are walking anywhere during the shooting season (roughly August to March); it pays to be noticed. ● *1km SW of Groffliers, off D940.* **S**

BUIRE-LE-SEC

ⓘ Mairie, Rue de Maintenay (tel: 03 21 90 33 49 fax: 03 21 86 27 27)

This small village 10km SE of Montreuil-sur-Mer offers a number of things to see and do. Check out the crafts and paintings at the Cité des Artisans shop, investigate bargain knitwear in the factory outlet, or give the family the slip in Buire's giant maize maze. There are fishing lakes strung along the Authie river and, across the water, the dazzling gardens of Valloires (see page 118).

➤Labyrinthe Géant des 7 Vallées Allow three hours to work your way into (and out of) this surprisingly disorientating, 8-hectare maize maze, which provides plenty of opportunity to lose yourself among its "walls" of 3-metre-high vegetation. There's a new design and new theme each year, with clues to search for and questions (in English as well as French) to answer. Wear sunhats and other protection if it's hot, and bring pencils for the quiz. O *Mid July-early Sept, daily 11am-7pm; early to mid Sept, Sun 11am-7pm; evening openings mid Aug, 8pm-midnight (bring a torch). Closed in heavy rain. On D130, NE of village (tel: 03 21 90 75 25/ 06 14 65 83 51). 9€, children under 12 7€, under-4s free.* **S**

➤Cité des Artisans A village-centre barn contains an assortment of hand-made decorative items in glass, wood, metal, silk, leather, wax & pottery. There are also jars of *potjevleesch* and other regional food specialities, including products from the Ferme St-Christophe, of Argoules—which can also be found on the shelves of Fortnum & Mason, in London. ◐ *1 Apr-30 Nov, Sat, Sun & public holidays 2.30-7pm (1 June-30 Sept, daily 2.30-7pm; 1 July-31 Aug & 1-31 Dec, daily 10am-noon & 2.30-7pm). 2 Rue de la Place (tel: 03 21 81 83 94).* **S**

➤Moulin de Maintenay A charming setting on the Authie river for this attractively restored

watermill. The present owners, whose family have been millers here since 1852, show the process of turning corn into flour and then into bread (using a wood-fired bakery across the road). The guide shows how grain is poured through a wooden chute to the four sets of millstones, which are at present driven by an electric motor, and explains the *bluterie*, the giant sieve that separates the flour from the bran. The water power also drove a bandsaw, on show in the first room. There's a delightful *crêperie* and tea-room across the road, with a terrace overlooking the water. ◐ *1 Apr-30 Sept, daily 2-7pm; 1 Oct-30 Nov, Sat, Sun 2-7pm. Bakery open from 11am, crêperie from noon. 25 Rue du Moulin, Maintenay, 2km SW of Buire (tel: 03 21 90 43 74). 3€, children 2€.*

■ **Wheel of fortune: the Moulin de Maintenay.**

BUIRE EXTRAS

Crafts: Poterie du Val d'Authie Eric Debruyne makes glazed stoneware bowls, plates & other items at his waterside studio. 1 Feb-31 Dec, Wed-Mon 9am-noon & 2-6pm (1 July-31 Aug, daily 9am-noon & 2-6pm). 1 Rue de la Vallée de l'Authie (D119), Roussent, 5km SW of Buire (tel: 03 21 81 25 15).

Factory shop: Saint-Kilien Knitwear for all tastes & ages. Mon-Sat 10am-noon & 2-7pm; Sun 2.30-7pm. Chemin de la Houssoye, 1km NW of Buire.

DESVRES

ⓘ 41 bis Rue des Potiers (tel: 03 21 92 09 09 fax: 03 21 92 22 09)
www.paysfaiencedesvres.fr
ot@cc-regiondesvres.fr

DESVRES EXTRAS

Market: Tues, Desvres. Mon,
Samer, 8km SW of Desvres.
Speciality: Pottery. Tarte au
papin (tart filled with prunes
& custard). Strawberries.
Factory & studio shops
(all selling local pottery):
Les Artistes Faïenciers
Mon-Sat 10am-noon
& 2-6pm; Sun 2-6pm.
39 Rue Rodolphe-Minguet.
*Faïencerie Bruno &
Kristine Morel* Tues-Sat
9-11.45am & 2-6.30pm.
159 Rue Jean-Jaurès.
Desvres Tradition Mon-Sat
8am-12.30pm & 1.30-7pm,
Sun (mid Apr-Dec) 10am-
12.30pm.1 Rue du Louvre.
*Festival: Fête de la
Faïence* Pottery festival,
mid July.

This busy little pottery town 16km south-east of Boulogne is the focus of eight intersecting roads, and has a centre organised into a brain-twisting one-way system.

The first pottery at Desvres was established in 1764. After the Revolution, a host of new ones sprung up—the best known being those of Fourmaintraux and of Masse—employing thousands in the production of crockery and ornaments. But the items that made the name of Desvres (pronounced "dair-vr") were the one-off decorative compositions of wall-tiles. Look out for signed examples decorating older shops, cafés and restaurants in the town, and farther afield in places such as Le Touquet.

> **Maison de la Faïence** Tucked away behind the fire station on the south-east edge of town is an interesting museum devoted to Desvres' pottery industry, fronted by dramatically-positioned ceramic squares that look like wall tiles for a giant's kitchen.

The visit starts with an excellent 15-minute slide show on the history of pottery from its beginnings in Mesopotamia and ancient Greece (English version available on request). Early Desvres ware focused on rustic figurines, later diversifiying into tile decorations for offices and shops, porcelain pillboxes, pictorial tiles, and late-19th-century novelty items.

You emerge into a brightly-lit room showing the processes of pottery-making, with tastefully-illuminated tools and pots (explanatory panels have brief footnotes in English). You see the moulding operation used to mass-produce plates and bowls, and the painstaking cutting away of the clay to decorate "openwork" items. Among the sometimes rather garish output were many designs imitating those of Sèvres, Limoges, Rouen, and elsewhere. Items on display include ink-wells, model animals and wonderful shop and café signs, culminating in a monstrous creation made for the Paris Exhibition of 1900. You can buy some of the present production at the museum, or wait until you get to one of the factory shops (see Extras) and hope you will find a bargain. ● *Tues-Sun 2-6.30pm (1 Apr-31 Oct, Tues-Sun 10am-1pm & 2-6.30pm; 1 July-31 Aug, daily 10am-1pm & 2-6.30pm). Closed 1 Jan & 25 Dec. Rue Jean-Macé (tel: 03 21 83 23 23). 4.50€, children 3.80€.* ♿ ☎ ⊙

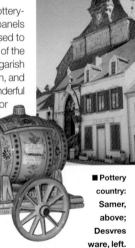

■ Pottery
country:
Samer,
above;
Desvres
ware, left.

> **Musée Jean-Charles Cazin** The pretty village of Samer (pronounced "sam-ay"), is noted for its strawberries and for its ancient church, almost hidden behind a cluster of houses that have been grafted onto it. In the *mairie*, across the square, a room off the entrance-hall displays paintings and drawings by Jean-Charles Cazin, born in Samer in 1841. There are also pieces by his sculptress wife, Marie Guillet, and studies of miners by their son Michel Cazin. ● *Mon-Fri 9-11.30am & 2-5pm. Mairie, Grand'Place, Samer, 8km SW of Desvres (tel: 03 21 33 50 64). Admission free.*

ETAPLES-SUR-MER

ⓘ La Corderie (Maréis building), Boulevard Bigot-Descelers (tel: 03 21 09 56 94 fax: 03 21 09 76 96)
www.etaples-tourisme.com
contact@ etaples-tourisme.com

There are lots of reasons to stop at Étaples, a fishing port lying on the Canche estuary, 27km south of Boulogne. Indeed, in high summer you may have more time to study its charms than you imagined since its pink stone bridge, known as "*le pont rose*", is a notorious bottleneck for Le Touquet-bound traffic from Boulogne, or from the A16.

Between 1880 and 1914, ease of railway travel made the Côte d'Opale a popular destination from Paris. Artists from as far afield as the United States and Australia, settled in Étaples, inspired by its scenery and its quaint fisherfolk. Some of

■ Spinning a yarn: a fisherman describes life at sea, at Maréis.

the paintings and sketches of sailors, fishwives and herring smacks created by these members of the "École d'Étaples" are displayed at the town's Musée de la Marine and Musée Quentovic, while a larger collection can be seen in the Le Touquet museum (see page 109).

Though silting of the Canche estuary has meant that its fleet now has to be moored up the coast at Boulogne, Étaples has a life that still revolves around fishing. There are two museums on the subject; fishing and pleasure-boat trips out into the Canche Bay; quayside stalls selling the freshest fish straight from the nets; and the renowned "Aux Pêcheurs d'Étaples" restaurant near the waterfront, owned by the fishermen's co-operative. For other foods, the large, twice-weekly market on the spacious main square, Place de Gaulle, has a mass of stalls offering everything from cherries to pumpkins, according to season.

North of the huge British war cemetery (see page 96) you can enjoy signposted walks in a duneland nature reserve that lies on both sides of the railway line. A few kilometres farther north still, past dunes ablaze with yellow gorse, lie the pleasant little seaside resorts of Ste-Cécile and St-Gabriel.

❯**Musée de la Marine** The pretty, late 19th-century building near the bridge, which was once the town's fish market, is now an interesting museum of Étaples' fishing history. (If you intend to visit both this and the more high-tech Maréis centre, it's probably best to do this rather simpler one first.) Exhibits are on three floors, and you could take an hour to see it all. Captions and information are in French only, but so much is visual that it's not hard to understand the rigours of this hard life. On the first floor is a recreation of a typical 1950s interior of a fisherman's house. In this society, couples usually married only once there was a baby on the way. Among the costumes, look out for the "*soleil*" or fan-shaped "sunburst" lace head-dresses, worn by the ladies of the coast from Berck to Calais—and which reached their apogee in Boulogne (see page 73). When the boats returned from their fishing trips, the wives were responsible for selling the fish their husbands caught.

On the second floor, there are models of sturdy *flobarts*, early trawlers and of an 1816 steam-powered Channel ferry, and displays of gnarled objects trawled from the depths, such as cannonballs, a whale's vertebra and mammoths' teeth.

A video in French shows the work on a *chalutier* (trawler). The men heave the net in over the stern, releasing a cascade of glittering mackerel onto the deck to be gutted, washed and sorted before the next catch is hauled in. Another section looks at emergency rations, rafts, lifeboats, flares and lifejackets—from old-fashioned cork to modern foam-filled ones. (The most important advance in lifejacket design has been the addition of the collar that maintains the wearer's head above water.) Alongside all this safety equipment is a copy of Victor Hugo's moving poem *Oceano Nox*, lamenting lives lost at sea. Back on the ground floor you can see splices and knots, the development of the ship's propellor in the late 18th century, and various trades ancillary to boatbuilding, such as shoe-, barrel- and sail-making, that were often carried out by disabled fishermen. ● *Tues-Sat 10am-noon & 3-6pm, Sun 3-6pm (1 May-30 Sept, Mon-Sat 10am-noon & 3-6pm, Sun 3-6pm). Halle à la Criée, Boulevard de l'Impératrice (tel: 03 21 09 77 21). 2€, children 1€. ("Pass'Port" ticket, admitting to the four main Étaples attractions, & valid for the rest of the year, costs 10€ & 8€.)* ☂

> ★ **Maréis** A brilliant place for a wet day—or for any other day—this indoor interpretation centre devoted to the fishing industry gives a great insight into the life of Étaples' fishermen today. Housed in a converted ropeworks near the waterfront, just north of the centre, it has a distinctive "sawtooth" roof. Imaginative display techniques ensure you emerge with a deepened understanding of trawling, drifting, line- and lobster-fishing, and dragging for scallops, and also of the camaraderie that binds a population linked by the fortunes of the ocean.

The visit kicks off with a "vox pop" film (13 minutes, in French), quizzing Parisians at Rungis (the capital's main wholesale food market) on the business of fishing. Their brief responses show the scant attention that land-dwellers normally pay to those who risk their lives at sea. (Apart from this first section, there are good English translations everywhere, including on the children's activities.)

A fascinating model demonstrates the action of wind on tide. Children love tickling rays and small turbots in a touch-tank, tying knots, and testing the size of mesh in fishing-nets (illustrating today's stringent rules).

You are plunged into the day-to-day work of the fishermen, as they set off before dawn for Boulogne, and sail in crews of six or seven, for days or weeks at a time, shooting nets, cleaning fish, and snatching sleep between shifts. Back home, their wives run the house, supervise the children's homework, and hope nothing will befall their spouses. You learn that, to build a new boat, a fisherman must not only find £1.4m to pay for it, but must also destroy its predecessor, or sell it abroad. Issues of over-fishing and of foreign competition are well explained, too, along with the effects of fishing quotas. Noisy dockside sounds accompany a 12-minute film of fishermen setting off to sea; you can step into a wheelhouse to see its high-tech GPS, radar and TV screens; a 3D film plunges you into the world of night fishing (special viewing glasses available); and you get to test your sea-legs during a simulated storm. This leads to a section on accidents and safety at sea, with charts of wrecks, displays of modern survival equipment and rations and information on the CROSS organisation (see page 87). ● *Tues-Sun & public holidays 9.30am-1pm & 2-6pm (1 Apr-31 Aug, daily 9.30am-1pm & 2-7pm). Closed 25 Dec & 1-19 Jan. La Corderie, Boulevard Bigot-Descelers (tel: 03 21 09 04 00). 7€, children 5€; family (2+2) 20€ (1 Apr-31 Aug, 8€, 5.50€ & 23€); & see "Pass'Port" details above.* ♿ ☂ ⛔

> **Maison de la Miniature** Alongside scaled-down model vehicles and boats are Ferraris, tanks, battleships, the *Titanic*, and ships in bottles, plus cutaway models of World War II German bunkers. A wonderfully detailed working model (that took 27 people eight years to build) shows

ETAPLES EXTRAS

Market: Tues & Fri.

Restaurant: Aux Pêcheurs d'Étaples The freshest of fish is on the menu at this smart first-floor restaurant, prominently sited on the quay above a wonderful fish shop. Menus 18-35€. Closed Sun evg (except Easter-Oct), & all Jan. Quai de la Canche (tel: 03 21 94 06 90).

Brocante: Grande Brocante Annual antiques fair, with stalls set up throughout town, early Aug.

Festival: Le Hareng Roi Herring festival, involving the barbecuing of hundreds of new season's fish (see picture, page 9), mid Nov.

■ **High and dry: work in the boatyard at Étaples.**

Étaples harbour in the early 1990s as a 1/87-scale representation. Its 2km network of cables causes the tide to ebb and flow, vehicles to dash around the streets—and even a "fire" to break out in one building. There's a "no touch" rule, so however tempting the displays may be to little fingers, you must supervise children. ● *Wed-Sat 10am-12.30pm & 2.30-6pm, Sun 9.30am-12.30pm & 2.30pm-6pm (1 July-31 Aug, Tues-Sat 10am-12.30pm & 2.30-6pm, Sun 9.30am-12.30pm & 2.30pm- 6.30pm). Closed 22 Dec-31 Jan. La Corderie, Boulevard Bigot-Descelers (tel: 03 21 09 78 24). 3.05€, children 1.52€; & see "Pass'Port" details, page 95.* ⑤

❯**Musée Quentovic** Taking its title from Étaples' name in the 7th century, the town's historical museum lies just off the main square. On the first floor, a map shows how France and Britain were joined by a large plain until global warming thousands of years ago caused the waters to rise and form the English Channel. The archaeology section features flint tools, Bronze and Iron Age pottery, Roman salt-making equipment, glass and bone beads, bronze rings, grinding-stones and a large collection of metal pins. Among geological finds are fossilised shellfish and some semi-precious stones. Panels describe how Quentovic was founded in the early 6th century and became an important trading place, before suffering many Viking raids in the mid 9th century.

One room is devoted to the impact on Étaples of World War I, when the town was effectively taken over by the British Army as a depot for supplies and ammunition, and a filtering point for new arrivals. Known to the Tommies as "Eat-apples", it was notorious for its training grounds, known as "bullrings", where soldiers were brutally drilled in bayoneting, grenade-throwing and trench-building before being despatched to the horrors of the front. There is information, too, on the week-long mutiny of September 1917, which followed the arrest of a New Zealand gunner. The duneland site of the present military cemetery (see below) contained a complex of 16 military hospitals, with a total of 22,000 beds. ● *Tues-Sun 2.30-6pm (1 July-31 Aug, Tues-Sun 10am-noon & 2.30-7pm). Closed during Ducasse (funfair) week in early Oct, & 25 Dec-1 Jan. 8 Place du Général-de-Gaulle (tel: 03 21 94 02 47). 2€, children 1€; & see "Pass'Port" details, page 95.* ⑤

❯**Cimetière Britannique** Visitors cannot fail to be moved at their first sight of this, the largest British military cemetery in France. The towering white stone arches designed by Sir Edwin

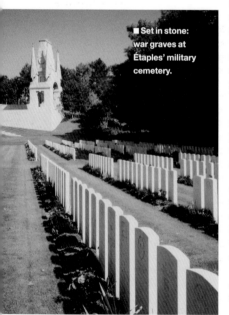

■ Set in stone: war graves at Étaples' military cemetery.

Lutyens look down on white headstones aligned with military precision on perfectly-groomed lawns that sweep down towards the sea. They commemorate 10,774 Allied troops from the 1914-18 war and also 658 Germans. The majority of those buried here during World War I would have died in one of the numerous hospitals on this site (see entry above). There are also 119 burials from World War II.

All Commonwealth war cemeteries have a visitors' book that you can sign, and a register showing the location of each grave. These are kept in a recess in one of the walls, behind a small bronze door. ● *On D940 Boulogne road, 2km NW of Étaples.* ⑤

❯**Opalaventure** Adventure trail among the pine trees, with high wires, scrambling-nets, swaying bridges and lofty platforms, open to adults, and to children measuring over 1m10 in height. Safety briefing given before starting. Participants must wear tough trousers and shoes. Booking is advisable, and all under-16s must be accompanied by an adult. ○ *1 July-31 Aug, daily 9.30am-7pm (last admittance 3.30pm). Chemin des Bateaux, St-Gabriel, 7km NW of Étaples (tel: 06 81 64 23 42). 21€, children 13€ (credit cards not accepted).* ⑤

■ Blast from the past: ruins of the medieval castle at Fressin.

FRESSIN

ⓘ 8 Grand'Rue (tel: 03 21 86 56 11 fax: 03 21 86 56 11)
www.fressin.com
assoc.patrimoine.fressin@wanadoo.fr

This pretty village set in the valley of the Planquette river, 10km south-west of Fruges, was the seat of the once-powerful Créquy family whose feudal castle controlled the passage of troops between the towns of Thérouanne and Hesdin.

Fressin was made famous in the early 20th century by French writer Georges Bernanos (1888-1948), who lived for 30 years in the village, and made it the setting for several books. His 1936 novel *Journal d'un Curé de Campagne*, published in English as *The Diary of a Country Priest*, was made into an award-winning film in 1950. Bernanos devotees come from afar to drink in the atmosphere though, sadly, the family's home was burnt down in 1940, leaving only an ancient, octagonal brick-and-stone dovecote.

❯ **Château Féodal** The leafy green site of the feudal castle built in the 15th century by the lords of Créquy makes a pleasant place to visit and to have a picnic. Keep an eye on children, though, as there are a few hazardous drops. Tickets are on sale opposite the gate, where you are given a map showing a series of commentary-points. (One button provides excellent descriptions in English of the various features.) A series of small formal gardens evokes Paradise, Evil and Good; a steep path leads along the far side of the now-dry moat, giving a view of the fortress's remaining parapets, their foundations made of alternating squares of flint and limestone. Scrambling down and up banks and following a series of arrows, you eventually find yourself in the rectangular inner courtyard where you can descend steps to peer into cellars and underground passages. (It's handy to take a torch.) Built in the days of archery, the castle eventually fell to cannon fire in 1658, when it was taken by French adventurer Balthazar de Fargues. The towering, ivy-covered walls, which are 7 metres thick in places, give an idea of its erstwhile grandeur. The visitor centre has a few cannonballs, fragments of glazed bowls, and models of the castle with examples of typical medieval

FRESSIN EXTRAS

Restaurants:

Auberge du Château
Friendly inn opposite the church, done out in red & gold. Menus from 18.20€. Closed Mon & Tues (open Wed & Thurs evgs on reservation only). 15 Grand' Rue (tel: 03 21 90 63 64).

Le Baladin Eccentrically-decorated estaminet (bits of furniture hang upside-down from the ceiling), serving traditional snacks. Menus from 16€. Open Fri, Sat from 6pm; Sun & public holidays from noon (1 July-31 Aug, Tues-Sat from 6pm, Sun from noon). Live music, Sat, from 10pm. 62 Rue Principale (D130), Torcy, 5km NW of Fressin (tel. 03 21 90 62 51).

Bar: Chés Deux Agaches
Family-friendly estaminet with a large selection of beers, & offering a go at traditional pub games made by the owner. Open Sun 4-8pm (Easter-Oct, Sat, Sun 4-8pm; 1 July-31 Aug, Tues-Sun 4-8pm). Rue de la Mairie (D154), Cavron-St-Martin, 3km SW of Fressin (tel: 03 21 81 49 16).

Festival: Le Château en Fête Annual festival of medieval entertainment around castle ruins, Aug.

siege machinery. ◑ *1 May-30 Sept, Sat, Sun & public holidays 2.30-7pm (1 June-31 Aug, daily 2.30-7pm). Rue Bernanos (tel: 03 21 86 56 11). 2.80€, children 1.50€.*

❯**Église St Martin** Largely rebuilt after a fire in 1525, this charming church is one of the most highly decorated of the Artois region. The stone-flagged floor is laid out in a dramatic chequer-board design, ornate sculpture embellishes the Gothic arches, and stone carvings of leaves and animals wind round the tops of its pillars. There's a primitive statue of St Martin cutting his cloak in two to give half to a freezing beggar (see page 113), and another of local saint St Benoît Labre (see page 164), whom Georges Bernanos nicknamed "*le pouilleux de Dieu*" ("God's flea-ridden down-and-out"). A small chapel dating from 1425 contains the tomb of one of Fressin's feudal lords, Jean IV de Créquy, and an exquisitely-carved altarpiece in Calais stone. ● *Grand'Rue.*

FRUGES

ⓘ **Hôtel de Ville, Place du Général-de-Gaulle (tel. 03 21 04 02 65 fax: 03 21 47 30 07) ot-fruges@pas-de-calais.com**

Seven roads converge on this small town on the D928, 21km north-east of Hesdin, drawing a constant stream of lorries that rattle the buildings and unnerve pedestrians. Fruges used to turn out cobblestones, bricks and roof-tiles for northern towns, and was also the hub of a now-vanished railway system that linked Aire to Montreuil and Berck, and Anvin to Lumbres and Calais. Today, the town is known for its wind farm, which will be the biggest in France on its completion in 2008. The 70 turbines are expected to produce 140 megawatts of electricity, enough to supply the needs of 150,000 households.

With the town's small museum almost always closed, there is not much to visit, but try and pop into the church of St Bertulphe at the crossroads. Inside the west door, an unusual memorial features enamel plaques bearing moving sepia images (pictured opposite) of those sons of Fruges who failed to return from the battlefields of World War I.

One of the brochures for walking routes available from Fruges tourist office is centred on the village of Verchin, 5km to the south-east, known for the corkscrew spire of its 17th-century church (pictured opposite). Legend says that the spire twisted in amazement on seeing the marriage there of a girl who was a virgin, and that it will only untwist when the same thing happens again! At Lisbourg, near Verchin, the source of the 214km-long river Lys is a point of pilgrimage for visitors from Belgium (where the Lys ends its journey, at Ghent). The British, on the other hand, are drawn to the battlefield of Agincourt, 6km to the south of Fruges, in the village known today as Azincourt.

❯**Musée Abbé Delétoille** Small museum near the bottom of the square, displaying pottery, copper, pewter, paintings, pipes and weapons, plus more than 200 old postcard views of Fruges. ◑ *1 Mar-31 May & 1 Sept-31 Oct, Wed 3-5pm; 1 June-31 Aug, Sun & public holidays 3-6pm. Fondation Boudenoot, 1 Rue du Maréchal-Leclerc (tel: 03 21 04 02 65). Admission free.*

❯**Jardin de la Lys** The river Lys runs through the tree-fringed parkland of an elegant country house that dates back, in part, to 1630. The walled garden is being lovingly restored by the château's owners to provide fruit and vegetables, herbs and flowers. Pear trees are trained against the 3.5m-high walls while paths of grass or gravel, edged with hedges of box and hornbeam, divide up areas devoted to roses, rhubarb, grasses, shade-loving plants, agapanthus or hollyhocks. ◑ *1 June-30 Sept; Sat, Sun 2.30-6pm (1 July-31 Aug, Thurs-Sun 2.30-6pm). Château de Verchin, Verchin, on D93 5km SE of Fruges (tel: 03 21 04 41 38). 5€, children 3.50€.*

❯ ★ **Dennlys Parc** Families with children up to 10 or 12 will love this well-designed amusement park, which even has rides for parents and grandparents, and offers excellent value for money. There are plenty of swings, slides and roundabouts for smaller family members, who are often too young or too short to use the rides at more sophisticated parks. Older children enjoy the roller-coasters, multi-seater rocking logs, haunted house, and bumper boats. The only extras are a few slot machines for inveterate gamblers. Take swimming-costumes if you want to use the water flume. (Boys should wear proper trunks, not "shorts"-style, nor cut-off trousers.) It's very picnic-friendly, with shady areas to sit and eat; you can leave your food in the car, and return to collect it at lunchtime. In peak season there may be queues for the most popular rides so the best strategy is to arrive early, as the gates open, or to head for the most popular rides at midday, when French visitors are settling down to a large lunch. ◑ *Easter holidays, daily 11am-6pm; 1-31 May, Wed, Sat, Sun & public holidays 11am-6pm; 1-30 June, daily 10am-6pm; 1 July-31 Aug, daily 10am-7pm; 1-30 Sept, Sun 11am-6pm. Moulin de la Tour, Dennebroeucq, 8km N of Fruges (tel: 03 21 95 11 39). 10.50€ (includes all rides), children 8.50€, under-3s free.* ◉

> ★ **Centre Historique Médiéval** Shakespeare's rousing words have ensured that few British can resist a visit to the site where Henry V led his 8,000 English soldiers to a victory on St Crispin's Day, during the Hundred Years War. In an attempt to assert his perceived right to the French crown and to seize as much French soil as possible, Henry invaded Normandy, captured the port of Harfleur, and set out north towards English-held Calais. The French blocked his main river-crossing-points, obliging Henry to swing his troops east as far as Péronne before turning north-west. Here at Azincourt he did battle with an army three times the size of his own, commanded by Constable Charles d'Albret.

Today this modern interpretation centre helps put into perspective the events leading up to the Battle of Agincourt on 25 October 1415. At the entrance desk you are issued with headsets providing English translations of the various videos, which are activated when you face the screen in question. (Disconcertingly, they switch to another commentary entirely if you turn your head.) This first, fact-filled part is probably not great for young children; however, they may be more interested in aspects of daily life that are exhibited in the room at the end. Twice an hour (on the hour and at half-past), in an enclosed central area, there is a 15-minute multi-media show in English, in a series of three rooms. The first has two life-sized animated figures representing Henry V and Constable d'Albret, musing (painfully slowly) in Shakespeare's words on the eve of the battle; the next room uses a model of the battlefield to explain tactics; the final one looks at the myth of Agincourt in English history.

Far more entertaining is the upstairs floor (picture on page 100), where there's a chance for some great hands-on experiences of the weapons and the protective clothing used by knights and foot-soldiers. You can pick up a broadsword; feel the weight of chain mail; look through a visor to appreciate a knight's limited field of vision; and heave on a rope to gauge the force exerted by England's archers as they despatched the arrows from their longbows. (Their firing-rate of 10 arrows a minute was 10 times that of the French crossbow-men, and a decisive factor in Henry's victory.) ● *Wed-Mon 10am-5pm (1 Apr-31 Oct, daily 10am-6pm). 22 Rue Charles VI (D71), Azincourt, 6km S of Fruges (tel: 03 21 47 27 53). 6.50€, children 5€.* ♿ ☎ ◉

■ **Twisted: Verchin spire.**

■ **Local heroes: war memorials in Fruges.**

FRUGES EXTRAS

Market: Sat.

Specialities: Sire de Créquy cheese.

Accommodation:

La Gacogne *3-épi B&B near Agincourt battlefield. Rooms from 54€. La Gacogne, 1km E of Azincourt & 6km S of Fruges (tel: 03 21 04 45 61). www.gacogne.new.fr/*

Restaurants:

Le Fournil *Sophisticated cooking, popular with businessmen at lunchtimes. Menus 16-39€. Closed Sun evg & Mon; & Tues evg Oct-Apr. 2 Rue de St-Omer (D928), Coupelle-Vieille, 2km NW of Fruges (tel: 03 21 04 47 13).*

Le Charles VI *Elegant restaurant serving excellent food. Menus from 13€. Closed Sun evg & Wed. 12 Rue Charles VI, Azincourt, 6km S of Fruges (tel: 03 21 41 53 00).*

Brocante: Brocante de Tante Mathilde/Tilly's Tea-Room *An eclectic antique collection, from jewellery to stuffed birds, on sale, alongside a pretty farmyard café dispensing scones & Darjeeling tea. Wed-Mon 2-7pm. 23 Rue Principale, Ambricourt, 6km SE of Fruges (tel: 03 21 41 93 80).*

■ Knight vision: get a feel for armour, swords and chain mail in the Agincourt battlefield centre.

❯ **Champ de Bataille d'Azincourt/Agincourt Battlefield** Life-sized cut-outs of archers line the roads bordering the site of the 1415 battle. The English position was in the south-east corner, with their adversaries flanked by woodland to the north-west. In the first 90 minutes, 8,000 French knights and foot-soldiers were slaughtered by the more agile English longbowmen. A cross on the D104, near the Tramecourt road, marks the burial ground of 10,000 French. (English casualties totalled fewer than 500.) At the English end of the road, a discreetly-sited *table d'orientation* has a tiled map illustrating the progress of the battle. Each July, a "living-history" medieval encampment reproduces the atmosphere. ● *4km circuit by D71E3/D107E2/D104/D71, Azincourt, 6km S of Fruges.* ◯

HARDELOT
ⓘ 476 Avenue François-1er (tel: 03 21 83 51 02 fax: 03 21 91 84 60)
www.hardelot-tourisme.com
contact@ville-neufchatel-hardelot.fr

This pleasant seaside resort, 11km south of Boulogne, is surrounded by woods and dunes, and is more understated than its better-known neighbour, Le Touquet. Hardelot's two 18-hole courses lure golfers from across the Channel, while its extensive sands and its "Station Kid" designation (see page 13) make it an ideal place for families.

In 1905 John Whitley followed up his development of Le Touquet (see page 106) with the creation of this sports-orientated resort. Tennis, bowling and golf attracted well-heeled British and Parisian visitors. Among designers of the imposing villas that sprang up was Louis Marie Cordonnier, later responsible for rebuilding many northern towns after the devastation of World War I. He designed a 32-room house for aviator Louis Blériot (who is credited with the invention of sand-yachting, on Hardelot's beach). Cordonnier built himself a splendid villa, too: named "Hurtebise", it stands among a group of others just off the seafront.

■ Distinctive: Hardelot villas by Louis Marie Cordonnier.

This golden era was interrupted by World War I. But an even greater blow was dealt by the next war, during which Allied bombing, and the building of Hitler's Atlantic Wall, destroyed many of the handsome villas.

>Château d'Hardelot The remains of a turretted, 13th-century castle among the trees strike an incongruous note. Largely dismantled on orders from Louis XIII's minister, Cardinal Richelieu, it was transformed into a Gothic mansion in the 19th century. Today the château stands closed up and crumbling, at the hub of a network of footpaths. One can imagine that Charles Dickens might have strolled this way with his mistress Nelly Ternan—whom he installed with her mother at nearby Condette in the 1860s. ● *Exterior only. Rue des Lacs, 3km NE of Hardelot.* **S**

>Aréna You could spend a happy hour or more in this modern, wood-built visitor centre among the dunes. It gives a good introduction to the fragile environment bordering the coast (its name comes from *arena*, the Latin word for sand). An introductory film shows how, in Jurassic times, this area was at the same latitude as Morocco. (English-speakers are well catered for, with surtitles on the film, and English captions on exhibits.) Displays show how shrubs, trees, animals and insects have adapted to this environment. You learn about the uses of sand in railway-building and glass-making, and can can look through microscopes at grains from cliffs and beaches. There are examples of flint, amethyst and other stones found near the shore; a slide show about the flora of the dunes; and a section on animals and birds, showing how to identify wildlife from footprints, droppings or toothmarks. Interactive games encourage you to work out who uses the dunes wisely and who does not. (Here's a clue: hikers and animals come out a lot better than footballers and quad-bikers!) A final film stresses the dangers of global warming and the need to preserve this fragile ecosystem. ❶ *1 Mar-31 Oct, Mon-Fri 8.30am-12.30pm & 1.30-5.30pm; first weekend of month, Sat, Sun 10am-12.30pm & 2-6pm (school-holiday periods Tues-Sun 10am-12.30pm & 2-6pm). Route de la Warenne, 1km W of Écault & 3km N of Hardelot-Plage, well signposted from the D119 (tel: 03 21 10 84 30). 4€, children 3€; family (2+2) 11€.* ♿ ❧ **S**

>Aire des Falaises de Widehem Southbound travellers on the A16 motorway can enjoy a surprisingly close encounter with a wind turbine. From the car park at the *aire*, or rest area, between junctions 26 and 27, near a large wind farm, you can climb a slope and come almost eye-to-eye with the rotating blades. ● *A16, 12km SE of Hardelot. Admission free.* **S**

>Mont St-Frieux There are three signposted walks up and around this hill, ranging from a route leading to the 151-metre high summit, which affords magnificent views over dunes and countryside, to a path around the foot of it that is accessible to wheelchairs. ● *Chemin de la Mer, 2km W of Dannes & 8km SE of Hardelot.* ♿ *(one route).* **S**

■ **Tee-time: Les Dunes golf course at Hardelot is popular with British visitors.**

HESDIN

ⓘ Place d'Armes (tel: 03 21 86 19 19 fax: 03 21 86 04 05)
www.tourisme7vallees.com
contact@tourisme-7vallees.com

The river Canche flows right through this pleasant town 40km south-east of Le Touquet, famous for its Thursday-morning market.

Hesdin was built as a Spanish stronghold in 1554 by the emperor Charles V a year after he had ordered the destruction of a nearby village of the same name (now reborn as "Vieil-Hesdin", or "old Hesdin"). The town was retaken in 1639 by the French king Louis XIII.

Some interesting old buildings take you back to these times, particularly the church, and a house at number 10 Rue Daniel-Lereuil. This was the birthplace in 1697 of Abbé Prévost, author of the romantic novel *Manon Lescaut*.

■ Honey trap: the bee museum near Hesdin.

Hesdin is on the eastern edge of the area known as "Les 7 Vallées", for which it is the main tourist office. These "Seven Valleys" are those of the rivers Authie, Bras de Brosne, Canche, Créquoise, Planquette, Ternoise and Lys, whose sparkling waters run past pretty villages and small farmhouses. The plateaux between them offer wonderful views, too. (See page 89 for suggested driving routes.)

The climate here is good for gardens. Green-fingered villagers plant drifts of flowers, and some even welcome visitors to their private plots (see page 15).

❯**Musée Municipal** Behind a curtain in the tourist office, a couple of tiny rooms that once served as prison cells contain the town's pocket-sized museum. On show are cannonballs and pictures of Louis XIII's siege of 1639. Other objects from the past include pewter measuring-jugs, ancient nails, thimbles, spurs and scraps of pottery, plus souvenirs of Victor Jacquemont (a renowned botanist, born in Hesdin in 1801). ● *Mon 2-5pm, Tues-Sat 9am-noon & 2-5pm (1 Apr-mid Sept, Mon 2-6pm, Tues-Sat 9am-noon & 2-6pm, Sun & public holidays 10am-noon & 3-5pm). Hôtel de Ville, Place d'Armes (tel: 03 21 86 71 69). Admission free.* ◉

❯**Église Notre-Dame** One of Hesdin's oldest buildings is the large church, with its tile-hung tower and ornate Renaissance sandstone porch. Consecrated in 1585, it has withstood the siege of Hesdin, the French Revolution and two world wars. Its interior contains an extravagant wooden canopy above the altar, a painting of St John thought to be by the Spanish artist Murillo, carved wooden choir stalls dating from 1607, and a scene representing the Virgin, Child and angels, sculpted with a depth and perspective that make it seem like a theatre set. ● *Rue de la Paroisse.* ◉

❯**Musée de l'Abeille d'Opale** Behind the honey shop on the busy Hesdin to Montreuil road, you can wander out into the garden of bee-keeper Robert Therry, where insects buzz around the nectar-rich flowers. Indoors, a small museum contains equipment for extracting honey, and an interesting glass-sided hive. A 15-minute video (in French only) is a rerun of a television programme

HESDIN EXTRAS

Market: Thurs.

Restaurants:

Les 3 Fontaines Delicious lunches at 2-star Logis hotel. Menus 17-32€. Closed Mon lunch & Sat lunch. 16 Rue d'Abbeville, Marconne, 1km SE of Hesdin (tel: 03 21 86 81 65).

Ferme-Auberge du Prieuré Fantastic five-course meal, based on home-produce, in child-friendly farm-restaurant. Menu 25€ (includes drinks); children 5-10€. Open Fri lunch to Sun lunch; booking essential. 2 Rue du Prieuré, Chériennes, 6km S of Hesdin (tel: 03 21 86 50 44).

Le Clos de la Prairie Chic restaurant in prettily renovated farm. Home-smoked fish & meat, & elegant desserts. Menus 15-38€. Closed Wed, & Thurs lunch. Gouy-St-André, 12km W of Hesdin (tel: 03 21 90 39 58).

Estaminet La Plume d'Oison Jolly atmosphere in Flemish-style restaurant serving a single set menu for around 15€, & offering pub games. Open Fri-Sun. Closed Jan. 1395 Route Nationale (D349), Bouin-Plumoison, 3km W of Hesdin (tel: 03 21 81 59 62).

Brocante fair 600 stalls in town streets, mid Aug.

Anglican services: Eucharist, 3rd Sun of month, 5pm. Parish church, Huby-St-Leu, 1km NW of Hesdin.

on Therry, in which he talks about his 5 million bees, and is seen at work extracting honey from the hives. A Fête du Miel (honey festival) is held here in early September. ● *1 Feb-31 Dec, Sun & public holidays 3-6pm (mid Apr-late Oct, Tues-Sat 2-6pm, Sun & public holidays 3-6pm). 923 Route Nationale (D349), Bouin-Plumoison, 3km W of Hesdin (tel: 03 21 81 46 24). Admission free.*

MERLIMONT-PLAGE

ⓘ **Place du Marché (tel: 03 21 94 32 90 fax: 03 21 09 63 27)**
www.merlimont.info
ot.merlimont@wanadoo.fr

Beyond the attractive old villas on Merlimont's seafront promenade, wild dunes stretch towards Le Touquet, 8km to the north. It's a small, family-friendly resort—old-fashioned in the best sense of the term—offering sailing, as well as sand-yachting, and jet-skiing.

Just 3km to the north, the resort of Stella-Plage is a little more brash, with colourfully-painted modern shops, bungalows and apartment buildings. The wind here is constantly redistributing the sand, sculpting dunes that are higher than some of the houses, but it's welcomed by the fly-surfers, whose activities are a dramatic sight on a breezy day.

➤**Parc Bagatelle** The long-established amusement park set in woodland 3km south of Merlimont has more than 40 thrills and spills for children and adults. Popular with the French since 1955, it includes exhilarating roller-coaster, watersplash and "rafting" trips; scaled-down adventures for the slightly less bold; a special area of gentler rides for the very young; and a cinema, mini-golf, pedaloes, a small farm, and a spectacular acrobatic show. On the minus side, admission is expensive, car-parking costs extra, toilets are malodorous, and queues for some rides can last 30 minutes in peak season. Disconcerting to British sensibilities, too, the park also offers performances by elephants and a troupe of lions and tigers. However, there is plenty of shade for hot days, and you are allowed to take picnics in with you. ◑ *Mid Apr-late Sept, Sat, Sun 10am-6.30pm (1 July-31 Aug, daily 10am-7pm). 21.50€ (includes all rides); over-60s, handicapped & children under 12 16€; children under 3, or less than 1 metre high, free (1 July-31 Aug, 22€, children under 12 17€); parking 4€. On D940, 3km SW of Merlimont (tel: 03 21 89 09 99).* ♿ *(half of the attractions).* ☯

■ **Outlook fine: traditional villas at Merlimont-Plage.**

Market: Mon & Fri (both 1 July-31 Aug), Place de la Gare. Wed & Sun (both 1 July-31 Aug), Place Royale, Stella-Plage, 3km N of Merlimont-Plage.
Specialities: Oysters.
Restaurant: Brasserie de la Plage: Les Pieds dans l'Eau Great fish restaurant in shack-like building overhanging beach. Menus 14.50-19.50€. Bd de la Manche (tel: 03 21 94 67 53).
Brocante: Dépôt-Vente de la Côte d'Opale Large junk emporium on Stella-Plage's main street. Tues-Sat 2.30-6.30pm, Sun 3-7pm. 1112 Bd Edmond-Labrasse (D144), Stella-Plage, 4km N of Merlimont-Plage (tel: 03 21 94 75 76).
Factory shop: Isambourg: Scènes de Vie Huge warehouse selling beads, stationery, soft toys, disposable tableware, & supplies for crafts—from candlemaking to embroidery. Mon-Sat 9am-noon & 2-7pm. Place de la Gare, Capelle (junction of D143 & D144E), 2.5km E of Merlimont village.

➤**St-Josse** This pretty, flower-filled village grew up around a monastery founded in the 7th century by St Josse (St Jodoc in English). He is said to ensure safety from fire, hail, plague and storms at sea. Fishermen seeking divine protection for their vessels as they head off on long trips have carved the names and registration numbers of boats into the stonework outside; you can see these on the church's north wall. ● *On D144, in village centre, 6km E of Merlimont.* Ⓢ

MONTREUIL

ⓘ 21 Rue Carnot (tel: 03 21 06 04 27 fax: 03 21 06 57 85)
www. tourisme-montreuillois.com
accueil@tourisme-montreuillois.com

★ An incredibly pretty fortified town, Montreuil is understandably popular. Located on the coast until the sea receded (it is still officially "Montreuil-sur-Mer"), it now stands 15km inland on a rocky spur.

Relics brought back from the Holy Land and dispersed among its eight churches brought pilgrims to the town, leading to the construction of a Hôtel-Dieu to receive the sick who came hoping for cures. In 1299 a treaty was signed here between Edward I of England and Philippe le Bel of France agreeing to the marriage of Edward's son (the future Edward II) with Isabelle, daughter of the French king. This union was at the root of the English claim to the French throne, which led to the Hundred Years War.

Having spent just half a day here, on 4 September 1837, the French writer Victor Hugo was so enchanted by Montreuil's old

Montreuil

Map of Montreuil showing streets including Citadelle, Porte de Boulogne, Porte de France, Hôtel Acary-de-la-Rivière, Chapelle de l'Hôtel-Dieu, Chapelle Ste-Austreberthe, Abbatiale St-Saulve, Haig statue, Station, and roads to Boulogne, Hesdin, and Abbeville.

■ Built to last: Montreuil's citadel, right, and walled old town, above.

■ Inspirational: Montreuil's picturesque Cavée St-Firmin suggested an episode in *Les Misérables*.

cobbled streets, that he made the town the setting for a major part of his epic 1862 novel *Les Misérables*. In the story, the reformed convict Jean Valjean—who has become a philanthropic factory-owner and mayor of the town—saves the life of an old man by lifting a heavy wagon that had collapsed on him, on the steep hill known as Cavée St-Firmin. The novel is the basis for an enjoyable *son-et-lumière* show performed in the citadel in July and August.

It's a delight to browse among the shops, take a walk around the ramparts, or wander the twisting streets looking at the ancient houses with their steeply-pitched roofs. Don't miss Rue Clape-en-Haut and Rue Clape-en-Bas, once the poorest areas of town but today reckoned the most picturesque. Main shopping areas are Place de Gaulle, known as "Grand'Place", Rue Pierre-Ledent and Place Darnétal. (Members of The Wine Society will find the Society's shop on Rue Tripot, behind the Hermitage hotel.)

For more active pleasures, you can canoe on the river Canche, or set out on signposted walks from beside the tourist office.

❯**Citadelle** Some 50 metres above the valley of the river Canche, the town's star-shaped fort was constructed in the 16th century. There is more to see than you might think—though some steep stone steps and scarily unguarded drops make it unsuitable for children or for those who have difficulty climbing. A descriptive leaflet (English version available) leads you to gunpowder magazine, chapel and arsenal, and up to the sentry-way and sturdy towers. One of the most interesting features is the series of five interlinked, semi-underground chambers, down a flight of steps signposted "*casemates*". During World War I they housed the communications centre for the 5,000-strong British GHQ, based in Montreuil from 1916. (The equestrian statue of Field Marshal Haig on the town's Grand'Place is a reminder of that time.) ● *Wed-Mon 10am-noon & 2-5pm (1 July-31 Aug, Wed-Mon 10am-noon & 2-6pm). Esplanade Vauban (tel: 03 21 06 10 83). 2.50€, children 1.25€.* ⚅

❯**Abbatiale St-Saulve** Statues line the porch of Montreuil's imposing abbey church while, inside, the fan-vaulting is colourfully illuminated by light streaming through the south windows. The pulpit is decorated with

MONTREUIL EXTRAS

Restaurants:

Le Darnétal *Imaginative food, with a modern twist. Menus from 16€. Closed Mon & Tues. Pl Darnétal (tel: 03 21 06 04 87).*

Le Jéroboam *Chic modern brasserie beside the Hermitage hotel. Menus 15-58€. Closed Sun & Mon, & Jan. 1 Rue des Juifs (tel: 03 21 86 65 80).*

Auberge de la Grenouillère *Characterful rural place with great food, below town walls. Menus 33-75€. Closed Tues & Wed (except July & Aug), & Jan. Pretty rooms from 105€. La Madelaine-sous-Montreuil, 3km W of Montreuil (tel: 03 21 06 07 22). www.lagrenouillere.fr/*

Brocante:

Au Fil du Temps *Two rooms full of small ornaments & quirky objects for collectors. Sun-Wed, 3-7pm; Thurs, Fri 10am-noon & 2.30-7pm; Sat 2.30-7pm. 27 Rue Pierre-Ledent (tel: 06 70 37 16 94).*

Vide-grenier *Enormous annual car-boot & bric-a-brac fair, 14 July.*

carved figures of the four evangelists, Matthew, Mark, Luke and John. All but one were decapitated during the Revolution; curiously, the missing heads have been replaced with those of chubby-cheeked cherubs. ● *Daily 9am-noon & 2-6pm. Mass: Sun 11am. Place Gambetta.* **S**

>Chapelle de l'Hôtel-Dieu   Much restored in 1865, this chapel alongside the Hermitage hotel was part of a hospital founded in 1200 and which functioned until 1992. Its sculpted 15th-century façade gives an idea of its original splendour. Carved panelling inside depicts the evangelists; above the ornate marble-and-gold altar, a series of stained-glass windows relate biblical stories. O *1-31 July, daily 3-6pm. Place Gambetta (tel: 03 21 06 04 27). 1.50€, children free.*

>Hôtel Acary de la Rivière   Bequeathed to the town in 1978, this former private residence opens briefly for temporary exhibitions. Apart from its elegant fireplaces and painted panelling, the house contains only a very few items of furniture. Its rear windows look out at a 1930s mansion (now the Château de Montreuil hotel), which was built by the last owners after they found this house too small. O *1 July-31 Aug, Wed-Mon 3-6pm. Parvis St-Firmin (tel: 03 21 06 04 27). 2€, children 1€.*

>Chocolaterie de Beussent   Once you have tasted the output of this tiny chocolate factory in the valley of the Course, you will be hooked on Bruno and Alain Derick's top-quality products. The irresistible aroma wafting from the building is the only hint that you have not arrived at a private house. The shop and factory entrances are down a flight of covered wooden steps (or by a ramp). Chocolates of various delectable flavours are in ready-to-buy packs at 6€ each, or you can have a selection made up. If you can't wait to get to the factory, you will find Chocolats de Beussent shops at Berck, Boulogne, Dunkerque, Montreuil, St-Omer, Le Touquet & Wimereux. ● *Shop: Mon-Sat 9am-noon & 2-7pm.* O *Visits: Mid July-31 Aug, Mon-Sat 3.30-4.30pm. 66 Route de Desvres (D127), Quesnoy, 1km N of Beussent & 8km N of Montreuil (tel: 03 21 86 17 62). Admission free.* ♿

LE TOUQUET-PARIS-PLAGE

ⓘ Palais de l'Europe, Place de l'Hermitage (tel: 03 21 06 72 00 fax: 03 21 06 72 19)
www.letouquet.com
office-tourisme@letouquet.com

The French love what they describe as the "so British" style of Le Touquet, though to those arriving from across the Channel this chic resort may not look quite foreign enough!

The 1,600 hectares of sandy heathland south of the Canche estuary were bought in 1837 by two business associates called Daloz and Alyon. After an initial agricultural project

■ Eccentric designs: Le Touquet's market-hall, right, and a quirky villa, below.

■ Making a splash: Aqualud is a favourite with the children.

on the site failed, Alyon withdrew; but Daloz persevered—planting thousands of trees instead. As these grew into an attractive forest, he decided to turn the area into a seaside resort (still a relatively new concept), and by 1894 there were 173 houses and hotels. However, the resort really took off with the arrival of an English entrepreneur, John Whitley, towards 1900. He targeted a wealthy British clientele with superb facilities for golf, tennis, polo and horse-racing. Parisians, too, were quick to appreciate the delights.

The hedonistic way of life that developed here was halted by World War I. However, a new golden age began in the 1920s, as international high society returned to Le Touquet's hotels, casino, restaurants, bars and sports fields. Architects built luxurious villas for writers, politicians, film stars and royalty. But with the outbreak of World War II the resort's fortunes changed again. The author PG Wodehouse was among British residents captured at their homes here in 1940 and interned in Germany for the rest of the war. To deter invasion, the Germans built blockhouses along the coast and laid mines among the sands. The Allies, too, inflicted damage with bombing raids against the town's airfield.

Today, sporting facilities and buildings have been restored to their original glory. Le Touquet's famous 1920s and 30s villas and public buildings feature an unusual blend of Arts & Crafts and Art Deco styles, with a deliciously Gallic spin. The smartest restaurants, art galleries and designer shops are in the Place de l'Hermitage area, which lies about 1km east of the beach. The most elegant houses lie inland, too, on roads radiating like a spider's web from Place de l'Hermitage (see plan, page 109), or around the golf club to the south. The *Promenades-Découverte* leaflet from the tourist office guides you past 15 discreetly-sited villas with names like *Balmoral*, *Sunny Corner* or *Glenwood*. (Confusingly, the tourist-office plans are orientated to show the west, seafront, side of town at top or bottom rather than in the conventional way, to the left.)

The streets near the seafront are, in contrast, laid out on a rigid grid system. As everywhere along the Opal Coast, the sands are vast—especially at low tide when the water can seem a very long

LE TOUQUET EXTRAS

Market: Mon (1 June-15 Sept); Thurs, Sat (all year). All in Pl du Marché Couvert.

Specialities: Ratte potatoes. Herrings. Fish soup from Chez Pérard.

Accommodation:

Hotel Westminster Grandest of the 4-star hotels. Rooms from 185€; menus from 50€ (brasserie from 26€). Parking. Ave du Verger (tel: 03 21 05 48 48). www.westminster.fr/

Mercure Grand Hotel Modern 4-star hotel, with beauty spa & indoor pool. Rooms from 141€. Parking. 4 Bd de la Canche (tel: 03 21 06 88 88). www.mercure.com/

Le Manoir Hotel 3-star hotel right on the golf courses; also with tennis court. Rooms from 118€; menus from 31€. Parking. Ave du Golf, 2km S of centre (tel: 03 21 06 28 28). www.opengolfclub.com/

Airport: Le Touquet-Côte d'Opale International (see page 11). Ave de Picardie, 2km SE of town centre (tel: 03 21 05 03 99).

■ On the wild side: the unspoilt dunes of the Canche estuary.

walk away. Car-parking is easiest near the extreme north or south of the beach promenade. Pedestrianised Rue St-Jean is the focus of this area. Rue de Metz has the edge for the best shops and restaurants, and also has the town's fanciful Art Deco post office, decorated inside with tiles from Desvres (see page 93). A little farther south along Rue de Metz you come to the extraordinary, horseshoe-shaped market hall, known as the *marché couvert* (pictured on page 106), designed in 1932 by Henry-Léon Bloch.

There is plenty of activity year-round on the sports and entertainment front. You can rent one of the tennis club's 40 clay courts, or (if you hold a golfing handicap) enjoy a round on one of the resort's three golf courses. For either of these, it's advisable to book in advance. There are riding stables near the *hippodrome* (race track), and a sailing base near the mouth of the river Canche. Speed-sailing and sand-yachting are organised at the southern end of the main beach, also the location of the town's "*thalassothérapie*" sea-water spa (see page 109). The lively night-time scene includes bars, discos, clubs and two casinos (but note that you need to show a passport to enter the gaming rooms).

❯**Aqualud** A prominent glass pyramid (pictured on page 107) shelters the indoor part of this seafront leisure-pool complex, keeping the water at a pleasant 29 degrees for its wave-pool, hot-tub, "Magic River" and waterslides. In summer the pyramid opens up and the fun extends into an outdoor pool, with more chutes (including some for younger children) and a big favourite, an inflatable octopus to scramble over. Safety rules don't always seem as rigidly applied as back home, so keep an eye out for your own children among the mêlée. Swimming-trunks compulsory; no beach-shorts or T-shirts allowed. ◑ *Feb-Apr, Sat, Sun & school-holiday periods, 10.15am-5.45pm; 1 May-30 June, Wed-Sun 10.15am-5.45pm; 1 July-31 Aug, daily 10.15am-6.45pm (Fri, Sat also 8pm-midnight); 1 Sept-mid Nov, Sat, Sun & school-holiday periods 10.15am-5.45pm.*

Boulevard de la Plage (tel: 03 21 90 07 07). All day 14€; 4 hours 13€, 3 hours 12€ (1 July-31 Aug, 16.50€, 15.50€ & 14.50€; Fri, Sat evenings 13€); children under 1 metre in height free. 🏃 🕓

➤**Musée du Touquet** This handsome 1930s villa, with its original panelling and polished floors, makes an ideal setting for works of late 19th- and early 20th-century artists of the "École d'Étaples". The name "Étaples School" was coined for those who—spurred on by easy railway access from Paris and the picturesque quality of the local fishermen—set up their easels in the village of Étaples (see page 94), just across the Canche estuary. On the ground floor the Côte d'Opale's lighthouses, farms, dunes and villas feature in dozens of paintings, together with portraits of brawny fisherfolk pushing shrimping-nets through the shallows. French artists include Eugène Boudin and Henri Le Sidaner, and the renowned actress Sarah Bernhardt, who was also an accomplished painter. Others came from farther afield: Myron Barlow and Fred de Forrest Schook from the US; Lee Hankey from Britain; Paul Graf from Sweden; and Iso Rae from Australia. The first-floor rooms contain more recent works by Édouard Pignon, Arthur Van Hecke, Jean Dubuffet, Sonia Delaunay, Serge Poliakoff and Victor Vasarely. ● *Mon & Wed-Sat 10am-noon & 2-6pm, Sun 10am-noon & 2.30-6pm. Villa Way Side, junction of Avenue du Golf & Avenue du Château, 1km SE of tourist office (tel: 03 21 05 62 62). 3.80€, over-60s 2€, children 1€.* 🕓

➤**Thalassa Le Touquet** As a *découverte* (discovery), you can enjoy a sybaritic half-day's exhilarating treatments in a sea-water spa at the south end of the seafront. (Packages, including stay at adjoining Novotel and Ibis hotels, also available.) ● *Mon-Sat 8.30am-6.30pm, Sun 8.30am-12.30pm. Novotel, Boulevard Jules-Pouget (tel: 03 21 09 85 00). Half a day: four treatments 95€; three treatments & massage 120€. http://france.spa.touquet.thalasso-line.com/* 🏃 🕓

➤**Horse-racing** Race meetings (*courses hippiques*) are held at Le Touquet's racecourse, which is endowed with two magnificent 1920s grandstands. The programme usually consists of a succession of flat, steeplechase and trotting races; bets (*gagnant*=to win; *placé*=each-way) can be placed through a Tote system. ○ *Late May-mid Aug, Sun & 14 July from 4pm. Hippodrome du Touquet, Avenue de la Dune-aux-Loups (tel: 03 21 05 07 98). 5€.*

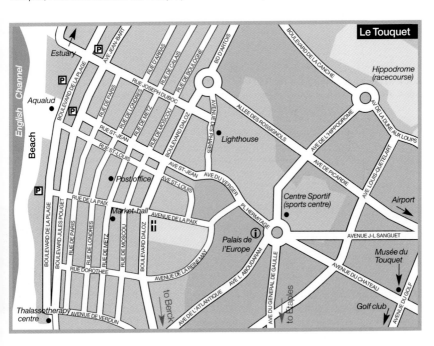

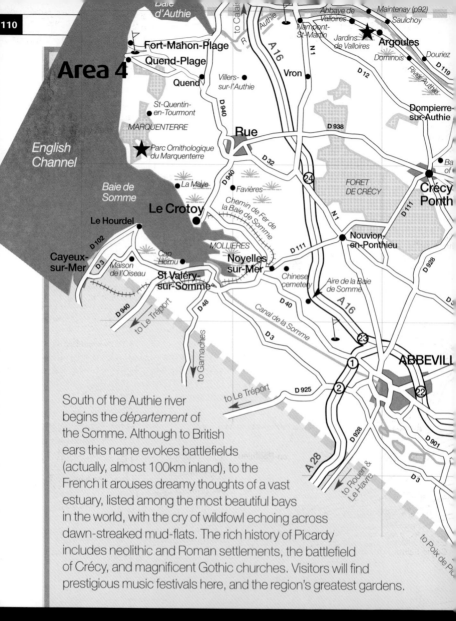

Area 4

English Channel

Baie d'Authie

to Calais

to Le Tréport

to Gamaches

Fort-Mahon-Plage
Quend-Plage
Quend
St-Quentin-en-Tourmont

MARQUENTERRE

★ Parc Ornithologique du Marquenterre

Baie de Somme

Le Hourdel

Le Crotoy

Cayeux-sur-Mer

Maison de l'Oiseau

Cap Hornu

St Valéry-sur-Somme

MOLLIÈRES

Noyelles-sur-Mer

Chinese cemetery

Canal de la Somme

Villers-sur-l'Authie

Rue

La Maye

Favières

Chemin de Fer de la Baie de Somme

Abbaye de Valloires
Jardins de Valloires
Nampont-St-Martin

Vron

Maintenay (p92)
Saulchoy

Argoules

Dominois

Douriez

Rivière/Authie

Dompierre-sur-Authie

Crécy Ponth

FORET DE CRÉCY

Nouvion-en-Ponthieu

Aire de la Baie de Somme

ABBEVILL

to Rouen & Le Havre

to Poix de Pi

South of the Authie river begins the *département* of the Somme. Although to British ears this name evokes battlefields (actually, almost 100km inland), to the French it arouses dreamy thoughts of a vast estuary, listed among the most beautiful bays in the world, with the cry of wildfowl echoing across dawn-streaked mud-flats. The rich history of Picardy includes neolithic and Roman settlements, the battlefield of Crécy, and magnificent Gothic churches. Visitors will find prestigious music festivals here, and the region's greatest gardens.

Amiens, Crécy, and the wildlife of the Somme Bay

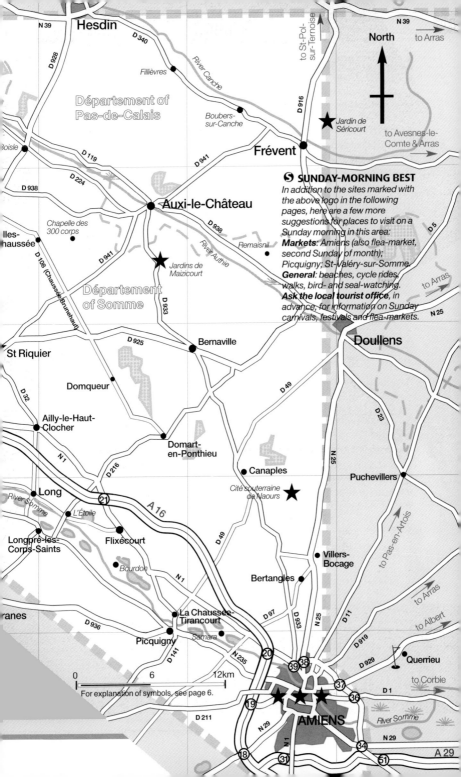

N 39

Hesdin

to St-Pol-sur-Ternoise

N 39

to Arras

North

Département of Pas-de-Calais

River Canche

Fillièvres

Boubers-sur-Canche

Jardin de Séricourt

to Avesnes-le-Comte & Arras

Boisle

Frévent

Auxi-le-Château

Chapelle des 300 corps

Remaisnil

les-haussée

Jardins de Maizicourt

Département of Somme

River Authie

D 108 (Chaussée Brunehaut)

☉ SUNDAY-MORNING BEST
In addition to the sites marked with the above logo in the following pages, here are a few more suggestions for places to visit on a Sunday morning in this area: **Markets:** Amiens (also flea-market, second Sunday of month); Picquigny; St-Valéry-sur-Somme. **General:** beaches, cycle rides, walks, bird- and seal-watching. **Ask the local tourist office**, in advance, for information on Sunday carnivals, festivals and flea-markets.

St Riquier

Bernaville

Doullens

Domqueur

Ailly-le-Haut-Clocher

Domart-en-Ponthieu

Canaples

Puchevillers

Long

L'Étoile

River Somme

Cité souterraine de Naours

Longpré-les-Corps-Saints

Flixécourt

Bourdon

Villers-Bocage

Bertangles

to Arras

to Albert

La Chaussée-Tirancourt

Samara

Picquigny

Querrieu

to Corbie

ranes

0   6   12km

For explanation of symbols, see page 6.

AMIENS

River Somme

A 29

ABBEVILLE

ⓘ Place de l'Amiral-Courbet (tel: 03 22 24 27 92 fax: 03 22 31 08 26)
www.ot-abbeville.fr
office.tourisme.abbeville@wanadoo.fr

A fragrant odour of cooked beet is a reminder that Abbeville, 45km north-west of Amiens, has been one of France's centres of sugar production since 1872. More than 9,000 tonnes of sugar-beet are processed here each day.

Independent since 1184, the town is capital of the historic area of Ponthieu. In 1665 King Louis XIV offered incentives to a Dutch cloth manufacturer, Josse van Robais, to set up a textile industry in France. Guaranteed a monopoly, huge tax advantages and freedom to practise his Protestant religion, van Robais brought 50 Dutch workers to Abbeville and started a golden age for the town; by 1709 the company employed 2,000 people. But the financial privileges were gradually withdrawn, and the factory closed in 1788. Most of the town's medieval buildings were destroyed in World War II bombing raids, though you can still see its collegial church, belfry, and a handful of ancient houses.

Between junctions 23 and 24 of the A16 motorway, the Baie de Somme service station offers views of the Somme estuary from a tall tower and from a reed-fringed marshland boardwalk.

❯ **Collégiale St-Vulfran** The principal treasure of Abbeville's Gothic church, built in 1488 to contain the relics of 8th-century bishop St Vulfran, is the sculpture on its west façade. Among the fine carvings, look for St Eustace fording a river to rescue his children, who are being snatched by wild animals. ◑ *Mid Apr-late Sept, Mon-Sat 2-6pm. Mass: Sun 11am. Parvis St-Vulfran.*

❯ **Château de Bagatelle** This little jewel of a château, in brick and white stone (pictured, page 34), was built in 1750 by Abraham van Robais, grandson of Abbeville's first textile manufacturer. Tours of the ground floor (with an English-speaking guide) lead you through the summer *salon*, dining-room and pretty music-room, all featuring original panelling, Flemish porcelain and 18th-century furniture. The charming gardens are partly formal French, and partly the less structured design known as a "*parc à l'anglaise*". In front of the house is a sunken area of lawn called "*le boulingrin*" (a French attempt at the English words "bowling green"). The back garden—predominantly in shades of green, punctuated with white flowers—has a long, rectangular, formal pool that reflects the perfect lines of the house. ◑ *Gardens: Mid May-mid Oct, Mon-Fri 2-4.30pm (15 July-31 Aug, Wed-Mon 2-6pm); closed public holidays except 14 July & 15 Aug. ○ Château: 14 July-31 Aug, Wed-Mon 2-6pm. 133 Route de Paris, on SE side of Abbeville & 1km W of J22 of A16 (tel: 03 22 24 02 69/06 86 01 18 12). Gardens 4€, children 2.50€; château & gardens 8€, children 4€.*

■ **Testing time: St Gengoulf and his wife at Abbeville's Musée Boucher-de-Perthes.**

❯ **Musée Boucher-de-Perthes** Inside Abbeville's 13th-century bell tower is an eclectic museum named after a 19th-century resident famous for his studies of the region's prehistory. A small room on the first floor is filled with gory medieval works: little St Cyr being martyred in a barrel of nails at the age of three; his mother, St Julitte, being sawn in half; St Laurent being roasted alive; and, in an adjacent room, a statue of St Gengoulf—patron saint of cuckolded husbands—preparing to stab his unfaithful wife as she plunges her arm into boiling water. (If it scalds her, she will be proved guilty.) In the archaeology section you find mammoths' teeth, bronze bowls, flint tools and some sophisticated Gallo-Roman objects. There is a permanent collection of paintings and sculptures by artists of northern France, Flanders and Holland. Alongside its traditional still-lifes and 16th-century portraits are a couple of works by Frans Hals, colourful altarpieces, and pottery from Delft, Italy and France. ● *Wed-Mon 2-6pm. Closed 1 Jan, 1 May, 14 July, 1 Nov & 25 Dec. 24 Rue Gontier-Patin (tel: 03 22 24 08 49). 1€, children free. Ascent of belfry, 1€.*

AMIENS

ⓘ 6 bis Rue Dusevel (tel: 03 22 71 60 50 fax: 03 22 71 60 51)
www.amiens.com/tourisme
ot@amiens-metropole.com

Astride the river Somme, the capital of the *département* and of the region of Picardy is celebrated for its magnificent cathedral, the largest Gothic church in France. Amiens was already an important focus of civilisation in paleolithic times. The Romans built a town of 25,000 inhabitants, named Samarobriva ("crossing-place of the Somme") and maintained a large garrison here. Among its soldiers was a young officer named Martin who, one cold day in 336AD, gave half his cloak to a beggar and then had a vision of Christ wearing it. This incident, which caused the future St Martin to give up the army and devote himself to the church, is commemorated by a plaque on the site (on today's Rue Lesueur).

The leaves of the woad plant ("*waid*" in the Picard dialect), that flourishes in the area's chalky ground, impart a deep, rich blue to fabric that used to be known as *"bleu d'Amiens"*. As a colour associated with the Virgin, and with royalty, this dye enjoyed high status in the 11th century, creating the fortune of the city and helping to fund the construction of its cathedral. Amiens' textile industry specialised in fine serge and, later, in velvet—enjoying a monopoly in France that came to an end with the Revolution. However, textile manufacture continued to be important here until the 1960s.

Amiens was heavily shelled in World War I during the German advance of 1918. (Plaques in the cathedral pay tribute to soldiers of many nations who died in the city's defence.) It fared even worse in the next war, suffering 60 per cent destruction—though the cathedral miraculously survived. As a result, the town contains some resolutely modern architecture, including a 29-storey skyscraper designed by Auguste Perret, who was nicknamed "the poet of concrete".

Among the few remaining buildings from Amiens' past are the Logis du Roy and Maison du Sagittaire, near the Rue des Trois-Cailloux, the half-timbered Maison du Pélerin opposite the cathedral,

■ **Strung up: the "Ché Cabotans" puppets.**

and the 14th-century belfry beside the market-hall. Behind the cathedral, the venerable Rue de Metz-l'Évêque leads down towards the Somme; turn left to reach ancient Place du Don, full of cafés; and then cross the river to the deliciously pretty canalside St-Leu district (pictured, page 33), once inhabited by weavers and woad-producers.

A long-standing local tradition is that of the marionettes known as "Ché Cabotans", of which the most notable character is a cheeky servant called Lafleur. You might glimpse some of them in the workshop of puppet-maker Jean-Pierre Facquier at 67 Rue du Don.

Shopping streets radiate from Place Gambetta and include Rue des Trois-Cailloux (with a branch of Galeries Lafayette department store at No 12). A large student population ensures that there are plenty of reasonably-priced sandwich bars, pizzerias and *crêperies* for lunch stops. On-street parking meters give two hours extra over lunch time, and free parking on Sunday, public holidays, and—unusually—on Monday morning.

> ★ **Cathédrale Notre-Dame** The city's 13th-century, Unesco-listed cathedral (pictured opposite, and on page 36) was built as a repository for its famous relic, the head of John the Baptist, brought back from the Crusades in 1206. Its freshly-cleaned west front is a marvel of the medieval stone-carver's art. The three statue-encrusted archways celebrate, respectively, St Firmin (the cathedral's first bishop), "le Beau Dieu" (God), and "la Mère-Dieu" (the Virgin Mary).

Inside, the columns supporting the 42-metre-high roof seem so tall that you wonder how the building can stay upright. Underfoot, the floor is a mixture of black and white designs with, in the centre (often obscured by chairs), the cathedral's maze—a 234-metre trail of black flagstones along which the faithful would shuffle on their knees as a substitute for making a pilgrimage to Jerusalem. Around the outside of the choir are two series of painted, high-relief sculptures, created between 1490 and 1530. Packed with lively details of medieval life, those on the south side tell the story of St Firmin; those on the north recount the life and death of John the Baptist. (Opposite this last, the blackened skull of St John is sometimes displayed on the north wall.) The wooden choir-stalls (visible on guided tours only) are decorated with thousands of exquisitely-carved figures on Biblical and domestic themes.

At the far east end, opposite the richly-decorated chapel of Notre-Dame de la Drapière, is one of Amiens' best-loved sights: Nicolas Blasset's sculpture of a weeping cherub, decorating the tomb of a cathedral canon. During World War I, troops from 30 nations sent postcards bearing images of the little stone angel back to their distant homelands.

From the shop just outside the cathedral you can rent audioguides in English, or book a visit up to the lofty terrace of the north tower. The tourist office organises regular cathedral tours. ● *Daily 8.30am-12.15pm & 2-5.15pm (1 Apr-30 Sept, daily 8.30am-6.30pm). Mass: May-Oct, daily 9am & 10.30am; Nov-Apr, 9am & 11.30am. Parvis Notre-Dame.* Ⓢ

> ★ **Son-et-lumière: *La Cathédrale en Couleurs*** At certain times of year, the cathedral's west front is illuminated by a state-of-the-art projection system. Inspired by traces of colour discovered in 1992, lighting experts "paint" each statue, bringing to life the medieval faces and costumes. Pink-cheeked, and clad in robes of every hue, the figures emerge with unbelievable clarity. People jostle for position on the stepped pavement opposite for the 45-minute show; try and pick a spot in the middle for the best view. After a 20-minute commentary about the discovery of

■ Concrete plan: the Tour Perret skyscraper.

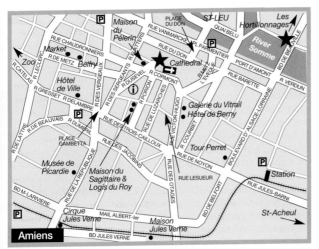

Amiens

■ Awe-inspiring: the cathedral of Amiens.

the paint and the meaning of certain panels, the lights remain on for about an hour so you can move in for a closer look. ◑ *1-30 June, daily 10.45pm; 1-31 July, daily 10.30pm; 1-31 Aug, daily 10pm; 1-30 Sept, daily 9.45pm; mid Dec-6 Jan, daily 7pm. Parvis Notre-Dame. Admission free.*

❯**Beffroi** Amiens' present belfry, near the covered market, dates from 1742. An interesting 90-minute guided tour, with a bilingual guide, shows its prison cells, ancient graffiti, early toilets and monumental fireplaces. From the roof-top terrace, there are wonderful views over the city. ◑ *1 Apr-30 Sept, Sun 10.30am. Place au Fil (tel: 03 22 71 60 50). 6€.* ⑤

❯**Musée de l'Hôtel de Berny** This grand brick town house dating from 1633 was restored in the 20th century by Gérard de Berny. He left it and his large collection of furniture, paintings, tapestries and Amiens pottery to the town as the basis for a museum of local history. At present closed for extensive refurbishment, it contains panelling from the Château de Long (see page 124), decorated with a series of 18th-century works depicting signs of the zodiac. *Closed till 2012. Admission details not available at time of writing. 36 Rue Victor-Hugo (tel: 03 22 97 14 00).*

❯**Galerie du Vitrail** Almost next to the Musée de Berny, on three floors of a tall 17th-century house, is an interesting museum of stained glass, attached to a working glass studio. Once-daily tours (in French only) lead to vaulted cellars for a look at ancient examples, collected by master glassmaker Claude Barre and his wife. Crisply illuminated, the vivid yellows and reds of the stained glass shine out in contrast to the more muted techniques of glass-painting, or of near-monochrome *grisaille.* On the first floor are more modern glass pieces, from 1900 to the present, evoking fountains, flowers and exotic birds. Back on the ground floor, you watch today's glass-workers busy on the creation of new windows or on the restoration of ancient examples from churches throughout France. ● *Mon-Sat 3pm prompt. Closed public holidays. 40 Rue Victor-Hugo, enter through workshop in courtyard (tel: 03 22 91 81 18). 4€, children 2€.*

❯**Musée de Picardie** Built in the mid 19th century, this palace-like museum is a monument to Picardy. In the basement, archaeological treasures are beautifully displayed. Alongside antiquities from Egypt and Greece—glowing alabaster beads, Cypriot vases and gold jewellery—is a large neolithic collection, including discoveries from a south-eastern suburb of Amiens, called St-Acheul. Quarrying in this district in 1850 revealed around 20,000 "biface" tools (shaped on two sides, rather than on just one), dating from neolithic times and revealing a new level of sophistication in manufacture. Since then, all such "biface" tools are referred to as "acheulean" after this area, no matter where in the world they are found.

Farther on are Bronze Age weapons and jewellery; gorgeous Gallo-Roman goblets and vases; Gaulish statuettes; and skeletons found at the Iron Age site of Ribemont-sur-Ancre (see page 140).

Displays on the ground floor start with the Middle Ages. (A dispenser in each room has boards with notes in English.) Ninth-century ivory carvings from Rheims stand beside stone capitals from the cloister of Corbie Abbey (see page 139). You see painted wooden figures of St Blaise, of the Virgin, and of St John alongside delicate, carved religious scenes in Nottingham alabaster. En route to a room of Classical-style marble statues, you pass through a brightly-coloured rotunda painted in zingy geometric stripes by American artist Sol LeWitt in 1992.

The main staircase and first floor are decorated with 14 works by Pierre Puvis de Chavannes (1824-98). Succeeding galleries (temporarily closed for renovation from 2007) contain Flemish, Dutch and Italian paintings from 16th to 20th centuries, including works by El Greco, Hals, Van Dyck, and Tiepolo, and some large canvases of leopard, tiger, elephant and crocodile hunts by François Boucher. There is also a small collection of 20th-century paintings. ● *Tues-Sun 10am-12.30pm & 2-6pm. Closed 1 Jan, 1 & 8 May, 1 & 11 Nov & 25 Dec. 48 Rue de la République (tel: 03 22 97 14 00). 4.50€, children 2.50€ (free on first Sun of month).* ♿ *(at 2 Rue Puvis-de-Chavannes).* 🎧 Ⓢ

❯ Zoo d'Amiens You could spend a good couple of hours visiting this unexpectedly pleasant zoo, north-west of the town centre. Winding

■ **Neolithic treasure: 4,500-year-old vase from archaeological displays in the Musée de Picardie.**

Jules Verne: father of science fiction

Born in Nantes in 1828, Jules Verne moved to Paris to study law. Early play-writing success and a passion for the work of Edgar Allan Poe caused him to abandon a legal career and to write *Un Voyage en Ballon* in 1851, which became in English *Five Weeks in a Balloon*. From his fertile imagination, Verne drew 62 novels and 18 short stories, in which he anticipated many modern inventions. Revelling in the age of railways and steamships, he imagined ever faster and more futuristic journeys, by space rockets and submarines.

In 1857 he married a young widow from Amiens. The couple left Paris in 1867 and settled in the seaside village of Le Crotoy (see page 121), where Verne continued to produce stories in his successful *Voyages Extraordinaires* series, among them *Vingt Mille Lieues sous les Mers* (*20,000 Leagues under the Sea*), in which he conjured up the legendary Captain Nemo. Three years later the family moved to Amiens, where they led a comfortable bourgeois life, with Verne serving as a city councillor from 1888 to 1893. He died in 1905, and is buried in the town's Cimetière de la Madeleine.

❯ Maison de Jules Verne The unusual three-storey town house, with its tall brick tower, was home to the Verne family for 18 years and now re-creates the world of this visionary writer. Starting among exotic foliage in the conservatory, the visit takes in dining-room, drawing-room and smoking-room, filled with heavy furniture, thick rugs and, occasionally, with murmuring recorded voices. Captions are in English throughout. A hallway contains references to Verne's successful career as a playwright, and to his voyage to the United States on the *Great Eastern* in 1867, alongside newspaper cuttings that inspired his adventure-packed tales. Up the spiral stairs is an area devoted to his relationship paths lead you to sheep and goats, past stripey zebras, cackling kookaburras, cavorting monkeys and some stunningly colourful macaws. The zoo has a big breeding programme, and you may be lucky enough to see juvenile sea-lion, gibbon or other young with their mothers.

There are shady trees, lots of benches, and excellent toilets near the entrance building. Animal feeding-times are posted near the ticket-office. Paths are of hard earth, so may become difficult for pushchairs after heavy rain. Keep an eye on adventurous children as some of the barriers might not be sufficient to hold them back. ● *Wed, Sat, Sun 2-5pm (school-holiday periods, daily 10am-5pm; 1 Apr-30 Sept, Mon-Sat 10am-6pm, Sun & public holidays 10am-7pm). Allée du Zoo, Esplanade de la Hotoie; car park is off Avenue Salvador-Allende (tel: 03 22 69 61 00). 4€, students & children 3€, under-5s free; family (1+1) 5.50€, (2+2) 8€.* ❺

❯ ★ **Les Hortillonnages** The starting-point for the enchanting, 50-minute guided boat trips through the narrow waterways off the river Somme is about 20 minutes' walk north-east of the cathedral. In the height of summer, or at weekends, it's wise to turn up early (about 1.30pm), otherwise you might have a long wait for a place. The traditional, black-tarred open boats, or *barques à cornet*, seat 12 people and are powered by silent electric motors. Productive vegetable plots once lined the canals, but today there are only seven remaining *hortillons*, or market-gardeners, still taking their goods to market. The waterside sites have mostly been given over to modest holiday retreats whose owners fill the gardens with flowers and eccentric sculptures, and line the banks with cascades of roses or nasturtiums. ◗ *1 Apr-31 Oct, from 2pm. 54 Boulevard de Beauvillé (tel: 03 22 92 12 18). 5€, children under 18 4.20€, under-11s 2.50€.*

Jules Verne

with his publisher (the English captions refer to him as "editor"), Jules Hetzel—also the publisher of George Sand, Victor Hugo and Honoré de Balzac. The fruitful partnership endured from 1862 until Hetzel's death in 1886.

The second-floor landing has a nautical theme, reflecting Verne's passion for his yacht, the *St Michel II*. It leads to a large room with displays about global travel in the 19th century. At the time, the Press was speculating how a trip round the world might be accomplished in less than three months using new engineering marvels: the 1869 Suez Canal; the 1869 east-to-west-coast railway across America; and the 1871 Mont-Cenis tunnel under the Alps. Inspired by this, in 1871 writer Edmond Plauchut published *Le Tour du Monde en 120 Jours*. Twelve months later Verne had improved on the idea, invented Phineas Fogg and his servant, Passepartout, and serialised *Le Tour du Monde en Quatre-Vingts Jours*, published as a book in 1873 (which appeared in English as *Around the World in 80 Days*). His readers took up the challenge. American journalist Nellie Bly completed her own tour in 72 days,

and came here to the house to tell Verne about her exploit.

Like *Vingt Mille Lieues sous les Mers*, this novel inspired many spin-offs, reflected in displays of themed plates, stereoscopic images, lantern slides, tobacco jars, puzzles, postcards and matchboxes. Finally, in the top of the tower, you come to an area displaying some wonderful posters that advertise films based on Jules Verne's works, the first dating from 1902. From 1916 to 1919, some of the screen adaptations were produced by Verne's son, Michael.

A few hundred metres west, along what is now Boulevard Jules-Verne, stands a large round theatre building called Le Cirque, which was officially opened by Verne in 1889. ● *Maison Jules Verne: Tues-Fri 10am-noon & 2-6pm; Sat, Sun & public holidays 2-6pm. 2 Rue Charles-Dubois, on the corner of Boulevard Jules-Verne (tel: 03 22 45 37 84). 5€, students & children 2.50€, under-8s free; family (2+2) 12€.* ♿ ❧

ARGOULES

ⓘ Mairie, 10 Rue Verte (tel: 03 22 29 91 15)

This village alongside the river Authie, 24km north of Abbeville, is known for its beautiful abbey and, especially, for the magnificent gardens of Valloires. Pretty villages strung along either side of the Authie include Saulchoy, Dominois, Douriez and Dompierre.

❯**Abbaye de Valloires** Founded in the 12th century, this Cistercian abbey—burial place of many French nobles slain at Crécy in 1346—was destroyed in the 1618-48 war against the Spanish. Rebuilt in its present form, it was sold off after the French Revolution, and is now a children's home. The hour-long guided tour takes in the arcaded cloister, the stone chapter-house, and luxurious withdrawing-rooms for high-ranking priests. The latter are lined with 18th-century wood-panelling, carved over a period of six years by Baron Pfaff von Pfaffenhoffen (see page 128). In the tall baroque chapel (where summer concerts are given), papier-mâché angels hang from the ceiling above a Pfaffenhoffen-decorated organ and a delicate ironwork screen bearing the arms of the abbey's bishops and benefactors. An English leaflet is available to help you keep up with the guide's explanations. ◑ *1 Feb-31 Mar, tours Mon-Fri, 3.30pm; 1 Apr-30 Sept, tours daily 11.30am, 2.30pm, 3.30pm, 4.30pm (1 June-31 Aug, also 10.30am & 5.30pm; organ concerts Sun 6pm); 1 Oct-mid Nov, tours daily 11.30am, 2.30pm, 3.30pm (Sat, Sun also 4.30pm). On D192, 1km NW of Argoules (tel: 03 22 29 62 33). 6.50€, children 4€.* ◎

❯★ **Jardins de Valloires** Visible from the grounds of the abbey, but a separate visitor attraction, are these wonderful botanical gardens, designed by Gilles Clément in 1989. Laid out around a lawn edged with pyramid-trimmed trees, they incorporate shady gravel walks, colour-themed borders, bog garden, and wildflower meadow. A "garden of the five senses" encourages children to sniff perfumed flowers, listen to rustling leaves, taste fruit, touch prickly stems and admire colourful foliage. Visit in April for cherry blossom; May for lilacs; June onwards for roses; August for hydrangeas; September and October for autumn colour. There's a well-written leaflet in English, a plant-sales area, shop, and a good café (serving dishes made from garden produce). ◑ *Mid Mar-11 Nov, daily 10am-6pm; last admission 5pm (mid May-mid Sept, daily 10am-7.15pm; last admission 6pm); occasional opening during Christmas holidays. On D192, 500m NW of Argoules (tel: 03 22 23 53 55). 6.50€, children 4€ (1 May-15 Sept 7.50€ & 4.50€).* ♿ ◎

■ Blooming marvellous: Valloires gardens

AUXI-LE-CHATEAU

ⓘ Hôtel de Ville (tel: 03 21 04 02 03 fax: 03 21 04 10 22)
www.ville-auxilechateau.fr
mairie.auxilechateau@wanadoo.fr

The picturesque little town of Auxi, 24km north-east of Abbeville, has a delightful mixture of architecture, with crow-stepped gables, an astonishingly flamboyant, brick *hôtel de ville*, and shops that advertise themselves with attractive, traditional-style hanging signs.

■ Secret gardens: a corner of Maizicourt.

❯ Musée des Arts et Traditions Populaires Opposite the church, In the old presbytery, local language and traditions are kept alive, with texts in Picard *patois* adding flavour to relics of a bygone age. Presented in glass-fronted rooms, exhibits are grouped by themes covering Auxi's agricultural, saddlery, shoe and enamelware industries. There are re-creations of kitchen, bedroom, laundry and a dental surgery. Other displays cover childhood, military service, religious observance, and death (porcelain wreaths for the graves of the rich; simple enamel plaques for burial places of the poor). Outside is a garden laid out with medicinal plants. ○ *1 July-31 Aug, daily 2.30-6.30pm; 1-30 Sept, Sat, Sun 2.30-6.30pm. Rue du Presbytère (tel: 03 21 04 02 03). 2€.*

❯ ★ Jardins de Maizicourt The romantic 8-hectare gardens around a mellow brick mansion are laid out with constantly-changing vistas, hidden enclosures and trim dovecotes. Surfaces vary, from cobbles to grass; spy-holes in hedges offer glimpses of a pool and pretty pavilions; stepping-stones lead through drifts of hostas and decorative grasses; and foxgloves provide muted colour in woodland glades. May is the time for the wistaria; June for rampaging roses; July and August for the best hydrangeas. There are no labels and no map, just an irresistible appeal to the senses. ◑ *1 May-30 Oct, Mon-Fri 2-6pm (1-30 June & 1-30 Sept, daily 2-6pm). On D933, Maizicourt, 5km S of Auxi-le-Château (tel: 03 22 32 69 64); parking near village church. 10€, children under 12 free.*

AUXI EXTRAS

Market: Sat.

Accommodation: Château de Remaisnil This 18th-century country house was the French home of Laura Ashley. Rooms from 195€; evening meal (on reservation) 45€. Remaisnil, 9.5km SE of Auxi (tel: 03 22 77 07 47). www.remaisnil.com/

LA CHAUSSÉE-TIRANCOURT

ⓘ Mairie, Place de l'Église (tel: 03 22 51 45 98)

This quiet village in the Somme valley, 12km north-west of Amiens, has been touched by history from many eras. Prehistoric finds here include the discovery, in 1967, of a 4,000-year-old grave, burial place of more than 300 people. Just across the Somme, in Picquigny, English claims to the throne of France were finally renounced by Edward IV in 1475, bringing an end to the Hundred Years War. A more recent conflict is evoked in the peaceful German military cemetery at Bourdon, 7km north-west of La Chaussée, where 22,187 World War II dead lie buried beneath its grass and its sombre green trees.

❯ Samara "Life-sized prehistory" is the subtitle of this enjoyable historical attraction on a 30-hectare site near the banks of the Somme. ("Samara" is the ancient name for the river.) You could spend a good half-day here learning about life from paleolithic to Gallo-Roman times. At the entrance you pick up a map and a schedule of the day's crafts displays. A winding path leads through an arboretum to a botanical garden full of herbs and flowers. From here, you have two options. The first is to continue on a nature theme, wandering around a swampy landscape typical of that inhabited by early man. (This could take an hour or more.) It demonstrates the origins of wetland, showing its evolution into beds of reed and willow, and its value to early man as a place for hunting, reed-gathering and peat-cutting. Admission to this "nature" part of the park is free.

The second route from the botanical garden takes you across the road, by a short tunnel, to a molehill-like structure known as the *"Pavillion"* for the prehistoric displays. (From here on, keep your ticket handy to prove you have paid.) Inside the building, you can join a free guided tour (in French), or pick up an English audioguide (1.50€) and follow numbered panels around the ground-floor displays; pressing a button near each video usually produces English subtitles. You learn about early prehistory and the historians who studied it; see flint tools, and bone-carvings; and read about funeral rites. Towards the end, near the statue of a Celtic horseman, is an area devoted to the Ribemont-sur-Ancre burial site 30km east of here (see page 140). On the lower floor are reconstructions of early dwellings, and explanations of the discoveries of bronze (from melting copper with tin) and iron (from heating iron ore). From these metals could be made weapons and jewels, feeding a sense of power that led to outbreaks of war and an end to the pastoral Stone Age life.

Outside, full-sized thatched buildings reproduce typical habitats of our ancestors: a longhouse, and some smaller constructions representing neolithic,

■ Ancestral home: Bronze Age at Samara.

Bronze and Iron Age dwellings. Nearby, craftsmen make pots, knap flints or kindle flames. Steep steps lead up to the site of a Gallo-Roman hill fort, or *oppidum*, from which there is a wonderful view across the Somme valley.

Take drinks and sunhats in hot weather; if wet, you need tough shoes for the marshland. There are toilets by the car park, and in the Pavillion. ◑ *Mid Mar–mid Nov, Mon–Fri 9.30am–5.30pm; Sat, Sun & public holidays 9.30am–6pm (1 May–30 June, Mon–Fri 9.30am–5.30pm; Sat, Sun & public holidays 9.30am–7.30pm; 1 July–31 Aug, daily 10am–6.30pm). On D191, 2km SE of La Chaussée (tel: 03 22 51 82 83). 9€, students, children & disabled 7.50€, under-6s free; family (2+2) 25€, extra children 6€. (Arboretum & marshland areas free.)* ♿ *(most).* ⓢ

LA CHAUSSÉE EXTRAS

Accommodation: Les Prés du Mesnil Simple 3-épi B&B near village church, with immaculate ground-floor rooms & copious breakfasts. Rooms from 49€; evening meal (on reservation) 20€. 1 Rue à l'Avoine (tel: 03 22 51 44 37/ 06 81 96 37 59).

CRÉCY-EN-PONTHIEU

ⓘ 32 Rue du Maréchal-Leclerc (tel: 03 22 23 93 84 fax: 03 22 23 93 84)
www.crecyenponthieu.com
sicrecy80@free.fr

This attractive village 12km north-east of Abbeville is the Crécy one learns about at school. To underline his claim to the French throne (see page 104), English king Edward III confronted Philippe VI of France just north of here, on 26 August 1346—the first major encounter of the Hundred Years War. France's heavily-encumbered knights and untrained infantry were no match for the well-disciplined English archers; by the end of the day a reputed 15,000 French had been slain, against English losses of a few hundred. There's a 10km signposted walk around town and battlefield; the tourist office has maps of other circuits that ramble through the ancient forest that lies to the south of the village.

❯**Musée Emhisarc** Near the village crossroads, a small museum presents a mixture of items, from mammoth bones to World War II helmets. The main room contains lovely Gallo-Roman glass, 6th-century funerary pots, glass beads, and fragments of pottery excavated at the site of Crécy's long-vanished castle. Most items have excellent English descriptive notes. Along the corridor are memorabilia from both world wars. In a further room, draped like a battlefield tent, a new permanent display about the Battle of Crécy is under construction. ● *Wed–Sat 10am–noon & 2–6pm (2 May–15 Oct, Wed–Sun 10am–12.30pm & 2–6.30pm). Closed 1–30 Apr. 4 Rue des Écoles (tel: 03 22 23 93 84). Admission free.* ⓢ

❯**Site of the Battle of Crécy** On a windswept plateau above the town, a wooden viewing-tower has been built at the site of the windmill from which Edward III watched the progress of the fighting and saw his son, the Black Prince, win his spurs on the battlefield. A faded panoramic picture helps to work out the disposition of English and French troops. After his victory, Edward marched his English soldiers north to lay siege to Calais (see page 75). ● *Route de Wadicourt (D111), 1km N of Crécy.* ⓢ

CRÉCY EXTRAS

Market: Mon.

Crafts: Vannerie du Boisle Large shop selling baskets of all shapes & sizes (those made on the site have a red label). Sun–Fri 2–6pm; Sat 10.30am–12.30pm & 2–6pm (1 Apr–31 Dec, daily 10am–12.30pm & 2–7pm). Le Boisle, on D928 8km NE of Crécy (tel: 03 22 29 65 66).

> **Chapelle des 300 Corps** In the midst of fields stands a curious roadside chapel with a steeply-pitched roof. In the churchyard around it are said to be buried 300 valiant French knights who fell at Crécy. ● *(exterior only). On D56, 2km E of Noyelles-en-Chaussée & 10km SE of Crécy.* **S**

LE CROTOY

ⓘ 1 Rue Carnot (tel: 03 22 27 05 25 fax: 03 22 27 90 58)
www.tourisme-crotoy.com
contact@tourisme-crotoy.com

The enchanting little seaside resort of Le Crotoy, 25km north-west of Abbeville, has the only south-facing beach of the Côte d'Opale. As sea-bathing increased in popularity during the 19th century, and the railways made travel easier, this picturesque fishing port began to draw the smart set. Paris perfumer Pierre Guerlain built a hotel and a house here in the 1850s and writer Jules Verne (see page 116) lived with his family in a villa called "La Solitude" (now No 9 Rue Jules-Verne) from 1869 to 1872. Seurat and Toulouse-Lautrec painted at Le Crotoy, and novelist Colette was a regular visitor to the resort.

Joan of Arc was held here for a month in 1430, en route to her trial, and death, in Rouen. A quayside monument above the beach pays tribute to her: "abandoned by those whom she had saved".

The tourist office has details of boat trips, fishing, tennis and riding, and of guided outings on foot or by bike—including the popular, muddy "*transbaie*" walks from Le Crotoy to St-Valéry, on the other side of the bay. At low tide the sea goes out a staggering 14km, and comes in exceedingly quickly once it turns. Currents are dangerously strong around the estuary, so always be aware of tide times.

Low water is an exceptionally beautiful time on the Somme estuary, when the glistening mud-flats reflect the muted blues and greys of the sky. From late August to February, the dawn silence is punctuated by the crack of guns, as wildfowlers—who have often spent the night in floating *huttes* (purpose-built hides, see page 92)—fire shots at migrating ducks and geese. Seals (see page 129) can be seen in the harbour during the two hours either side of high tide; or, at low water, off La Maye beach, 3km north-west of town.

Not quite as wild as these are the 2,000 sheep that graze on the *mollières*, or salt-meadows. Their delicately-flavoured meat has recently been awarded the super-status of an *appellation d'origine contrôlée*. If you want to try some, look for the "Estran" label in butchers' shops or on restaurant menus from June to February. Early October sees the annual "*transhumance*", when the flock is driven along the beach, through Le Crotoy, to its winter quarters. The event is marked with a day of sheepdog and sheep-shearing demonstrations and, of course, a feast of delicious grilled lamb.

Market: Tues (15 June-15 Sept), Rue de la République. Fri, Place Jeanne-d'Arc.
Specialities: Salt-meadow lamb. Cockles. Samphire.
Accommodation/food:
Les Tourelles *Pretty 2-star seafront hotel, with red-brick pinnacles. Rooms from 49€; menus from 21€. 2-4 Rue Pierre-Guerlain (tel: 03 22 27 16 33). www.lestourelles.com/*
Chez Mado *Friendly restaurant overlooking the sea. Three rooms, from 68€; fishy menus 16-36€. 6 Quai Léonard (tel: 03 22 27 81 22). www.chezmado.com/*
Café: Relais de la Baie *Breakfasts, English-style sandwiches & teas; plus art exhibitions. Open mid Mar-end Sept, Tues-Sun. 1 Rue du Crotoy, Noyelles-sur-Mer, 8km SE of Le Crotoy (tel: 03 22 23 50 20).*

■ **Watery world: low tide on Le Crotoy mud-flats.**

> **Chemin de Fer de la Baie de Somme** A classic steam train offers passengers wonderful views over salt-meadows and mud-flats during an hour-long journey around the perimeter of the bay. After closure in 1969, the line reopened to tourist traffic in 1971. The pristine engine and its restored carriages run between Le Crotoy and St-Valéry-sur-Somme by way of Noyelles-sur-Mer (the journey can continue farther west to Cayeux-sur-Mer). You can take a return ticket, or do one leg by bike

(cycles are carried free), or on foot (combined with a guided, cross-bay walk). Maintenance issues might occasionally mean a steam engine is not available. ❶ *1 Apr-30 Sept, Sat, Sun, Wed (1 July-31 Aug, daily); 1-31 Oct, Sun; plus occasional other dates. From 10.15am (exact times vary). Avenue de la Gare, off D104 Route de Rue (tel: 03 22 26 96 96). Le Crotoy to St-Valéry return: 10€, children 8€, under-4s free.* ❺

❯**Cimetière Chinois** Beyond a traditional Chinese gate lies one of the more unusual of the Commonwealth War Graves Commission's immaculately-tended cemeteries. This is the burial place of around 700 Chinese, part of a 100,000-strong labour force employed in France during World War I to load and unload equipment at docks and depots. In April each year, members of France's Chinese community come here to remember the dead, bringing enormous floral wreaths to mark the festival of Qingming. ● *Nolette (off D111), near Noyelles-sur-Mer, 9km SE of Le Crotoy.* ❺

■ Chinese memories: graves at Nolette.

FRÉVENT

ⓘ **12 Rue du Président-Wilson (tel: 03 21 47 18 55 fax: 03 21 41 99 96)**
www.ternois-tourisme.com
ot.frevent@wanadoo.fr

This market town 24km south-east of Hesdin, in the upper valley of the Canche, enjoyed an industrial boom in the 19th century, with wool and linen mills and the manufacture of agricultural machinery. However, during World War II the occupying Germans used a local foundry for manufacturing weapons, and the surrounding countryside for launching V1 attacks (see page 70), making Frévent a target for much Allied bombing. Rebuilt today, it is a thriving modern shopping centre. To the north-west, towards Fillièvres, pretty flower-filled villages (notably that of Boubers-sur-Canche) lie along the valley of the river.

❯**Musée Ducatel** Staff from the tourist office will step next door to open up this interesting museum of art and archaeology on request. Its ground-floor displays are based around a gift of colourful paintings left to the town by their creator Louis Ducatel (1902-99). An accomplished artist, this native of Frévent was also a brilliant civil engineer, manufacturer of oil pipelines, writer, politician (he stood for the French presidency in 1969), and the inventor of a flexible, thermoplastic paint. Upstairs is a collection of Gallo-Roman and Mérovingian coins, ancient pottery, and medieval floor tiles. ● *Tues-Fri 10am-noon & 2-4.30pm, Sat 10am-noon & 2-6pm, Sun 9.30am-noon & 2-6pm. 12 Rue du Président-Wilson (tel: 03 21 47 18 55). 3.10€, children 1.55€.* ❺

❯**Moulin-Musée Wintenberger** An old corn mill in the municipal garden contains a museum on Frévent's agricultural heritage. A good English brochure guides you up and down wooden stairs around 24 rooms packed with models, photographs, tools and machines. You can finger a bunch of flax, and feel the differences in texture between bran, cornflour and rye flour. There is much on the history of the Établissements Wintenberger, the company that was the town's major employer for a century, from 1837, manufacturing root-cutters, grain-crushers, seed-drills and other agricultural equipment. ❶ *Mid Mar-30 Nov, Fri-Sun 2-6pm (1 July-31 Aug, Tues-Sun 2-6pm). Place du Château, Rue Leclerc (tel: 03 21 41 31 26). 5€, children 2€.* ➤

❯ ★ **Jardin de Séricourt** This magical garden in a sheltered valley is deservedly classed "*jardin remarquable*". Designer and plant-breeder Yves Gosse de Gorre has created a series of surprises around his elegant house, based on a passion for contrasts and a mischievous sense of humour. Visitors pass from light to shade, from open lawns to enclosed woodland, and hear their footsteps on gravel, pebbles, wood blocks, crushed slate or mown grass. A palette of green foliage includes junipers, viburnums, hostas and grasses, with occasional injections of pink from lilacs and white from roses or wistaria. Moods can be sombre, as in the *"jardin guerrier"* (a "battlefield" garden in which armies of yews have snipped-out faces like warrior masks). They can be entertaining, as in the giant topiary "armchairs"; or inventive, as in the *"bois des ombres"*, an area of deep shade between colour-washed tree trunks. You can buy plants to take away, including the home-bred, white "Rose de Séricourt". ● *Tues-Sat 10am-12.30pm & 2-6pm (1 July-31 Aug, Tues-Sat 10am-12.30pm & 2-6pm; Sun, Mon 3-6pm). Closed 14 July, 15 Aug & 25 Dec-1 Jan. 2 Rue du Bois (Nuncq road), Séricourt, 2km NE of Frévent (tel: 03 21 03 64 42). 6.50€, children free.*

➤ **Pépinière Hennebelle** The late Jean-Pierre Hennebelle was a legendary figure to plant-lovers in France, creating many new varieties and displaying old ones in unusual ways. Since 2002, his sons have taken over his nursery and still provide keen gardeners (such as regular customer Catherine Deneuve) with a living catalogue of rare trees and shrubs. You can place orders, but plants will not be dug up and despatched until autumn. ● *Mon-Fri 8.30am-12.30pm & 1.30-6.30pm, Sat 9.30am-12.30pm & 2.30-6pm. 4 Rue du Marais, Boubers-sur-Canche, 5km NW of Frévent (tel: 03 21 03 77 26). Admission free; donations of 1€ per person welcome.*

FRÉVENT EXTRAS

Market: *Tues.*

Accommodation:

Le Moulin de Fillièvres
Welcoming 3-épi B&B in old watermill on the Canche. Riverside garden, convivial evening meals. Rooms from 48€; evening meal (on reservation) 19€. 16 Rue de St-Pol, Fillièvres, 11km NW of Frévent (tel: 03 21 41 13 20). www.moulindefillievres.com/

Brocante: **La Boutique**
A blue line painted on the floor leads from ground floor to attics of a shop devoted to furniture & knick-knacks. Tues-Sun 2.30-7pm. 8 & 12 Rue de St-Pol (tel: 03 21 03 61 23).

LONG

ⓘ **5 Grande Rue (tel: 03 22 31 82 50 fax: 03 22 31 71 88)**
www.long.fr
officedetourisme.long@wanadoo.fr

One of the most attractive villages along the Somme, 13km south-east of Abbeville, Long (pictured on page 35) earned so much from the sale of peat in the late 19th century that it became, for a time, the richest village in France. Peat financed the imposing Hôtel de Ville, two schools and the church. It even funded the construction of a tiny hydro-electric station that supplied every home with running water and electric light, earning Long the nickname of *"ville de lumière"* ("town of light"). Deposits of peat, a vital source of fuel in areas where there are few trees, are created by decomposition of vegetable matter. To extract the combustible lower layers, peat-cutters used a spade called a *louchet*, which

was fixed to a 7-metre-long pole and driven down, vertically from the water's edge. This constant cutting into the banks formed large *entailles*, or gashes in the landscape that account for many of the lakes along the river Somme (see picture, page 124). Once dug, the peat was pounded, formed into bricks, and stacked up to dry.

➤ **Centrale Hydro-Électrique** The village's water-driven power-station is in a small brick building straddling the river. From 1902 it furnished each house with a cold-water supply and energy for one light bulb—then considered the height of luxury. But, as locals installed bathrooms and washing-machines, demand outstripped capacity and activity ceased in 1974. Inside, the fragrant smell of engine oil hangs over the dials and circuit-breakers. While you view a short video about the history of Long and its peat-digging (in French, with some challengingly strong Picard accents from older interviewees), the guide opens the sluices, and gears up for the electricity demonstration. Gradually, power builds up from the force of

■ Symphony in green: topiary at Séricourt.

■ For peat's sake: many lakes on the Somme were dug out for fuel.

the river below, until a solitary light bulb begins to burn, recalling Long's brilliant past. ◗ *2 May-30 Sept, Tues-Sun 2-6pm. Chemin de Halage, signposted off D32 S of bridge (tel: 03 22 31 80 21). 2€, under 7s free.*

❯Château de Long This pretty brick and stone mansion in the village centre was built in 1733. Twentieth-century owners have restored it, and today you can take a guided tour (in French only) of the ground floor. The visit takes in the bright hallway; a bedroom lined with flower-painted panels; and the airy music-room, in which a lifelike, costumed automaton "plays" a selection of Viennese waltzes on a baby grand piano. The walls of the dazzling "zodiac" *salon* are decorated in tones of grey and gold, with reproductions of paintings showing fanciful versions of the 12 zodiac signs; the originals are in the Hôtel de Berny museum, in Amiens (see page 115). Outside, there's a delightfully informal garden, and temporary exhibitions in the stables. ○ *Late June-early Sept, Mon-Sat 2-6pm (timings subject to change). Rue du 11 Novembre (tel: 03 22 31 34 53). 4.50€.*

NAOURS

ⓘ Mairie, 5 Rue de l'Église (tel: 03 22 93 30 77 fax: 03 22 93 71 95)

Naours (pronounced "nah-oor"), 18km north of Amiens, is famous for its subterranean "village", or hiding-places, carved out of a network of tunnels. The main village, known for cider production, is more conventional, with farmhouses and crumbing earth-walled barns. Built in a rather grander architectural style of stone and brick, is the village of Bertangles, 8km to the south (pictured, page 29). Its graveyard was the first burial place of World War I flying ace Manfred von Richthofen, the "Red Baron" (see page 140).

❯ ★ Cité Souterraine de Naours Brochures for this family attraction hardly do justice to the amazing labyrinth of underground passages found here. (If you are visiting any of the other tunnel systems in the area, save this one until last; beside it, others pale into insignificance.) These man-made caves are the result of stone-quarrying since the 3rd century. Under constant threat of raids by Vikings, English, Spanish and Dutch, the population of up to 3,000 would withdraw below ground for a few days, with their rabbits and poultry, until the danger passed. ("They disappeared under the earth like ants", wrote a bewildered 8th-century invader.) The 2km of tunnels hewn into the chalk are arranged on three levels, comprising 300 "rooms" and some larger spaces used as chapels or for public assemblies. Six exits provided escape routes to the surface, and cunning pitfalls made entry hazardous for attackers. The guide points out fossils in the ceilings, ledges for oil lamps, and an ingenious evacuation system that diverted smoke into the chimney of a distant house. The caves were filled in after the Revolution, and rediscovered in 1887. In 1916 the site became a hospital for Australian troops, many of whom scrawled now-historic graffiti on the walls. Under the occupation of 1940, it was used as a munitions store, and as a German command post. The 45-minute tour involves steps, low ceilings and uneven surfaces. Wear flat shoes, and bring a jacket or sweater as, even on a hot day, it can feel chilly below ground. Tours can be given in English if numbers warrant; otherwise you can ask the guide for a written description to read en route.

NAOURS EXTRAS

Speciality: Cider.

Shop: **Cidrerie de la Garenne** *Cider, apple juice, cider vinegar & home-made jams. Mon-Sat 9am-noon & 2-7pm (1 Apr-30 Sept, daily 9am-noon & 2-7pm).* 18 Rue de la Croix *(tel: 03 22 93 71 89).*

Outdoors, on the surface, you find lawns and woodland; enclosures full of pygmy goats, fallow deer and fat-bellied black pigs; and old-fashioned playground rides for younger children (swings, wobbly walkway and so on) included in the admission charge. A family could spend half a day here—especially if you try the 18-hole mini-golf (3.50€) or sample the home-cooking in the café. You are not allowed to take food or drinks into the grounds, but you can leave to eat, and return later. (There is a covered picnic area above the car park.) ◑ *1 Feb-15 Nov, daily 10am-noon & 2-5.30pm (1 Apr-31 Aug, daily 9.30am-6.30pm). 5 Rue des Carrières (D60), 1km E of Naours (tel: 03 22 93 71 78). 10€, under-13s 8€ (without tunnel tour, both 5€), under-4s free.* ◉

❯Château de Bertangles The façades of this 18th-century mansion are decorated with carvings, and its magnificent main gates are adorned with designs on a hunting theme. A guided tour takes you inside some of the ground-floor rooms: the sunlit hall, the wood-panelled drawing-room, and the tapestry-hung dining-room. It ends outdoors, in an ancient farmyard that resembles a Brueghel painting, with crumbling outbuildings, a dovecote, and a medieval stone gateway. ○ *Mid July-mid Aug, daily guided tour 5.30pm prompt. Meet at campsite office, 10 Rue du Château, Bertangles, 8km S of Naours (tel: 03 22 93 68 36). 4€, children 2€.*

QUEND-PLAGE

ⓘ 1 Place du 8 mai 1945 (tel: 03 22 23 32 04 fax: 03 22 23 62 65)
www.office-tourisme-quend-plage.com
contact@office-tourisme-quend-plage.com

Quend-Plage, 10km north-west of Rue, and its neighbour Fort-Mahon-Plage are small family resorts on the sandy coast south of the Authie estuary. Launched at a similar time to Le Touquet and Hardelot, they have quite a different character from their high-society cousins. Both have Blue Flag awards for water quality, dozens of campsites, and a host of wind- and sand-related sports, as well as mini-golf, cycle-hire and lake-fishing.

Quend-Plage, to the south, offers modern shops and apartment blocks brightly painted in ochre, turquoise and dusky pink. There's a concentration of pizzerias and *friteries* (chip stands), plus *gaufre* (waffle) and candy-floss stalls. Activities include jet-skiing and a popular treetop trail; nightlife revolves around bars, disco, cinema and casino.

Fort-Mahon-Plage is quieter and less colourful than its neighbour, with a wide avenue of tamarisk plants leading towards the seafront. The beach has a *"handiplage"* designation; as part of this disabled-friendly policy, it offers free loan of Tiralos (see page 12) from the lifeguard station. There are plenty of sailing-related activities and, on dry land, a climbing wall *(mur d'escalade)* on a local water-tower.

❯Aquaclub de Belle-Dune Amid the pine forest is a water park with open-air pools, slides and playground as well as covered wave pool, flumes and waterfall. Adults can also use hot tubs, sauna and Turkish baths. No swimming "shorts" allowed. Take 2€ coins for the cloakroom lockers. ◑ *Mid Mar-mid Nov, & school holidays: Mon-Wed & Fri 2-7pm; Sat, Sun 11am-7pm (1 June-31*

■ Zipped up: children swing through the trees at Quend-Plage.

QUEND EXTRAS

Market: Mon & Thurs (both 15 June-15 Sept), Quend-Plage. Tues & Fri (both 1 June-30 Sept), Fort-Mahon-Plage, 2km N of Quend-Plage.
Speciality: *Mussels.*
Festival: Fête de la Moule *Mussel festival, Fort-Mahon-Plage, mid Sept.*
Golf: Golf de Belle-Dune *One of France's top courses, by JM Rossi. Promenade du Marquenterre, 2km NE of Quend-Plage (tel: 03 22 23 45 50). www.golfdebelledune.com/*

Aug, daily 11am-7pm). Promenade du Marquenterre, 2km NE of Quend-Plage (tel: 03 22 23 73 00). Pools: 10€, children 8.40€, children under 1m in height free; family (2+2 or 1+3) 35.40€ (1 June-31 Aug, 12.50€, 10€; 4.40€ & 45€). Espace détente (sauna, hot tubs etc) 3.50€. Ⓢ

➤Arbre et Aventure Swaying bridges, scrambling-nets and zip-wires link the platforms in the pine trees on a 3-hectare site that provides five entertaining treetop trails of varying degrees of difficulty. Trainers and tough clothes are essential; wire harnesses and gloves provided. Unusually, there are routes for younger children (parental supervision necessary). ◑ *Easter-mid Nov, Sat, Sun & public holidays 10am-5pm (1 July-31 Aug, daily 10am-5pm). 6 Avenue Henri-Renard, Quend-Plage-les-Pins (tel: 03 22 23 90 99/06 89 89 42 32). 18€, children under 12 13€.* Ⓢ

RUE

ⓘ 54 Rue Porte de Bécray (tel: 03 22 25 69 94 fax: 03 22 25 76 26)
www.ville-rue.fr
officedutourisme.rue80@wanadoo.fr

Once a major seaport, this quiet market town 20km north-west of Abbeville has a number of fine religious buildings. A *crucifix miraculeux,* washed up on the shore in 1101 and said to have floated from Jerusalem, made Rue a focus of pilgrimage in medieval times. The town is the capital of Marquenterre, a flat area of sand, water and woodland between the Somme and Authie estuaries, ideal for exploring by bike. The bird reserve here is an internationally important breeding-ground for avocet and spoonbill.

Just north of Rue, the Domaine de Marcanterra organises guided nature walks and rides, on bikes or on horseback. Its hardy small horses are a new breed created here in the mid 1970s. Called "Hensons", this cross between Norwegian ponies and thoroughbred horses spend their early years grazing on the reserve, and are rounded up each autumn.

➤Musée des Frères Caudron The town's ancient belfry contains a fascinating museum about two brothers, pioneers of aircraft-building in Picardy. Inspired by the success of the Wright brothers in the US in 1903, Gaston and René Caudron constructed a glider that became airborne after being towed by a horse. By 1910 they had made a biplane that flew 10km, and over the next 30 years built more than 10,000 aircraft, including many used during World War I and for the French airmail service. They opened factories at Rue, Lyon and near Paris, and flying schools at Rue and in China. Pictures of their graduate pilots include one of American Bessie Coleman who, in 1921, became the world's first licensed black aviator. In contrast, the large pictures on the top half of the walls in the main room depict the region's traditional occupations of sugar-production, cattle-rearing and peat-cutting. They were painted in 1901 by a local artist, Albert Siffait de Moncourt. ◗ *Mid Feb-1 Nov, Mon 2.30-6pm; Tues & Thurs-Sat 10am-noon & 2.30-6pm; Sun & public holidays 10am-12.30pm (1 July-31 Aug, Mon-Sat 10am-noon & 2.30-6pm; Sun & public holidays 10am-12.30pm). Beffroi, Rue du Colonel-Tetart (tel: 03 22 25 01 57). Admission free.* ◉

❯**Chapelle du St-Esprit** This flamboyant Gothic chapel was built between 1440 and 1514 to cope with the ever-more-numerous pilgrims flocking to the original church (the adjacent St-Wulphy's) to see the famous crucifix. The chapel's façade is decorated with Biblical scenes, so finely executed that they appear to be made from lace rather than stone. From the narthex, or inner porch, you can peer into the chapel, but in the summer the tourist office's guided tours take you inside for a closer look at the vaulted ceiling and at the large 19th-century canvases by Siffait de Moncourt (see Caudron Museum, above), depicting the arrival of the crucifix. The last remnant of it—a wooden hand of Christ—is on display in a glass-fronted box behind the altar. ◗ *Early Feb-31 Oct, daily 9.30am-5.30pm, narthex only (1 July-31 Aug, guided tours daily 10.30am, 11.30am, 4pm, 5pm & 6pm). Rue du Colonel-Tetart (tel: 03 22 25 69 94). Narthex admission free; guided tour 2€.* ◉

❯**Chapelle de l'Hospice** Guided tours of the St-Esprit chapel (see above) include a visit to this very different 16th-century building, which was once the chapel for the town's hospital. Beneath its high wooden ceiling, the walls are decorated with carvings of animals, and emblems of saints. ○ *1 July-31 Aug; guided tours only (see above). Rue du Colonel-Tetart.* ◉

❯ ★ **Parc Ornithologique du Marquenterre** This wonderful bird reserve on the Somme Bay is one of Europe's most treasured wetlands. More than 300 species pass through each year, including sandpipers, plovers and barnacle geese. Birds that breed here include herons, storks and egrets. At the ticket office you are issued with a map of the 2km, 4km and 6km trails, and an information sheet in English. Before starting out on a route, climb up to the platform among the pine trees to orientate yourself with a view over the lakes, reedbeds and walkways. Trails are marked with coloured arrows (for the red, 2km, walk, start by following the blue and green arrows). Multilingual panels provide information along the way.

The various rules (don't stray off the paths, make a noise, pick flowers or frighten the birds) mean the reserve is probably not an ideal place to bring young children until they have an interest in the subject. There are picnic areas by the car park and toilets in the visitor centre. It's a good idea to take your own binoculars; you can hire them (3.50€), but may have to queue on a busy day. The visitor centre is free, and you can drop in to enjoy its bird-themed shop, log fire and hot snacks. ● *Daily 10am-5pm (1 Feb-11 Nov, daily 10am-5.30pm; 1 Apr-30 Sept, daily 10am-7.30pm); last admission 3pm, 4pm & 5pm respectively. Closed 1 Jan & 25 Dec. Chemin des Garennes, St-Quentin-en-Tourmont, 6km W of Rue (tel: 03 22 25 68 99). 9.50€, children 7.10€, under 6s free.* ◉

RUE EXTRAS

Market: Sat.

Speciality: Bisteu (potato & bacon pasty).

Restaurant: **La Clé des Champs** Charmingly restored village farmhouse, serving sophisticated food. Menus 14-33€. Closed Sun evg-Tues. Favières, 5km S of Rue (tel: 03 22 27 88 00).

Festivals:

Ars Terra International piano festival, featuring rising stars of the keyboard. Villers-sur-Authie, 7km N of Rue, late July. www.arsterra.fr/

Fête du Henson The local herd of horses is moved to winter pastures, Domaine de Marcanterra, early Nov.

ST-RIQUIER

ⓘ Le Beffroi (tel: 03 22 28 91 72 fax: 03 22 28 02 73)
http://perso.orange.fr/off.tourisme.saint.riquier
off.tourisme.saint.riquier @wanadoo.fr

★ The mixture of building styles in St-Riquier, 9km north-east of Abbeville, is astonishing: some houses in brick, some in stone, and one having a gable shaped like Napoleon's hat. However, this delightful village is justly famous for its magnificent Gothic abbey church. A map from the tourist office shows a one-hour route past this and other interesting features.

❯Abbatiale St-Riquier The Benedictine abbey dates back to the time of Charlemagne (754-814) when its influence spread throughout the Christian west. Ravaged by Norman invasions, it was destroyed in 1131 in feudal wars and rebuilt in the 13th century, only to be gutted in the Hundred Years War, and again by Louis XI. The 16th-century, flamboyant Gothic church you see today has a façade ornamented with more than 50 statues. In contrast, the interior is plain, with stone pillars and sculptures, and clear glass windows. You can take guided tours (in French) of the church, and also of the "treasure room", which contains holy relics and a series of 16th-century wall-paintings. ◑ *1 Apr-late Oct, daily 10am-5pm (guided tours Tues-Sat 10am, 11am, 2pm, 3pm, 4pm & 5pm; Sun 2pm, 3pm, 4pm & 5pm; 1.50€, children 0.75€). Closed during July music festival, & during services. Mass: Sun 11am. Place de l'Église.* ☉

❯Musée Picard Alongside the church, the former monastic buildings contain an enjoyable museum of rural life in the region. It shows domestic interiors, and tools and techniques of sowing, reaping, cider-making, eel-catching, peat-cutting and game-trapping, and puts on excellent temporary exhibitions. Outside, are three superb Picardy barns. ◑ *Mid Mar-late Nov, Mon-Fri 2-6pm; Sat, Sun & public holidays 10am-noon & 2-6pm (1 May-30 Sept, daily 10am-noon & 2-6pm; 1 July-31 Aug, daily 10am-6pm). Place de l'Église (tel: 03 22 28 20 20). Admission free.* ☉

❯Chapelle de l'Hôtel-Dieu The panelling of this small 18th-century chapel was carved by Baron Pfaff von Pfaffenhoffen, an Austrian who settled in St-Riquier in 1750, having fled his own country after killing a man in a duel. The guided tours also take in the cloister that lies behind. ◑ *1 Apr-31 Oct, Sat-Thurs, 2-6pm. Rue de l'Hôpital (tel: 03 22 28 92 92). 2€.*

❯Les Muches de Domqueur/Maison Picarde Two rooms of a typical Picardy farmhouse show the simple life of its former inhabitants. Beneath it lies a 17th-century network of underground passages that sheltered the population from marauders. An entertaining 90-minute tour (in French) leads you through 120 metres of the tunnels, past some 30 hollowed-out chambers. Low headroom and uneven surfaces make the visit unsuitable for those with mobility problems or any tendency to claustrophobia. ◑ *1 Apr-30 Sept, Sat, Sun 3-6pm. 4 Place de l'Église, Domqueur, 8km SE of St-Riquier (tel: 03 22 28 09 17). 3.50€, children 2.50€.*

ST-RIQUIER EXTRAS

Accommodation: Hotel Jean de Bruges Tastefully restored stone mansion alongside church. Rooms from 99€. Light lunches & teas. 18 Place de l'Église (tel: 03 22 28 30 30). www.hotel-jean-de-bruges.com/ *Festival: Festival de Musique de St-Riquier* Classical music concerts by international musicians, July. www.festival-de-saint-riquier.fr/ *Brocante: Antiquités Brocante Cabuzel* Small shop crammed with furniture, glass & objects. Tues-Thurs 2-6.30pm, Fri-Sun 10am-noon & 2-6.30pm. 2 Rue de Gaulle (tel: 03 22 28 49 05).

■ **Emperor's hat: some of the varied architecture in the village of St-Riquier.**

ST-VALÉRY-SUR-SOMME

ⓘ **2 Place Guillaume-le-Conquérant (tel: 03 22 60 93 50 fax: 03 22 60 80 34)**
www.saint-valery-sur-somme.com
officetourismesaintvalery.80@wanadoo.fr

With its yachts, restaurants, chic little shops and trendy cafés, St-Valéry, 20km north-west of Abbeville, is one of the most picturesque spots on France's Opal Coast. Its mixture of architectural styles ranges from medieval ramparts to 19th-century villas.

A monument near the waterfront commemorates the invasion of England by William the Conqueror (or Guillaume le Conquérant, as he is better known here), who waited at St-Valéry for a favourable wind to convey his 700 ships across the Channel. The town passed back and forth between English and French during the Hundred Years War, was burnt down by Louis XI in 1475, and was taken first by Protestants and then by Catholics in the 16th-century Wars of Religion. A signposted 7.5km walking route leads from quaysides to viewpoints, via the old fishermen's quarter called Le Courtgain and the twisting streets of the medieval upper town.

You can take a steam-train ride around the estuary to Le Crotoy (see page 121), or west to Cayeux-sur-Mer, or join a guided walk across the mud-flats, to Le Crotoy. A stroll along waterside Quai Jeanne-d'Arc, lined with attractive villas, leads to the town beach and to Cap Hornu, where the bay begins to widen. Around high tide, some of the 100-strong colony of common seals that live in the estuary venture inshore as far as St-Valéry's harbour. At low water, they can be seen farther away, basking on sandbanks off the village of Le Hourdel. Here, where the Somme joins the sea, you can eat oysters, or look for the rare plants that grow on the shingle strand.

➤ **Écomusée Picarvie** This comprehensive and enjoyable museum shows almost every aspect of early 20th-century rural life in Picardy. Ask for a sheet in English to explain the old shops, crafts, room-settings and building styles. You find equipment for shoeing horses and oxen, making boots and galoshes, churning butter, ironing bonnets and lifting beet. There are reconstructions of a schoolroom (with posters warning of the evils of drink), and of the workshops of cooper, wheelwright, locksmith and saddler. A 10-minute video (in French) explains the cultivation of flax, and the soaking, crushing and carding that produces the soft threads for weaving into linen. ❶ *1 May-30 Sept, Wed-Sun 10am-6pm. 5 Quai du Romerel (tel: 03 22 26 94 90). 5.25€, children 3€.* ❺

➤ **Herbarium des Remparts** The rather dull-sounding name doesn't prepare you for the vivid hues of poppies, roses and pinks that await behind the blue door of this walled garden. It has been planted by Nicole Quillot, who rescued the former convent garden from 40 years of neglect. Around a gnarled apple tree are laid out beds for medicinal, dye, food and herbal plants—and even for poisonous varieties. Hemp, flax and nettles represent plants used for clothing; "war vegetables" (such as Jerusalem artichokes, swedes and soapwort) show what French families survived on during the privations of World Wars I and II. Look out for witty displays of flower-pots: as edging, as plant-labels and as hanging decoration. You can buy sprigs of herbs, or pretty little packets of seeds gathered here to take home and plant. ❶ *1 May-15 Nov, Mon-Fri 10am-6pm; Sat, Sun 10am-12.30pm & 3-6pm. 36 Rue Brandt, off Rue du Comte-Robert (tel: 03 22 26 90 72). 5€, children under 12 free.* ❺

➤ **Maison de l'Oiseau** In the flat landscape south of the Somme estuary a typical Picardy farm has been turned into a bird-related visitor centre. Large glass cases with painted backgrounds show 250 stuffed birds and their habitats: razorbills, gannets and curlews on cliffs; oystercatchers, avocets and redshanks on mud-flats; jays, hawks and woodpeckers in forests and fields. A good 10-minute film illustrates the effects of farming and of the tides. During summer there are flying demonstrations by birds of prey (known in French as *rapaces*); check times on arrival. Buzzards, hawks, owls and eagles skim above the heads of the audience. (To avoid uncomfortably close encounters with the performers, you are warned to turn off mobile phones, and not to eat or smoke.) ● *Daily 10am-5pm (early Apr-early Oct, daily 10am-6pm). Closed 25 Dec. Flying displays early Apr-31 Aug, daily 11.30am, 2.30pm & 4.30pm; 1 Sept-early Oct, daily 3.30pm. Carrefour du Hourdel, Lanchères, on D3, 6km W of St-Valéry (tel: 03 22 26 93 93). 6.30€, children 4.60€, under-6s free; family (2+2) 19.80€ (early Apr-early Oct, with flying display, 9.90€, 7€ & 30.20€).* ♿ ❺

ST-VALÉRY EXTRAS

Market: Sun, Place des Pilotes; Wed, Place du Jeu-de-Battoir.

Accommodation/food: *Relais Guillaume de Normandy* Distinctive old waterfront house, now a 2-star Logis. Rooms from 55€; menus 18-40€. Closed Tues, except mid July-31 Aug. 46 Quai du Romerel (tel: 03 22 60 82 36). www.logisdefrance.com/

Restaurant: Bistrot St Val' Great fish, plus local dishes like ficelle picarde (stuffed pancake). Menus from 15€. 5 Place des Pilotes (tel: 03 22 60 82 54).

Festivals: *Fête Guillaume le Conquérant* Weekend of medieval entertainment & festivities, June.

Transbaie Annual running race at low tide from St-Valéry to Le Crotoy & back, across the estuary, June.

■ **Top garden: Herbarium on St-Valéry's ramparts.**

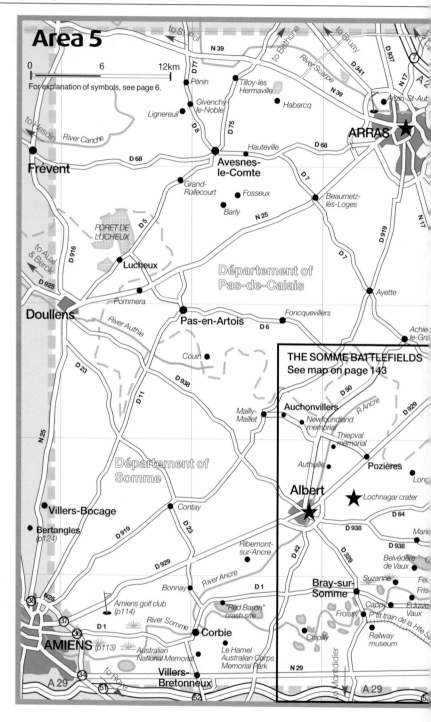

Area 5

0   6   12km

For explanation of symbols, see page 6.

N 39

to St Pol

D 77

to Béthune

River Scarpe

to Bruay

D 341

D 937

N 17

A 2

7

Pénin

Tilloy-lès-Hermaville

Habarcq

Arzio-St-Aub

Givenchy-le-Noble

Lignereuil

D 8

D 75

N 39

ARRAS

to Hesdin

River Canche

D 68

Hauteville

D 68

D 7

Frévent

Avesnes-le-Comte

Grand-Rullecourt

Fosseux

Beaumetz-lès-Loges

D 919

N 17

FORÊT DE LUCHEUX

D 5

Barly

N 25

D 7

Département of Pas-de-Calais

to Auxi & Berck

D 916

Lucheux

D 925

Pommera

Ayette

Doullens

River Authie

Pas-en-Artois

D 6

Foncquevillers

Achie-le-Gra

Couin

THE SOMME BATTLEFIELDS
See map on page 143

D 23

D 938

D 11

D 50

R Ancre

D 929

Mailly-Maillet

Auchonvillers

Newfoundland memorial

Thiepval memorial

N 25

Département of Somme

Authuille

Pozières

Long

Villers-Bocage

Contay

Albert

Lochnagar crater

D 64

Bertangles
(p124)

D 919

D 23

Marie

D 938

Ribemont-sur-Ancre

D 42

D 329

D 938

Belvédère de Vaux

Suzanne

Fe

Fris

38

N 26

Bonnay

River Ancre

D 1

Bray-sur-Somme

Cappy

Écluse

Vaux

37

D 1

Amiens golf club
(p114)

River Somme

"Red Baron"
crash site

Froissy

P'tit train de la Hte S

36

AMIENS (p113)

Australian National Memorial

Corbie

Chipilly

Railway museum

34

Le Hamel
Australian Corps
Memorial Park

N 29

to Roye

51

Villers-Bretonneux

A 29

to Montdidier

A 29

52

First-timers visiting World War I sites might be apprehensive about plunging into an atmosphere of gloom and destruction. But, while the events of 1914 to 1918 are tragic in the extreme, visiting the museums, memorials and cemeteries can prove to be a serene and even uplifting experience. In the aftermath of the war, many of the shell-shattered French towns and villages were "adopted" by others overseas; street names, such as "Rue de Birmingham" in Albert, often commemorate this assistance. The city of Sheffield built workers' housing in Bapaume; Blackburn sent help to Péronne; and the Australian state of Victoria funded a school for Villers-Bretonneux. A result of all this 1920s' reconstruction in the region has been a new heritage of Art Deco buildings. The landscape, too, has been renewed, and today the beautiful rolling downland of the Upper Somme is smoothly cultivated. Farther north, in the peaceful Artois countryside, unblemished villages still contain ancient fortified farms and elegant 18th-century country mansions.

✪ SUNDAY-MORNING BEST

In addition to the sites marked with the above logo in the following pages, here are a few more suggestions for places to visit on a Sunday morning in this area:
Anglican service: *Arras (see relevant Extras column).*
General: *walks, battlefield sites, war cemeteries and memorials.*
Ask the local tourist office, *in advance, for information on Sunday carnivals, festivals and flea-markets.*

Arras, Albert, and the Somme battlefields

ALBERT

ⓘ 9 Rue Gambetta (tel: 03 22 75 16 42 fax: 03 22 75 11 72)
www.ville-albert.fr
ot.albert.ancre@wanadoo.fr

To British visitors, this small town 30km north-east of Amiens is known as the epicentre of Somme battlefield tourism. The tourist office—focus for the "Secteur du Souvenir", or Remembrance Trail—is well stocked with information on battlefield walks and on local companies offering short battlefield tours. It also rents out bikes.

You are likely to have seen photographs of the shattered town during the Battle of the Somme, particularly images of its "leaning Madonna" (see picture, page 141). Albert's vast neo-byzantine basilica had been completed only 18 years before it was destroyed by bombardment in January 1915. Its crowning, 5-metre-high statue of the Virgin dangled horizontally over the town, giving rise to a legend that when she fell the war would end. (The prophecy was almost fulfilled, as she fell in April 1918.) The church was rebuilt to the identical plan by Louis Duthoit, son of the original architect.

Local man Henri Potez made Albert famous in the 1920s and 30s for aircraft manufacture (a full-sized Potez 36 hangs inside the hall of the railway station). A link with this industry continues today, with the modern Aérospatiale factory on the south-east side of town.

> ★ **Musée: Somme 1916/Musée des Abris** Beside the basilica, an atmospheric museum is installed in a series of underground tunnels that were once air-raid shelters. The visit starts with a short video (screened alternately in French and English) about the Battle of the Somme. Then, along 250 metres of passages, you see relics from the trenches, letters, newspaper-cuttings and cartoons, and tributes to soldiers and workers from French and British colonies. A series of tableaux shows Allied and German dugouts; informative captions, in English, explain advances in gas protection, medical treatment and design of uniforms. (Steel helmets appeared only in September 1915.) There are trench mortars, bayonets, a cutaway shell-case showing the flesh-tearing shrapnel balls within, and examples of "trench art" (see page 167). Finally you walk through a barrage of battlefield noise and flashing lights, emerging into the peace of the museum shop. You can buy shell-cases and other war souvenirs, but make sure you obtain a receipt for anything you might take home (see page 22). ● 1 Feb-15 Dec, daily 9am-noon & 2-6pm (1 June-30 Sept, daily 9am-6pm). Rue Anicet-Godin (tel: 03 22 75 16 17). 4€, children 2.50€. 🎧 🅂

> ★ **Lochnagar crater** The scale of this hole in the ground, 90 metres across and 30 metres deep, renders most visitors speechless. It was created by an explosion timed for 7.28am on 1 July 1916, the largest in a chain of 19 massive mines that were set off beneath the German lines in the moments before the Allied attack. An annual ceremony is held here at 7.28am on 1 July. ● Off D929 (signposted "La Grande Mine"), La Boisselle, 2km NE of Albert, off D929. 🅂

■ Getting the low-down: Somme museum in Albert.

Fine art: gateway to the Beaux-Arts in Arras.

ARRAS

ⓘ Place des Héros (tel: 03 21 51 26 95 fax: 03 21 71 07 34)
www.ot-arras.fr
arras.tourisme@wanadoo.fr

★ The city of Arras, capital of the ancient province of Artois, is one of the region's most attractive towns. Following signposts to "Les Places" leads to its two, almost adjacent arcaded squares: Grand'Place (the larger), and Place des Héros. Their cobbled pavements are lined with a total of 155 gabled houses (pictured, page 135). It is amazing to realise that they were all faithfully reconstructed in the 1920s, after the devastation of World War I.

The Romans established "Nemetacum" at the confluence of the Scarpe and the Crinchon rivers. St Vaast brought Christianity to the area in the 6th century; the Benedictine abbey founded in his name became the largest in the kingdom. The cloth trade and, later, the production of tapestries, maintained the prosperity of Arras through the Middle Ages.

The 17th century saw a surge of new building in the town (including its two main squares); the 18th century was a time of cultural and scientific expansion, and also of the laying out of Place Victor-Hugo—an architectural delight hidden away in the "lower town". However, the Revolution swept away Arras's medieval cathedral, the original abbey of St Vaast and many other religious buildings.

The city is honeycombed with tunnels and cellars that have served many purposes through the centuries. Some of those beneath the tourist office in the Hôtel de Ville (town hall) can be visited; others, with a World War I connection, will be opening in 2008 (see page 135). Outside the town hall, a succession of silver-coloured pavement studs marks a 2km walking route around the main monuments. The tourist office rents out audioguides in English to enhance the visit, and organises guided walking tours in summer.

The area round the railway station is the place for modern hotels, and for restaurants that are likely to be open on a Sunday evening. Shoppers should make for the long thoroughfare called, variously, Rue St Aubert/Rue Ernestale/Rue Gambetta, a virtual style-book of Art Deco architecture. There are some quaint little shops in the side streets and a great Saturday market in the main squares. Most shops are closed on Monday.

➤ Musée des Beaux-Arts Beyond a cobbled courtyard, this elegant building on the site of the abbey of St Vaast houses an excellent historical and fine-arts museum. It contains Roman items unearthed from sites around the town, as well as jewellery, ancient seals, fragments of statues and frescoes, carved wooden angels and finely-etched funerary slabs. Other displays feature Arras lace, blue-and-white Arras porcelain, tapestries, altar panels and some skeletal 15th-century tomb figures. Upstairs are magnificent examples of French and Flemish painting, plus works by 18th- and 19th-century artists. Labelling is in French only, but in most rooms you find a leaflet in English describing the exhibits. ● *Wed-Mon 9.30am-noon & 2-5.30pm. Closed public holidays. 22 Rue Paul-Doumer (tel: 03 21 71 26 43). 4€, children 2€.* 🅺 🆂

➤ Les Dessous d'Arras: "Les Bôves" A highlight of a visit to Arras is this subterranean tour of tunnels hollowed out in the 10th century and used as stone quarries, depots for merchandise and refuge from invaders. The guided tour (hourly, and in English on request) lasts 40 minutes. With low headroom and uneven surfaces, it is not for the claustrophobic, the infirm or babes in arms.

From mid March to mid June, the visits take on a different aspect. Half is still on the history, but the rest features specially-illuminated subterranean gardens—the "Jardin des Bôves"—where orchids bloom and ferns flourish. ● *Mon 10am-noon & 2-6pm, Tues-Sat 9am-noon & 2-6pm, Sun 10am-12.30pm & 2.30-6.30pm (1 May-30 Sept, Mon-Sat 9am-6.30pm, Sun 10am-1pm &*

2.30-6.30pm). Closed 1 Jan & 25 Dec. Tourist office, Hôtel de Ville, Place des Héros (tel: 03 21 5 26 95). 4.70€, children 2.70€. 🔊

❯**Historama** In an underground room by the entrance to the *bôves*, you can view a 20-minute presentation about the city's history narrated, rather jokily, as if by the golden lion that looks down from the top of the belfry (English version on request). The Roman remains, medieval stone-carvings and Arras pottery shown on screen can be seen in the Beaux-Arts museum (see page 133). You can enjoy the lion's-eye view of the town yourself, later, with a guided visit to the first level of the belfry
● *Visiting information as above. Historama: 2.70€, children 1.80€. Belfry: 2.70€ & 1.80€.* 🔊

❯**Cathédrale** Daylight streams into the lovely neo-Classical cathedral, originally built as the church of St Vaast abbey. As it was restored in the 1920s, much of the furniture and bronze fitments have a strongly Art Deco feel. On display are an Aubusson tapestry, eight imposing sculptures of saints, and a series of golden caskets containing holy relics—including a scrap of the surplice said to have been worn by Thomas à Becket when he was assassinated, in 1170. ● *Mon-Sat 2.30-5.30pm (1 May-15 Oct, daily 10.30am-5.30pm. Guided tours mid June-mid Sept, Sat 3pm, 4.80€, children 3.20€). Mass: 1 July-31 Aug, Sun 10.30am. Rue Albert-1er de Belgique.* 🔊

❯**Cité Nature** This modern hymn to food has been installed in a former factory north of the town centre. In an enormous, airy space, glass panels display seeds and vegetables to hugely decorative effect. (It's as well that the museum is strong on visuals, because there are as yet no caption translations to help foreign visitors.) Ten thousand years of food history take in neolithic farming tools, medieval ploughing techniques, steam-powered farm machines and a real modern tractor. Grand tableware includes glass from Lille, and silver sugar-tongs. Panels compare the daily intake of a farmworker and a farm-owner (the first high on bread and soup; the second enjoying larger helpings of meat). There are displays on beer and wine, fruit and vegetables, fish, chocolate, coffee, tea and oil. Boxes of fragrant spices are laid out to be sniffed. ● *Tues-Fri 9am-5pm; Sat, Sun 2-6pm. Closed public holidays. 25 Boulevard Robert-Schuman (tel: 03 21 21 59 59). 7€, children 3€; family (2+2) 16€.* ♿ 🐾

❯**Musée du Compagnonnage/Maison Robespierre** Built in 1730, this town house was the home of statesman Maximilien de Robespierre from 1787 to 1789, just before his election to the *États Généraux*, or National Assembly. One corner of the main room contains exhibits on the life of this Arras-born barrister and poet, a major figure of the French Revolution, but who was himself overthrown and guillotined in 1794, at the age of 36.

The main part of the ground floor is given over to the subject of the brotherhood (*compagnonnage*, in French) of master builders. The organisation evolved from medieval livery companies, with the *maçon*, or stonemason, at the top of a hierarchy of building trades. It flourished after the Revolution (the brotherhood is at the origins of the trades-union movement in France) but, with other "secret" societies, was suppressed by the Vichy government during World War II. The Compagnonnage reformed in 1953 and is today active in helping young tradesmen develop their building skills. Photographs, certificates and silk sashes illustrate the Masonic-style ceremonies that surrounded a *compagnon's* progress, which also involved a year working in different corners of France. The elaborate structures on display show off the craftsmen's abilities. ● *Tues, Thurs 2-5.30pm; Sat, Sun & public holidays 3.30-6.30pm (1 May-30 Sept, Tues-Fri 2-5.30pm; Sat, Sun & public holidays 2.30-6.30pm). Closed 1 Jan & 25 Dec. 9 Rue Maximilien-de-Robespierre (tel: 03 21 71 33 94). Admission free.*

❯**Église Notre-Dame-des-Ardents** This small, 19th-century brick church celebrates an appearance of the Virgin in May 1105. During

■ **Intricate craftsmanship: the skill of the Compagnons.**

■ Arras reborn: the Grand'Place.

an epidemic of a plague called *les ardents* (identified today as ergotism) she revealed herself to two troubadours, telling them that on Whit Sunday she would give them a holy candle. They were to light it, drip its wax into water, and give sips of the liquid to the afflicted. Miraculously, the 144 people treated recovered. ● *Daily 2.30-4.30pm. Rue Aristide-Briand.*

❯**Site Archéologique de Nemetacum** Excavations for a new town-centre building development in the 1990s uncovered remains of the 2,000-year-old city of Nemetacum, or Roman Arras. Behind a set of unprepossessing metal gates, guided tours (in French) take you around the site, across metal walkways, for a close look at the wall-footings outlining the houses and roadways. (The artefacts found are in the Beaux-Arts museum, see page 133.) In July and August you can also just walk in and view the site from a platform. ❶ *Mid June-mid Sept, guided tours Sat, Sun 3pm & 4pm, 3€, children free. 1 July-31 Aug, access to viewing platform Tues-Sun 2.30pm-5pm, admission free. 77 Rue Baudimont.*

❯**Carrière Wellington/Wellington Quarry Memorial** This new attraction will take visitors 60 metres below ground to hear about the Allied plan, in 1916, to link and extend the city's warren of cellars, quarries and tunnels eastward until they reached the German lines. Located near the railway station, the "Wellington" quarry is named in honour of the New Zealand miners who dug through the chalk for almost a year to accomplish this. More than 20,000 British troops were concealed underground for several days before launching a surprise attack on 9 April 1917 towards the Germans' Hindenburg Line, in what became known as the Battle of Arras. ● *Opens 2008. Days, times & admission charge not known at time of writing. Information from tourist office (tel: 03 21 51 26 95).*

❯**Citadelle** The imposing fortress, completed in 1672, still has a military function as a barracks for the Gendarmerie so visits are only possible on 90-minute guided tours (in English, if requested). You book through the tourist office, and need to show passports on arrival to confirm identity. The brick ramparts were built in the classic star-shaped design by military engineer Vauban (see page 46). A model of the citadel helps you to understand how defenders could protect every part of its exterior walls. At its heart is a large parade-ground surrounded by arsenal, gunpowder-store, governor's house and a small baroque chapel. Ironically, the shifting of France's frontier northwards in 1659 meant that Vauban's magnificent stronghold never had to withstand attack. ❶ *Mid June-mid Sept, guided tours (pre-booked only) Sun 3pm; meet outside main entrance, Boulevard du Général-de-Gaulle (tel: 03 21 51 26 95). 4.80€, children 3.20€.*

❯**Mur des Fusillés** The little road between the citadel and Arras's large British military memorial and cemetery leads to one of the area's grimmest stories of World War II. A kilometre or so along the road, an iron gate gives access to the dry moat of the citadel in which, between 1941 and 1944,

ARRAS EXTRAS

Market*: Sat & Wed.*

Specialities*: Andouillette (tripe sausage). Arras china.*

Accommodation/food:

Hotel d'Angleterre *Small 4-star hotel opposite station. Rooms from 97€; menus 14-30€. 7 Place Foch (tel: 03 21 51 51 16). www.hotelangleterre.net/*

Hotel de l'Univers *3-star central hotel. Rooms from 93€; menus 19-53€. 3/5 Place de la Croix-Rouge (tel: 03 21 71 34 01). www. hotel-univers-arras.com/*

Restaurants*:*

La Faisanderie *Grand restaurant in vaulted cellars. Menus 23-62€. Closed Sun evg & Mon. 45 Grand' Place (tel: 03 21 48 20 76).*

Aux Grandes Arcades *Popular, traditional place. Menus from 15€. 8 Grand' Place (tel: 03 21 23 30 89).*

La Coupole d'Arras *Good brasserie near station. Menu 30€. Closed Sun evg, Nov to Easter. 26 Bd de Strasbourg (tel: 03 21 71 88 44).*

Brocante: Trouvailles *Large place on NE corner of town. Mon-Sat 2.30-7pm. 4 Rue Victor-Leroy (tel: 03 21 51 14 11).*

Factory shop: Sylvie Thiriez *Luxury household linen. Mon 2-7pm, Tues-Sat 10am-noon & 2-7pm. 70 Rue des Trois-Visages.*

Anglican services*: Holy Communion 2nd & 4th Sun 10.30am. 103 Rue d'Amiens.*

Golf: Golf d'Arras *18-hole course, laid out by JC Cornillot. Anzin-St-Aubin, 4km NW of Arras (tel: 03 21 50 24 24). www.golf-arras.com/*

218 members of the Resistance were shot. Plaques on the brick walls give names and occupations among the numerous coal-miners, many Polish names are a reminder that thousands of workers were brought from Poland in the 1920s to supplement a French labour force grossly depleted by World War I. ● *Avenue des Fusillés*. ♿ Ⓢ

➤Son-et-lumière: *Histoires et Rêves d'Artois* Epic 90-minute open-air show, presented as a slightly tongue-in-cheek patchwork of 20 centuries of local history. It covers the arrival of Christianity Arras's medieval cloth trade, coal-mining, and an emotive evocation of the trenches—jumbled up and interspersed with galloping horses, dancing villagers and brilliant tableaux. The jokey repartee between the presenters may be difficult for non-French-speakers to follow but, with its torchlit procession and dazzling fireworks, the spectacle is so visual that full understanding hardly matters. Wrap up warmly, as the show continues in almost all weathers. Booking in advance by credit card via phone or website. Ⓞ *First three weekends of Sept, Fri & Sat, 9pm. Anzin-St-Aubin, 4km NW of Arras (tel: 03 21 51 29 61). 15€, children under 12 5€. http://acnspectacle.com/*

AUCHONVILLERS
ⓘ see Albert (page 132)

Dubbed memorably by the British Tommy "Ocean Villas" (a fair stab at the proper pronunciation), this small village 13km north of Albert was almost on the Battle of the Somme front line. On 1 July 1916 the Allies unleashed their attack a few hundred metres to the east with the detonation of a huge mine at Hawthorn Ridge.

➤Mémorial Terre-Neuvien/Beaumont-Hamel Newfoundland Memorial
A life-sized bronze caribou appears to bellow mournfully across the ground over which so many men of Newfoundland went to their deaths on 1 July 1916. Off the Hamel road, the zigzagging Allied and German trenches—now gently grassed over—reproduce the bewildering maze from which the troops climbed, and a signposted trail re-creates their route across no man's land during the attack. After the first 30 minutes, three-quarters of the Newfoundlanders lay dead or wounded.

A little clapboard house contains a visitor centre recounting how Newfoundland, which was not yet part of Canada in 1916, had formed its own regiment to come to the aid of Britain. Of the 25,000 who temporarily relinquished their hard lives as fishermen and sailed for Europe, just 6,000 men returned home, many with missing limbs and shattered minds. The terrible losses have caused 1 July to become a national day of mourning in Newfoundland; a ceremony of commemoration is held here on that date. ● *Site: open at all times. Museum: daily 10am-6pm.*

■ The call of home: a caribou mourns the Newfoundlanders.

AUCHONVILLERS EXTRAS

Accommodation/food:

Les Galets English-owned B&B, located almost on the 1 July 1916 front line. Rooms 56€; evening meals (on reservation) 20€. Route de Beaumont (tel: 03 22 76 28 79). www.lesgalets.com.

Snacks & teas:

Ocean Villas Breakfasts (til 11am), hearty plates of chili & fish-&-chips, & home-made cakes. Open 9am-7pm. Trench excavations in back garden. Also B&B rooms from 66€; evening meal 20€. 10 Rue de Lattre (tel: 03 22 76 23 66). www. oceanvillas-tearooms.com.

Gare de Beaucourt

Snacks, ices, poppy-themed souvenirs & strong English tea served in a dilapidated railway station, once part of the German front line. Poppy crosses on sale. Open 11am-7pm (Sat, Sun until 10pm). Beaucourt, 2.5km E of Auchonvillers (tel: 03 22 83 00 02).

Closed 25 Dec-1 Jan. Guided visits in English available between May & Nov. D73 Hamel road, 2km SE of Auchonvillers (tel: 03 22 76 70 86). Admission free. ⓰ Ⓢ

➤HélicoSomme helicopter visits You can take an 18-minute flight over the battlefield areas of Beaumont-Hamel, Thiepval and Pozières. Special, longer Australian- or Canadian-themed trips are also available by arrangement. ● Mar-Nov. Departs from Newfoundland Memorial, as above (tel: 03 22 76 14 18/06 16 28 60 59). 90€ per person (minimum four people); longer trips 160-175€ per person. ⓰ www. ensomme.net/

➤Église St-Pierre It seems miraculous that, just 3km from the Somme front line, the extravagant 16th-century carving on the façade of this village church should have survived. Between the doors sits a sorrowing figure of Christ; above it, Adam and Eve are shown being expelled from Paradise. ● (exterior only). Mailly-Maillet, 1.5km W of Auchonvillers. ⓰ Ⓢ

➤Château de Couin In the centre of a sleepy Artois village, this stately home adorned with sculptures of chubby stone cherubs was built by a wealthy 18th-century politician. Closed up for 40 years after World War II, it is today being restored by its present owners. The 90-minute guided tours show off high-ceilinged, wood-panelled ground-floor rooms, now

■ **Chiselled features: Mailly-Maillet church.**

redecorated in hand-blocked wallpapers, luxurious fabrics and expensive trimmings. The disued basement has late-19th-century conveniences, including a kitchen range and majestic radiators. Outside, in the 1780s stable block, wrought-iron hayracks, marble mangers, moulded ceilings and gracious chandeliers demonstrate that, here, even the horses lived in style. ❶ 15 Mar-31 Oct, Mon, Thurs, Fri 10am-4pm; 1st & 3rd weekends of month Sat, Sun 11am-5pm (16 June-31 Aug, Wed-Mon 10am-6pm); guided tours 11am & 2.30pm. 11 Rue Principale (D25), Couin, 12km NW of Auchonvillers (tel: 03 21 58 98 67). 7.50€, children 4.50€; under-10s free. Ⓢ

AVESNES-LE-COMTE

ⓘ see Arras (page 133)

Avesnes-le-Comte is a slightly faded market town, 20km west of Arras. It lies at the heart of the Arras/St-Pol-sur-Ternoise/Doullens triangle, among hilly Artois countryside crammed with villages so frozen in time that you half-expect medieval knights on horseback to come clattering out of their courtyards. Some attractive places worth exploring include, anticlockwise from the south, Barly, Fosseux, Hauteville, Habarcq, Tilloy-lès-Hermaville, Pénin, Givenchy-le-Noble, Lignereuil and Grand-Rullecourt. On the way, you'll pass 18th-century country houses, crumbling wattle-and-daub barns, and grand 16th-century fortified farms of red brick or white stone, whose imposing gateways sometimes provide glimpses of ancient turrets and dovecotes within.

AVESNES EXTRAS

Market: Fri.

Accommodation:

La Solette Welcoming 3-épi B&B, with lots of home-made breakfast treats. Rooms from 50€. 10 Rue du Moulin, Hauteville, 4km SE of Avesnes (tel: 03 21 58 73 58). www.lasolette.com/

➤Château de Grand-Rullecourt This attractive 18th-century mansion stands behind magnificent ironwork gates in the heart of the village. The aristocratic owner (who speaks perfect English) gives guided tours of chapel, library and dining-room, and up the grand staircase to see some of the bedrooms that are let out as *chambres d'hôte* (B&B). There's a welcoming feeling about the house, augmented by books, paintings and family photographs. ○ 1 July-31 Aug, Fri-Mon 2-6pm. On D75, Grand-Rullecourt, 4.5km SW of Avesnes (tel: 03 21 58 06 37). 6€, children 4€, under-10s free.

➤Château de Barly Though it seems imposing at first glance, this charming 18th-century country house is just one room deep, with windows giving onto gardens front and back. The hour-long

guided tour (in French, but you can request an English leaflet) covers every detail of its history and architecture, from the tiny chapel to the beautiful *salon*. The château is at present being sympathetically restored by its antique-dealer owners. The prettily-painted ground-floor rooms are filled with period furniture, set off by ultra-modern ceramics. In the small landscaped garden at the rear, a long rectangular pool reflects the harmonious lines of the house. ○ *1 July-31 Aug, daily 1-7pm. On D8, Barly, 3km S of Avesnes-le-Comte (tel: 03 21 48 41 20). 5€, students & children 3€, under-10s free.*

■ Grand design, above: the château of Barly. Off the track, right: Cappy railway museum

BRAY-SUR-SOMME

ⓘ 1 Place de la Liberté (tel: 03 22 76 11 38); Oct-Apr, as Albert (page 132)
www.ville-braysursomme.fr
officedetourisme@paysducoquelicot.com

This small village of the upper Somme valley, 9km south-east of Albert, is one of the main crossing-points of the river. Following the meandering Somme eastward takes you through a string of pretty villages: Cappy (on the line of the steam railway, see below), Suzanne (with a grand private château), Éclusier-Vaux (known for its wooden eel-trap), Frise, Curlu, Feuillères and Cléry-sur-Somme. Divert briefly after Éclusier, up the lane towards Maricourt, for a stupendous panorama over the river and its lakes from the Belvédère de Vaux. To the south-west of Bray, an unusual World War I monument at Chipilly (pictured below) represents a British artilleryman comforting his wounded horse.

➤**Musée Historique** Behind the counter of the tourist office, an interesting little museum covers local history from the Celtic period to World War II. You can see the entrance to underground tunnels, or *"muches"*, where the inhabitants sheltered in time of war, and learn the finer points of peat-cutting and eel-trapping. Famous locals include General Louis Friant, who commanded a brigade of Napoleon's "Grande Armée", and Louise Marais d'Arc, a World War I nurse who later set up social services and home-nursing in the area. Well-made dioramas show the German airfield at nearby Cappy, including the distinctive aircraft of the "Red Baron" (see page 140), who was based there. Other reminders of the World War I German presence include photographs of "Big Bertha", a huge gun installed near Bray and trained on the city of Amiens. Labels are in French, but an English information sheet is available. ○ *Mid May-mid Sept, Wed-Sun 10am-noon (Fri, Sat 10am-noon & 2-6pm). Place de la Liberté (tel: 03 22 76 11 38). 2€, children 1€.* ⓢ

➤**Musée des Chemins de Fer Militaires et Industriels** The goods-wagon shape of the modern engine-shed, and the station-style clock outside it, put you in the mood for exploring this wonderful collection of 30 narrow-gauge locomotives and 100 wagons dating from 1915 to 1945. Claimed to be Europe's largest collection of 60cm-gauge railway material, it is a Mecca for rail enthusiasts. All notices and captions are in English. Among engines on display are an 040 Vulcan, and a 1917 ex-War Department 131 T Alco Cooke, both in working order. There are also hoppers, coal wagons and tip-trucks, plus a collection of French stationmasters' caps.

BRAY EXTRAS

Market: Wed pm (all day on first Wed of month).

Restaurants:

Marina Good plates of mussels. Closed Wed. 23 Rue G-Deremarque (tel: 03 22 76 16 60).

Les Étangs du Levant Try ficelle picarde (pancake) & local smoked eel. Menus 15-28€. Closed Tues. 25 Rue du 1er Septembre 1944 (tel: 03 22 76 70 00).

■ Fond farewell: Chipilly

Narrow-gauge railways were used in industry, mining and agriculture. This one was employed by the British army from 1916, transporting artillery, ammunition and fodder to the Somme battlefront. It later served the sugar factory at Dompierre-Bécancourt. ◑ *Open on steam days; details & admission times below. 5.50€, children 3€ (combined ticket with steam-train ride, see below).*

➤P'tit Train de la Haute-Somme Every summer since 1971, tourist trains have run on this 60cm-gauge line, which is twinned with Leighton Buzzard Railway in England. The whistle blows, steam hisses and, with a puff of coal smoke, the train creaks into life. Passengers sit in open-sided

carriages for the rocky 75-minute ride to Dompierre, a route that runs beside the Somme, via attractive woods and open fields, and through a long, dark tunnel. (Steeper bits of the route may be diesel-hauled.) ◑ *1 May-mid Sept, Sun & public holidays 2-7pm (mid July-late Aug, Tues-Sun 2-5.45pm); last departure 5.15pm & 4pm, respectively. Froissy, off D329 3km S of Bray (tel: 03 22 83 11 89). 8.50€ including museum, children 5.50€ (mid July-late Aug, Tues-Sat 7€ & 5.50€; Sun & public holidays 8.50€ & 5.50€).* ♿

CORBIE

ⓘ **30 Place de la République (tel: 03 22 96 95 76 fax: 03 22 48 47 07)**
www.mairie-corbie.fr
officetourismecorbie.80@wanadoo.fr

The centre of this small town 17km east of Amiens, clustered around a tree-lined market square, seems unchanged over the centuries. At the junction of the Somme and the Ancre rivers, it is dominated by two 55-metre-high Gothic towers, reminders of the rich abbey founded here in the 7th century. A smaller-scale ecclesiastical treasure is the little church of Notre-Dame de l'Assomption on the D30 at La Neuville, a northern suburb of Corbie. Though modest in size, it features over its door a huge 16th-century stone-carving, full of finely-observed detail, depicting Jesus riding into Jerusalem on Palm Sunday.

➤Abbatiale St-Pierre The church of the great Benedictine abbey founded in 657 by Queen Bathilde, towers above town and countryside. The name of Corbie became known in the 8th century for its missions to Westphalia and Scandinavia and—especially—for a new style of writing developed in the abbey's scriptorium. The lower-case letters that had been evolved for sacred texts were harder to read and to write than the capital letters that had previously been used. Corbie's monks invented a clearer lower-case script that became the standard for official documents throughout the Western world, until it was superseded in the 14th century by Gothic lettering. Originally called "Carolingian minuscule" (after the reigning emperor, Charlemagne), the style associated with the abbey is today known as "Corbie ab" (a reference to its distinctive lower-case a and b letters).

The abbey's palatial Porte d'Honneur on the main square (pictured page 140) was built in 1750. Soon afterwards, the Revolution forced the abbey's closure. The church's nave was shortened from 117 metres to the 36 metres you see today, its other buildings were destroyed, and the stones sold off. You can visit the church interior, accompanied by a member of tourist-office staff to see a plan and a model of the original abbey, statues of St Peter and of Queen Bathilde, and the relics of St Colette (see page 140). ● *Tourist office open Tues-Sat (1 July-31 Aug, Tues-Sun); hours subject to change. Church visit: 0.50€ (guided tour 2.50€, children free).* ○ *Guided ascent of towers: 1 July-31 Aug, Fri 10.30am; booking essential, via tourist office (tel: 03 22 96 95 76). 2€.*

> **➤Musée des Amis du Vieux Corbie** The history of the town and its abbey are explained (in English, if required) by a volunteer guide in this small museum off the main square. In the series of small rooms, filled with photographs and copies of documents rather than original pieces, you learn about the script developed by Corbie's monks (see page 139), and are shown reproductions of pages from the illuminated, 8th-century Corbie Psalter.

Upstairs is information on Picardy's greatest saint, Colette, born in Corbie in 1381. At 21 she chose a hermit-like existence, living in a tiny cell grafted onto one of the town's churches. Later, she travelled France, founding 17 convents. Other displays recount the 1636 siege of Corbie, by which Cardinal Richelieu expelled the Spanish from this, then frontier town, and recall Corbie-born aviator Eugène Lefebvre who, in 1909, became the first civil pilot to die in an air crash. ◑ *15 June-15 Sept, Tues-Sat 2.30-5.30pm. 13 bis Place de la République (tel: 03 22 96 43 37). Admission free.*

> **➤Point de Vue de Ste-Colette** To enjoy a wonderful view across the Somme and its lakes, take the D1 up the hill, past the large statue of St Colette (by Amiens sculptor Albert Roze), and turn off to the right at the picnic sign. The marshland below, popular today for fishing and wildfowling, was used over the centuries for the cultivation of woad and to provide peat for fuel. ● *On D1, 1km NE of Corbie.* **S**

> **➤"Red Baron" site** Farther along the D1, opposite a derelict brickworks, a roadside panel marks the place where the legendary German aviator Manfred von Richthofen was shot down, on 21 April 1918. The "Red Baron" was based 20km to the east, at Cappy (see page 138), and in two years had, alone, accounted for 80 Allied aircraft. He was buried by the Allies with full military honours at Bertangles, 20km north-west of Corbie (see page 124). His body was later removed, first to Fricourt German cemetery, near Albert; then to Berlin; and finally, in 1975, to his family's grave at Wiesbaden. ● *On D1, Vaux-sur-Somme, 3km NE of Corbie.* **S**

> **➤Centre Archéologique Départemental** Aerial surveys revealed evidence of a large Roman settlement between Corbie and Albert; subsequent excavations discovered an even earlier Gaulish sanctuary—the best-preserved in Europe. Although there is no public access to the site itself, some finds are displayed in a small museum (closed for refurbishment during 2007) at the archaeological laboratories.

A first-floor room contains aerial views and a plan of the site where three mass graves were found, each containing bones of some 200 people. The information panels are rather wordy, especially if you don't read French too well, but macabre illustrations of a 3rd-century-BC Celtic war show how prisoners had been decapitated and their bodies suspended inside a building until they fell to the ground (a scenario suggested by the jumbled arrangement of the bones). It is thought the heads were retained by the victors as trophies. Across the yard, a second building contains some of the finds, including a skeleton, bronze bangles, gold coins and weapons. Many more items are on display in the Musée de Picardie at Amiens (see page 115). ◑ *Due to reopen 2008. Mid Apr-31 Oct, Tues-Sat 9.30am-noon & 1.30-5pm. Closed public holidays. 9 Place du Général-de-Gaulle, Ribemont-sur-Ancre, 9km NE of Corbie (tel: 03 22 40 64 66). 4€, children 2€; under-10s free.*

■ **Heaven's gate: a remnant of Corbie's abbey.**

CORBIE EXTRAS

Market: Fri.

Accommodation:

Le Macassar *Perfectly-restored Art Deco interior for this luxurious boutique hotel. Rooms 120-225€. 8 Place de la République (tel: 03 22 48 40 04). www.lemacassar.com/*

Restaurant: Val d'Ancre *Elegant cuisine & waterside eating. Menus 20-41€. Closed Sun evg & Wed. 6 Rue du Petit Marais, Bonnay, 3km N of Corbie (tel: 03 22 96 99 50).*

■ Facets of war: clockwise, graves near Longueval; battlefield poppies; basilica at Albert; model plane in museum at Villers-Bretonneux.

The Somme battlefields

For those who have not visited battlefield areas before, it can be hard to know where to start. Sometimes the first experience is a chance halt at a wayside war cemetery; for others it is led by a desire to pay personal homage at the grave of a long-dead relative.

For first-time visitors, it is good to start with an overview. For this, the modern Historial centre at Péronne (see page 146) does an admirable job of setting World War I in context. The quirkier Somme 1916 museum, in Albert (page 132), uses battlefield relics and reconstructed bunkers to plunge you into the atmosphere of what took place here. Children would probably gain most from visiting a place with visible trenches, such as the Newfoundland memorial (page 136), or the Artois battleground of Vimy (page 168).

Concerned about France's alliance with Russia in the 1890s, Germany had begun planning to invade its neighbour. In August 1914 the German army swept south-west to within 40km of Paris. But the French repulsed the attack at the river Marne in September, and the invaders fell back, choosing strategic high ground along a 640km line that became known as the Western Front.

The Germans created underground fortresses of well-protected dugouts, and an equally strong second line (the Hindenburg Line) to which they could retreat. In contrast, Allied trenches were temporary structures intended to be abandoned as troops advanced. New technology was put to the test on all sides: the first gas was used in April 1915; first fighter planes in July 1915; and first tanks in September 1916.

In 1914 and 1915 the battlegrounds were mostly farther north, in Belgium and around Arras, Neuve-Chapelle and Loos. In February 1916 proposals were made for a large Anglo-French attack on the Somme in June, to break through the enemy front. However, the massive German assault on Verdun, 200km to the south-east, on 21 February drained French resources. The Somme plan, therefore,

■ **Not forgotten: French soldier in "bleu horizon" uniform. French and British lines met on the Somme.**

became much more heavily British than first intended. The French were limited to the sector south of Maricourt; the British spread along a 30km front to the north.

The notorious first day on the Somme, 1 July 1916, left more than 57,000 British killed, wounded or missing. By November 1916, when the battle petered out in atrocious weather conditions, the total number of casualties on all sides had reached 1.2 million. The painful progress is spelt out by four panels along the D929 between Albert and Bapaume, showing the position of the front line on 1 July, 1 September, 1 October and 20 November 1916. In four and a half months the Allies had gained less than 12km.

In March 1917 the Germans withdrew to their heavily-fortified Hindenburg Line, which stretched south-east from Arras towards Soissons. Twelve months later they staged a fresh offensive—sometimes known as the Second Battle of the Somme—retaking all the ground they had ceded in 1916, and pushing forward to within 16km of Amiens by April 1918.

In the face of catastrophe, the supreme command of the French, British and American armies was placed in the hands of France's Marshal Foch (see page 144). After detailed planning, the Allies launched a successful offensive on 8 August 1918, driving the Germans east and into eventual surrender.

The astonishing number of Commonwealth cemeteries stems from the British decision to bury soldiers where they died. German and American casualties tended to be assembled in a few, larger cemeteries, while French policy was to offer each one a war grave near home.

Commonwealth graveyards make a powerful appeal to the emotions. The rows of identical

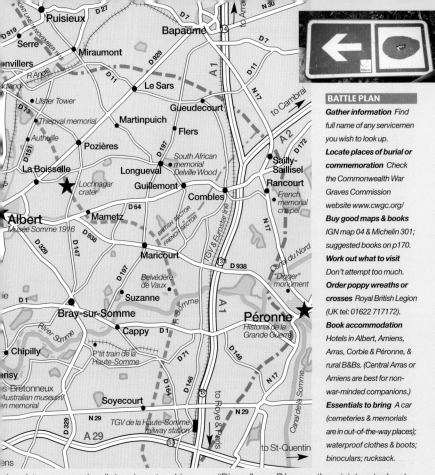

BATTLE PLAN

Gather information Find full name of any servicemen you wish to look up.

Locate places of burial or commemoration Check the Commonwealth War Graves Commission website www.cwgc.org/

Buy good maps & books IGN map 04 & Michelin 301; suggested books on p170.

Work out what to visit Don't attempt too much.

Order poppy wreaths or crosses Royal British Legion (UK tel: 01622 717172).

Book accommodation Hotels in Albert, Amiens, Arras, Corbie & Péronne, & rural B&Bs. (Central Arras or Amiens are best for non-war-minded companions.)

Essentials to bring A car (cemeteries & memorials are in out-of-the-way places); waterproof clothes & boots; binoculars; rucksack.

headstones, occasionally bearing a touching epitaph; the messages left in cemetery visitors' books; and the perfectly-tended lawns and flowers combine to produce a feeling of awe.

Rudyard Kipling's poignant phrase for the stone of each unidentified Commonwealth serviceman, "Known Unto God", is far less anonymous than "Unknown" (as in *"inconnu"* and *"unbekannter"*, the French and German equivalents). Winner of the 1907 Nobel Prize for Literature, Kipling selected or created many inscriptions for the Imperial War Graves Commission (as it was then called). His own son, Jack, was reported missing at Loos in 1915.

Memorials to the missing do not come more imposing than that of Thiepval (page 148), the world's largest military monument. There are some unusual smaller memorials, too. Look for the Welsh dragon at Mametz; a soldier and his dying horse at Chipilly (page 138); the Australian

"Digger" near Péronne; the miniature tanks at Pozières; and Newfoundland's caribous at Beaumont-Hamel (page 136) and Gueudecourt.

French village memorials often feature a *poilu*, the French equivalent of the Tommy. His clothes are sometimes painted a startlingly intense pale blue—the colour of French uniforms from 1915. Newer conscripts were nicknamed *"bleuets"*, or "cornflowers", by those who had worn the earlier, scarlet-trousered uniform, and the *bleuet*, like the poppy in the UK, became a symbol of remembrance. Fund-raising flowers, originally made by disabled ex-servicemen, are still sold on France's two armistice commemoration dates of 8 May (for World War II) and 11 November.

Whether you spend an hour or a week in the area, whether you prepare with detailed study of movements and tactics or simply by digging out a book of war poetry, you will find your visit a thought-provoking and rewarding experience.

■ Silent witness: the ancient belfry of Lucheux saw the passage of Joan of Arc, and invasions by English and Spanish.

DOULLENS

ⓘ Le Beffroi, Rue du Bourg (tel: 03 22 32 54 52 fax: 03 22 32 54 52)
http://doullenstourisme.free.fr
office-de-tourisme-doullens@wanadoo.fr

Much of this unselfconsciously-attractive town 32km north of Amiens seems to have emerged unscathed from the conflicts that have ravaged the region over the centuries. The mighty, 16th-century citadel on the south side of town dates from a time when Doullens guarded France's frontier. Today the centre has a pleasant mixture of old houses, smart shops, and an ancient brick belfry that houses the tourist office. There is an animated market each Thursday, with live geese, chickens and rabbits on sale alongside the vegetables.

Though it seems a long way from the battlefields of the Somme, Doullens was the scene of one of the most significant moments of World War I: the agreement to place the hitherto fragmented military control of Allied forces in the hands of one commander (see below).

❯**Salle du Commandement Unique** Inside the flamboyant town hall, signs point upstairs to the site of a historic meeting of 26 March 1918. The Germans had launched a dramatically-successful offensive towards Amiens, exploiting a gap between British and French armies and retaking all the ground they had lost since 1916. The top Allied political and military leaders gathered here, and formally handed to France's Marshal Foch the *commandement unique*, or supreme command, of Allied armies on the Western Front. A stained-glass window (right) immortalises the occasion; in front of it stands a table with places labelled for Haig, Clemenceau, Pétain, Wilson and other signatories. This action proved a turning-point. After meticulous planning and co-ordination,

■ United front: Allied chiefs at Doullens.

an Allied offensive of August 1918 forced the Germans back east—and towards the Armistice. ● *Mon-Thurs 8-11.45am & 2-5.45pm; Fri 8-11.45am & 2-4.45pm; Sat 10-11.45am. Closed public holidays. Hôtel de Ville, 2 Avenue du Maréchal-Foch (tel: 03 22 77 00 07). Admission free.*

➤ **Citadelle** The biggest citadel in France, this gigantic stronghold was started by French king François I, continued by his son, and added to by successive monarchs. After the Artois reverted to France in 1659, Doullens was no longer a frontier town and the citadel became a prison (a role it held intermittently until the 1950s). Encroaching vegetation almost swallowed up the abandoned fortress until volunteers began to clear it in 1974. Today they act as guides for visitors. On the hour-long tour, you see the exteriors of a comfortable-looking house built for the Duc du Maine (illegitimate son of Louis XIV), the governor's residence, a tall barrack block, and the bleak, derelict prison. You also visit the warren of passages that run between the inner and outer walls, enjoying an artilleryman's-eye view of the world outside. ◑ *1 May-30 Sept: Sat, Sun & public holidays 3pm & 4.30pm (1 July-31 Aug, Tues-Sun 3pm & 4.30pm). On S side of town, off N25 Amiens road (tel: 03 22 32 54 52). 3€, children 1.50€.*

DOULLENS EXTRAS

Market: Thurs.

Festivals:

Journées Doullennaises des Jardins d'Agrément Two-day garden show, June.

Foire de la St-Martin Big street fair, & special meals of tripe & chips, mid Nov.

LUCHEUX

ⓘ see Doullens (page 144)

The delightful village of Lucheux lies on the D5, 7km north-east of Doullens. Flowers spill over the verges, embellishing its mellow brick cottages. Lucheux's ancient buildings encapsulate the three orders of medieval civilisation in the region: the castle (representing feudal power), the church (ecclesiastical power) and the belfry (municipal power). All are normally closed to the public, but you can visit the château grounds and church interior during the summer on guided tours organised by Doullens tourist office.

Events during the village's packed history include the martyrdom of St Léger—adviser to the 7th-century King Childeric II—and the passage of Joan of Arc with her captors in November 1430. On the border between French and Spanish territory, Lucheux was the object of attacks by the English (in 1522), Burgundians (1552) and Spanish (1595). Burnt to the ground by the Duke of Marlborough in 1708, the village was rebuilt in the harmonious form you see today.

LUCHEUX EXTRAS

Restaurant: Auberge de Pommera Pretty lunch stop on main road, beside a conspicuous shop (see below). Menus 17-26€. Closed evgs, except Sat. 21 Route Nationale (N25), Pommera, 3.5km SE of Lucheux (tel: 03 21 58 91 30).

Shop: Deco Cailliau Land A bizarre collection of life-sized model cows, saints, gnomes, film stars & plastic birds on sale, from 15€ to 600€. Mon-Sat 9am-7pm, Sun 2-6pm. Pommera, on N25, 3.5km SE of Lucheux.

➤ **Château de Lucheux** As you walk up the steep cobbled street towards the entrance, you can appreciate the strategic position of the medieval castle. One of the largest fortresses in the region, it was started in 1120 and enlarged over successive centuries. But 16th-century firepower brought about its destruction. From the outside, you can still admire the 14th-century Porte du Bourg, flanked by defensive towers and a deep, dry moat once filled with prickly, protective undergrowth. The remains of the château have become a children's home, so there is no admittance to its grounds unless on a tour. During the visit (in French, but an English leaflet is available), the guide points out the mix of Romanesque and Gothic styles, and a ruined tower remaining from the chapel, beneath which the Knights Templar are said to have buried treasure. On one stretch of grass, a strangely isolated wall contains a range of arched windows—a vestige of the castle's banqueting-hall in which royal feasts could last 10 days. ◑ *Guided tours of grounds 1 June-mid Sept: Sat, Sun 3pm (1 July-31 Aug, daily 3pm). Meet at tourist-office hut, near belfry (tel: 03 22 32 54 52). 4€, children 2€.*

➤ **Arbre des Épousailles** A newly-wed couple would vie to see which of them could squeeze first through the narrow gap between two venerable lime trees that still stand on the green to the north-east of the belfry. Whoever won, it was said, would wear the trousers! ● *Off D5 Avesnes road.*

PÉRONNE

ⓘ 1 Rue Louis XI (tel: 03 22 84 42 38 fax: 03 22 84 51 25)
www.ot-peronne.fr
accueil@ot-peronne.fr

With a history of frequent destruction, it seems incredible that this pleasant little market town on the river Somme, 42km south-east of Arras, could present such a cohesive face today. Much pulled about in the Revolution, obliterated in the Franco-Prussian war of 1870-71, ruined by departing Germans in World War I, and 40 per cent destroyed in World War II, Péronne has a phoenix-like ability to rise again. Its troubled past has made the town an appropriate place to relate the events of World War I, at the informative Historial de la Grande Guerre. A little north of Péronne, particular tribute is paid to the Australians who fought so courageously here in 1918 with a statue of a sturdy "Digger" at Mont-St-Quentin. French deeds of valour are movingly commemorated at a chapel in Rancourt (see page 147).

> ★ **Historial de la Grande Guerre** Beyond the ancient gatehouse of Péronne's castle lies a large, modern interpretation centre that does an admirable job of describing the causes, events and consequences of World War I plainly, and even-handedly—in French, English and German. An expert might find it oversimplified, but anyone struggling to make sense of the conflict, which involved 30 countries, will be grateful to have things spelt out so clearly. Free audioguides are issued in your chosen language (a passport is required as security).

Maps show the positions of the military fronts at different stages of the war, explaining how England, France and Russia had formed the "Triple Entente", and Germany, Austro-Hungary and Italy the equally strong "Triple Alliance". Wall cabinets display domestic memorabilia of peacetime Germany, France and Britain—from rowing trophies and share certificates to hats, uniforms and electric fans.

Then, 50 etchings by German artist Otto Dix (1891-1969) plunge you into the horror of war through grisly portrayals of barbed-wire, crazed men and wounded horses. Next, recruitment posters and heart-wrenching personal letters give way to military equipment and uniforms, laid out in shallow pits in the floor and juxtaposed with soldiers' poems and works of art. There's a poignancy about the similarities in both sentiments and possessions: mess-kits, pay-books and much-creased photographs of loved ones. Maps and charts illustrate the movement of the battlefronts, enumerating the terrible French casualties at Verdun from February to December 1916, and the awful death toll of 1 July 1916, the first day of the Battle of the Somme. In a 20-minute film, a Northumberland veteran describes the hell he came through. (Pick up a special headset by the entrance to the screening; this moving account is, frustratingly, dubbed into French.) Further rooms show propaganda, the increasing mechanisation of "total war" and the coming of peace. The final section deals with war memorials, reconstruction—and battlefield tourism.

You could spend two hours here—more, if you view each of the many short videos. A good bookshop has battlefield maps, and English war-related publications. ● *Mid Jan-mid Dec, Tues-Sun 10am-6pm (1 Apr-30 Sept, daily 10am-6pm). Château de Péronne, Place André-Audinot (tel: 03 22 83 14 18). 7.50€, seniors 6€, children 3.80€.* 🚻 🐾 🚫

PÉRONNE EXTRAS

Market: Sat.

Specialities: Colvert beer. Smoked eel.

Accommodation/food:
Hotel St-Claude *3-star hotel opposite Historial. Two restaurants; parking. Rooms from 100€; menus 16-29€. 42 Place Louis-Daudré (tel: 03 22 79 49 49). www.bestwestern.com/*
Hostellerie des Remparts *2-star Logis in town centre. Dingy décor, but surprisingly delicious meals. Rooms from 60€; menus from 13/22€. 23 Rue Beaubois (tel: 03 22 84 01 22). www.logisdefrance.com/*
Le Prieuré *2-star Logis. Rooms from 62€; menus 19-40€. On N17, Rancourt, 11km N of Péronne (tel: 03 22 85 04 43). www.hotel-le-prieure.fr/*

■ **Machinery of war: on display at the Historial.**

■ Sleeping soldiers: German graves at Rancourt.

➤**Musée Alfred Danicourt** On the first floor of the town hall is a small, well-presented, museum of local history named after its founder, a 19th-century mayor of Péronne. A well-explained prehistory section shows stone axes, flint tools and grinding-stones. Its great treasure is Danicourt's collection of gold Gallo-Roman coins (one bearing the head of Gaulish general Vercingetorix). There are shards of Roman pottery, brightly-coloured glass beads, and a stone sarcophagus complete with skeleton and accompanying burial items. In the main room hang some large-scale pictures by celebrated local artists Francis Tattegrain (1852-1915) and Charles-Henri Michel (1817-1905). You learn about the cult of St Fursy, whose relics made Péronne a pilgrimage centre, and about the seige of 1536, when Péronne held out for 31 days against the Austro-Hungarian Emperor Charles V. ● *Tues-Fri 2-5.30pm; Sat 9am-noon & 2-4.30pm. Closed three weeks in May, & occasionally at other times. Hôtel de Ville, Rue St-Sauveur (tel: 03 22 73 31 10). Admission free.*

➤**Chapelle du Souvenir Français** This hilltop chapel in the French sector of the Somme battlefields was built by a couple in tribute to their officer son, Jean du Bos, who lies beneath a large slab detailing his many awards and citations. On the walls, other panels commemorate equally courageous soldiers from all levels of French society. At the caretaker's house, alongside, is a small museum containing World War I-related documents and relics. Adjoining the chapel is the largest French military cemetery in the Somme *département*, containing 5,326 graves. Across from it lie British and German cemeteries. ● *Daily 10am-5pm (1 June-30 Sept daily 8am-6pm). 2 Route Nationale (N17), Rancourt, 10km N of Péronne (tel: 03 22 85 04 47). 1€.* 🌀

POZIERES

ⓘ see Albert (page 132)

Pozières, a small village 8.5km north-east of Albert, saw intense fighting during the battles of the Somme. It proclaims particular gratitude to the Australians, who lost many men in the capture of this crest in 1916 and, again, in 1918 when Pozières was lost and then retaken. An obelisk dedicated to the 1st Australian Division stands at the southern edge of the village; the 2nd Australian Division is commemorated by a smaller memorial alongside the D929 at the north end, near the most recent tribute—a brightly-painted, Aussie-themed water-tower.

Opposite this, beside a prominent radio mast, is an unusual monument to the Tank Corps. Sited near the place from which these fearsome new weapons first set out into battle on 15 September 1916, it features four small, scale-model tanks around its base.

➤**"Le Tommy" Museum** You need a strong stomach to digest some of the gruesome sights in the reconstitution of British and German trenches in the back yard of this Pozières café. To the right is a section of Allied trench, with uniformed dummies, bits of machinery, jerricans and half-buried shells. On the wire-fringed parapet above lies a camouflaged sniper, while a disembodied hand sticks out from the mud. Round the other side, a German trench is laid out as a communications centre, with mess-tins, grenade-launcher and hundreds of rusty shell-cases. Inside the café, alongside the drinks and snacks, are many interesting old war photographs. ● *Daily 10am-5pm. Le Tommy, 91 Route d'Albert, D929 (tel: 03 22 74 82 84). Museum: 4€, children 2.50€.* **S**

❯ **Mémorial Franco-Britannique/Thiepval Franco-British memorial** Thiepval ridge was the strongest of German defences on the Somme, fortified and held since 1914. Dominating the British positions, it was one of the Allies' principal objectives for 1 July 1916, though it was not taken until September. Lutyens's colossal arch stands today on the original German front line; its 16 pillars bear the names of 73,367 British and Commonwealth dead who fell in the battles of the Somme from 1916 to 1918 and who have no known grave. A commemoration ceremony is held here on 1 July each year. ● *On D151, 200m S of Thiepval & 3.5km NW of Pozières.* **S**

❯ **Thiepval Visitor Centre** A modern, glass-fronted interpretation centre lies semi-hidden in the memorial's landscaped car park. Inside, panels and diagrams explain, in English, French and German, the strategic importance of Thiepval (pronounced "t'yepval"), showing clearly the structure of the British Fourth Army. Excellent animated maps demonstrate the shifting position of the front line during the various Somme battles. Two parallel history-lines look at the effect of the war on a British and a French family. A small cinema shows three 10-minute films on Somme-related themes. There are toilets, and a bookshop that stocks British publications on World War I, as well as a few Royal British Legion poppy crosses. ● *Daily 10am-5pm (1 May-30 Oct, daily 10am-6pm). Closed late Dec-early Jan. Thiepval, as above (tel: 03 22 74 60 47). Admission free.* ♿ **S**

❯ **Tour d'Ulster/Ulster Tower** The D73 north-west of Thiepval passes a remarkably Irish-looking structure, a replica of Helen's Tower, in County Down. It straddles the remains of the German front-line trench, which was taken by the 9th Royal Irish Rifles on 1 July. The tower itself is not open, but a small visitor centre has a tea-room, toilets, and a little museum.

Wall panels explain how Unionists and Nationalists set aside their differences to form the 36th (Ulster) Division, with 132,454 men enlisting to fight alongside Britain. Northern Ireland's factories produced 75 million shells for the war; Belfast ropeworks provided half the Navy's rope and cord; and farmers gave over land to the cultivation of flax, vital for making kitbags, lifejackets, and surgical thread. A 9-minute audiovisual show (with English commentary) describes how, on 1 July 1916, the Ulster Division went over the top 30 minutes before zero hour, pushed forward and captured its objective. However, as divisons either side had been less successful, the Ulsters were left trying to hold a salient—a dangerously-exposed bulge of territory, vulnerable on three sides to enemy fire. After waiting two days for reinforcements, they had to retreat. ◑ *1 Mar-30 Nov, Tues-Sun 10am-5pm (1 May-30 Sept, Tues-Sun 10am-6pm). Route de St-Pierre-Divion, Thiepval, 4km NW of Pozières (tel: 03 22 74 87 14). Admission free.* **S**

■ **Irish story: told at the Ulster Tower.**

❯ **Mémorial National et Musée Sud-Africains/South Africa (Delville Wood) Memorial and Museum** Opposite Delville Wood Cemetery, east of Pozières, stands a memorial, dedicated to South Africans who fell in all theatres of war.

On 14 July 1916, the 9th (Scottish) Division successfully attacked the village of Longueval. The 1st South African Infantry Brigade, attached to it, was ordered to capture adjacent Delville Wood "at all costs". At dawn next day 3,153 officers and men went in. After almost five days battling against heavy resistance, they were forced to withdraw from what had become a wasteland of shattered stumps. Only 780 of them survived, of whom just 143 were unscathed.

Today's memorial is surrounded by trees grown from acorns brought from the Cape, with one mighty hornbeam behind the museum having survived from 1916. The woodland is criss-crossed with paths along trench lines that still bear names such as Princes Street or Rotten Row. Through the memorial lies the museum, a circular building around a central courtyard. You set off clockwise, through different areas that explain South Africa's participation in both world wars and in the Korean War. Each has a similar layout: a huge, modern bronze wall sculpture, followed by displays on the same theme. Everything is described in French, English and Afrikaans. ◑ *1 Feb-10 Nov, Tues-Sun 10am-3.45pm (1 Apr-mid Oct, Tues-Sun 10am-5.45pm). Closed public holidays. Longueval, 5km E of Pozières (tel: 03 22 85 02 17). Admission free.* Ⓢ

VILLERS-BRETONNEUX

ⓘ **Mairie, 1 Place Charles-de-Gaulle**
(tel: 03 22 96 31 00)
www.villers-bretonneux.com
mairie@villers-bretonneux.com

Once known for its hosiery and its textile industries, this small town 13km south-east of Amiens has developed a very special relationship with Australia. On 25 April 1918, during a battle to defend Amiens, Australian troops retook Villers-Bretonneux from the Germans, who had seized it 24 hours earlier. In July 1918, Australians and Canadians captured a German trench at nearby Le Hamel; in August they formed an essential

■ **Australian memorial: on the ridge at Le Hamel.**

part of the Allied offensive that pushed the Germans back for good. The State of Victoria, from which many of the World War I troops had originated, contributed generously to the town's post-war reconstruction, as did the city of Melbourne (streets are named after both).

Australia suffered the highest proportion of casualties among Commonwealth countries. Of 413,000 men mobilised, 14.5 per cent did not return home. The unknown Australian World War I soldier buried at the national war memorial in Canberra was repatriated in 1993 from Adelaide Cemetery, 2km to the west of Villers.

❯ **Musée Franco-Australien/Franco-Australian Museum** The museum is located on the first floor of a school—itself a gift to the town from the children of the state of Victoria. Its collection of documents, letters, photographs and personal items creates an intensely moving picture of the Australians who arrived on the Somme in March 1916, having already experienced bitter fighting against the Turks at Gallipoli. Displays, captioned in English, give good explanations of the battles. There are slouch hats, flags, and uniforms of Australian soldiers and nurses. Some marvellous contemporary black-and-white photographs show life in and around the trenches, and there are touching mementoes entrusted to the museum by Australian families. Hanging from the rafters are models of early fighter planes (pictured, page 141), including a red triplane like that flown by Manfred von Richthofen. ● *Tues 2-6pm; Wed-Sat 10am-12.30pm & 2-6pm; first & third Sun of month 2-6pm. Closed public holidays (except 11 Nov), & last week of Dec & first week of Jan. 9 Rue Victoria (tel: 03 22 96 80 79). 4€, children 2.50€; under-6s free.*

❯ **Mémorial de Villers-Bretonneux/Australian National Memorial** A tall monument in a hilltop cemetery pays tribute to all Australians who fought in France and Belgium; the walls bear 10,797 names of those who died on the Somme and at Arras, and have no known grave. A ceremony takes place each year around Anzac Day (25 April). ● *On D23, 2km N of Villers-Bretonneux.* Ⓢ

❯ **Monument Australien/Australian Corps Memorial Park** In July 1918, before the Allied offensive, Australian and American soldiers captured a German trench system on this ridge in an impeccably-planned attack. A small sign points the way to a black marble monument (pictured above); from the car park (which has picnic tables and toilets) you reach the crest via a winding path lined with panels that recount the action. ● *Daily 10am-6pm. Le Hamel, 5km NE of Villers-Bretonneux.* Ⓢ

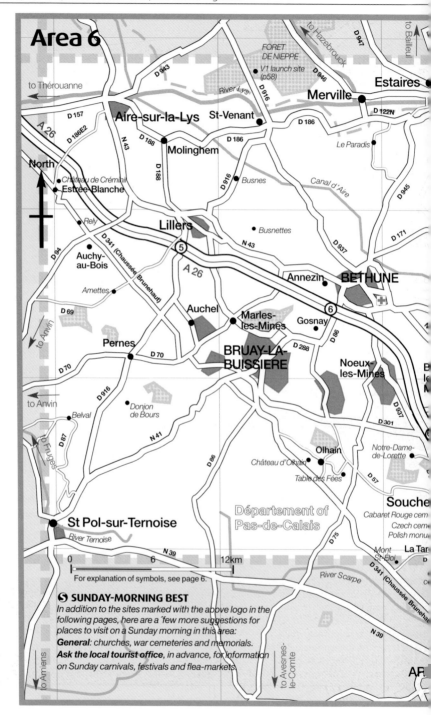

Area 6

to Bailleul

FORÊT DE NIEPPE

V1 launch site (p58)

to Thérouanne

Estaires

Merville

to Hazebrouck

River Lys

D 947

D 946

D 916

D 943

D 157

Aire-sur-la-Lys

St-Venant

D 122N

D 186

D 186E2

N 43

D 188

Molinghem

Le Paradis

D 186

A 26

North

Château de Créminil

Estrée Blanche

D 188

D 916

Busnes

Canal d'Aire

Rely

D 341 (Chaussée Brunehaut)

Lillers

Busnettes

D 945

D 171

⑤

N 43

D 937

Auchy-au-Bois

A 26

Annezin

BÉTHUNE

D 94

Amettes

Auchel

Marles-les-Mines

Gosnay

⑥

D 69

D 86

Noeux-les-Mines

Pernes

D 70

BRUAY-LA-BUISSIERE

D 288

to Anvin

D 916

Donjon de Bours

N 41

D 86

D 301

D 837

to Anvin

Belval

to Fruges

D 87

Olhain

Notre-Dame-de-Lorette

Château d'Olhain

Table des Fées

D 57

St Pol-sur-Ternoise

Département of Pas-de-Calais

Souche

River Ternoise

D 75

Cabaret Rouge cem
Czech cem
Polish monu

0   6   12km

For explanation of symbols, see page 6.

Mont St-Éloi

La Tar

N 39

River Scarpe

D 341 (Chaussée Brunehau

to Amiens

to Avesnes-le-Comte

N 39

AR

ⓢ SUNDAY-MORNING BEST

In addition to the sites marked with the above logo in the following pages, here are a few more suggestions for places to visit on a Sunday morning in this area:
General: *churches, war cemeteries and memorials.*
Ask the local tourist office, *in advance, for information on Sunday carnivals, festivals and flea-markets.*

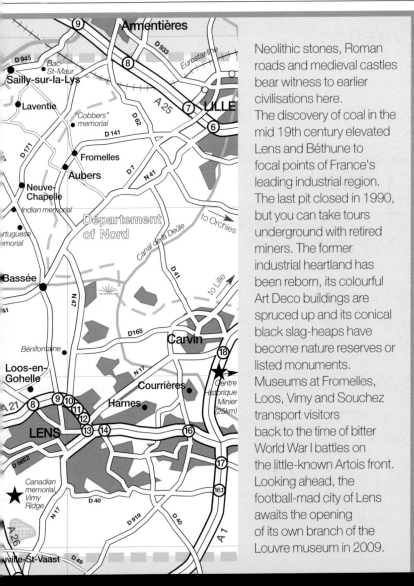

Neolithic stones, Roman roads and medieval castles bear witness to earlier civilisations here. The discovery of coal in the mid 19th century elevated Lens and Béthune to focal points of France's leading industrial region. The last pit closed in 1990, but you can take tours underground with retired miners. The former industrial heartland has been reborn, its colourful Art Deco buildings are spruced up and its conical black slag-heaps have become nature reserves or listed monuments. Museums at Fromelles, Loos, Vimy and Souchez transport visitors back to the time of bitter World War I battles on the little-known Artois front. Looking ahead, the football-mad city of Lens awaits the opening of its own branch of the Louvre museum in 2009.

Lens, Béthune, battles of the Artois, and the mining basin

AIRE-SUR-LA-LYS

ⓘ Grand'Place (tel: 03 21 39 65 66
fax: 03 21 39 65 66)
www.ville-airesurlalys.fr
tourisme.airelys@wanadoo.fr

Unselfconsciously old, the streets of this town 20km
south-east of St-Omer seem little changed from
pre-Revolutionary days. Aire was the subject of
numerous sieges over the centuries as Spain and
France disputed ownership. Its position on two

■ Barging along: the river Lys at St-Venant.

main canals, as well as on the 214km-long river Lys,
made it an important trading centre; the wealth this engendered
built Aire's churches, chapels and barracks. The grand houses
along today's ring road testify to another surge of prosperity in the
19th century, when foundries, breweries, sawmills and tanneries
sprang up along the banks of the Lys.

The focus is the Grand'Place, with its 18th-century merchants'
houses, huge, Classical-style town hall and the town's most
ancient building, Le Bailliage, built in 1600 for the local militia.
Today it houses the tourist office, which organises guided tours of
town and belfry and provides a selection of leaflets to lead you
around the most interesting corners of Aire.

❯**Collégiale St-Pierre** When you look up inside at the dizzyingly tall nave
of Aire's vast Gothic collegial church—founded by Count Baudouin the
Pious in 1059—it's hard to imagine that Allied bombing on 8 August 1944
reduced its centre to a pile of rubble. Off the side aisles, under a blue-
painted ceiling spangled with stars, is an assortment of chapels, one
containing 16th-century frescoes on the life of St James. ● *Daily 9am-6pm;
Mass: Sun 10am & 11.30am. Place St-Pierre (tel: 03 21 39 65 66).* ◐
❯**Château de Créminil** You might catch a glimpse of this exquisite little
17th-century castle at the end of an avenue of trees, if you turn off the
D341 (the Roman road known as "Chaussée Brunehaut") onto the
Witternesse road. Built of white stone and surrounded by water, it has a
fairy-tale quality unexpected in these parts. The owners are restoring the
château and parkland, and welcome summer visitors to the grounds and
to occasional outdoor events—particularly during the *Semaine des
Jardins* in early June. The medieval-style garden is packed with herbs,
flowers and neatly-labelled espaliered trees, and a wildflower meadow
unfurls like a colourful kilim. An annual medieval-themed weekend held in
June offers garden tours, a living-history encampment, children's cal-
ligraphy workshops, and some interesting displays of photographs,
traditions and old tools. ○ *1 July-31 Aug, Tues-Sun 1-7pm. First Sun in
June, & Sun of heritage weekend in mid Sept 10am-6pm. 5€, children
under 12 free. Estrée-Blanche, 6km SW of Aire on D186E2 (tel: 03 21 39 31 38/06 75 87 65 92).*
❯**St-Venant** Travelling on the D916 around the old fortifications, you might miss this pretty village on
the river Lys entirely. In the centre, an extraordinary church stands on a delightful cobbled square
surrounded by mellow-brick cafés and shops crowned with eccentrically-shaped roofs. Tourists are
welcomed with information panels, in English and French, on local legends, buildings and waterside
walks; pleasure-cruiser activity is concentrated around the lock and marina. ● *10km E of Aire.* ◐

AIRE EXTRAS

Market: Fri.

Specialities: Andouille
(chitterling sausage).

Accommodation/food:
Hostellerie des 3
Mousquetaires *Grand
dining & 4-star rooms in a
19th-century mansion.
Rooms from 55€; menus
from 32€. Château de la
Redoute, Route de Béthune
(N43), 1km W of Aire
(tel: 03 21 39 01 11). www.
loisirs-gourmets.com/*
Le Buffet *Top-class meals
served in an elegant,
conservatory, plus 2-star
bedrooms. Rooms from 64€;
menus from 30€. Closed
Sun evg & Mon. 22 Rue de
la Gare, Isbergues, 6km SE
of Aire (tel: 03 21 25 82 40).
www.logisdefrance.com/*
Festivals:
Notre-Dame Panetière
*Procession of the venerated
statue from Aire's
collegial church, mid Aug.*
Fête de l'Andouille,
*chitterling-sausage festival,
early Sept.*

AUBERS

ⓘ 34 Rue d'Houdringue (tel: 03 20 50 63 85 fax: 03 20 50 69 31)
http://paysdeweppes.free.fr
paysdeweppes@free.fr

Along with many other places in this quiet area known as the Weppes, Aubers lay on the front line during World War I. A ridge here, though only 6 metres in height, gave valuable views over the flat marshland. This strategic point, 17km north-east of Béthune, was heavily reinforced by the Germans, who held it from October 1914 to October 1918.

The Allies looked on its capture as a first step towards the liberation of Lille. At Neuve-Chapelle, 4km south-west of Aubers, a British offensive launched on 10 March 1915 gained just 800 metres of ground along a 3km front. Two months later, a battle for Aubers Ridge itself was fought to support French efforts at Notre-Dame-de-Lorette, 20km to the south-west. On 19 July the following year the Allies launched an unsuccessful attack on nearby Fromelles, 3km to the north-east. The casualties from these encounters were enormous, and have left a legacy in the form of unusual, and moving, memorials to Australian, Indian and Portuguese troops, as well as many war cemeteries.

Though Aubers and its neighbouring villages were bombarded to near-total destruction, they are reborn today, with pristine houses, bright flowers and a network of walking and cycling routes. An excellent little museum of World War I at Fromelles spells out the story of the battles; brochures of routes around the scenes of the fighting are available from Aubers tourist office.

> **Parc Australien/"Cobbers" Memorial** Following the D22 north from Fromelles church, and then Commonwealth War Graves Commission signs towards VC Corner cemetery, along the D22C, you come across this homage to the actions of Australian forces. On the old German trench line, among the remains of concrete bunkers, a life-sized modern bronze statue representing a soldier carrying an injured comrade dominates the landscape. Of the 3,000 Australians wounded here in July 1916, many owed their survival to heroic individuals such as Sergeant Simon Fraser, the inspiration for the sculpture. A hundred metres north, on the old Allied front line, VC Corner cemetery holds the remains of 410 Australians who perished during the the battle.

Unusually, this is a mass grave since, with no truce along this part of the front until the Armistice of 1918, many of these dead remained out on the battlefield for the best part of two years and could no longer be identified. Their names are among those of 1,299 Australians engraved on the wall, lost in the fruitless attack. ● *Rue Delval (D22C), 1.4km NW of Fromelles & 4km N of Aubers.* ♿ Ⓢ

■ **Australian cobbers:**
heroes at Fromelles.

> **Musée 14-18** In the second-floor attics of Fromelles' *mairie*, three rooms are devoted to World War I and a fourth to World War II. Crammed into this small space are relics of uniforms, equipment and personal items unearthed during excavations, or ploughed up (still) by farmers. The volunteer curators have labelled most objects in English, French and German. There are good reconstructions of bunkers and trenches; unusually macho-looking dummies stare disconcertingly at visitors; in one corner a stuffed rat adds an extra shudder. You see shelfloads of *pickelhaube* (German spiked helmets), and imaginatively displayed minutiae of daily life in the trenches: shaving-kits, binoculars, cigarette-papers, notebooks and playing-cards. Photographs and medals recall the Australian combatants. Down on the floor, among the ammunition

boxes and sandbags, are the pumps necessary to cope with the water-table—so high here that trenches had to be built *up*, with sandbag ramparts, as well as down. (One look at the water-filled ditches along the roads shows nothing has changed.) If you have an interest in the subject, you could probably spend two hours here. An English brochure gives information about the museum and about the 1916 Battle of Fromelles. The museum is due to move to larger premises from 2008, which should make access easier; it may also extend its opening by an extra day a month. ◑ *1 Jan-31 May & 1 Sept-31 Dec; second Sun of month 10am-noon & 2-6pm; closed 1 June-31 Aug. Mairie de Fromelles, D121/D22, 3km NE of Aubers (tel: 03 20 50 63 85). 4€, children 3€; disabled free.* ✎ ⑤

❯**Indian Memorial**   A pair of stone Bengal tigers stand guard over the names of 4,847 Indians who lost their lives

■ **Indian heritage: a salute to the fallen.**

between 1914 and 1918 and who have no known grave. This awe-inspiring stone construction near Neuve-Chapelle was designed by Sir Herbert Baker, architect of much of New Delhi. The carvings of animals and reptiles on the openwork wall are from Indian regimental badges. It pays tribute to Indians who served in all branches of the services, from the Ghurka Rifles to the Indian Veterinary Corps, including thousands of bearers, labourers, mule-drivers and grooms. ● *Carrefour de La Bombe, junction of D171 and D947, 5km SW of Aubers.* ⑤

❯**Portuguese Cemetery**   Two hundred metres along the road from the Indian Memorial, behind a decorative stone arch, is a large Portuguese burial ground. Portugal's World War I alliance with the British was in recognition of support lent by Britain against Napoleon during the Peninsular War of 1807-13. Here, in the Battle of the Lys (9-29 April 1918), the Portuguese lost a third of their fighting force on the first day, with 327 officers and 7,098 men killed, wounded or captured. ● *On D947, S of Carrefour de La Bombe, and 5km SW of Aubers.* ⑤

BÉTHUNE

ⓘ **Rue Aristide-Briand (tel: 03 21 57 25 47 fax: 03 21 57 01 60);**
42/48 Rue St Pry until Dec 2007.
www.tourisme-artoiscomm.fr
maisontourisme-bethune@laposte.net

For a place with such dignified buildings, Béthune—18km north-west of Lens—offers surprisingly little in the way of museums, so those that follow are located outside the town. The centre is worth a visit, though, for the variety of Art Deco buildings that fringe its cobbled main square, surrounding a sturdy stone belfry that dates back to 1388.

The slightly mystifying references all over Béthune to *"l'âne Buridan"* relate to a French philosopher, born in the town in 1300. Pointing out the difficulty of choosing between two equally attractive alternatives, Jean Buridan cited as an example that an *âne* (a donkey), given a choice between a pail of water and a bundle of hay, might hestitate so long between making a decision that it would die of both hunger and thirst. Today chocolates, cakes and even a local beer keep his name alive.

Béthune's wealth was originally based on the cloth trade and farming. Its position on the Aire canal made it a centre of trade, too, even before the discovery of coal deposits nearby in 1850. From then it developed as a port for the shipment of *"l'or noir"*, or "black gold".

Lying 8km from the front, and full of British troops during World War I, Béthune was a focus for enemy bombardment that inflicted 90 per cent destruction on the town. Rebuilt during the 1920s, it is today a business centre, with shopping focused on the streets around the Grand'Place, and a large out-of-town retail park to the south-west, near junction 6 of the A26. The tourist office, 100 metres south-east of the square, has brochures of walking routes around the town's main architectural features and organises regular guided visits (in English, if required) of town, belfry and church.

> **Grand'Place** Béthune's main square is edged with a dazzling collection of Flemish-inspired Art Deco façades. The post-1918 redesign was shared out between three architects: Jacques Alleman, Léon Guthmann and Paul Dégez. Between them they created this astonishing variety of gables, colourful paintwork, eccentric tiles and decorative stonework around the ancient belfry. ● *Grand'Place.* ♿

> **Église St-Vaast** A stone's throw from the Grand'Place, this byzantine-style brick church stands on the site of a chapel that St Vaast himself built. Today's edifice—light, yet slightly austere inside—was designed after World War I by the architect Louis Marie Cordonnier. On the south side, nearest the main door, one of the stained-glass windows features Cordonnier himself, standing to the right of St Vaast. ● *Mon-Sat 8am-6pm, Sun 10am-noon. Mass: Sun 11am. 45 Rue Louis-Blanc.*

> **Confrérie des Charitables** The origins of the town's brotherhood of the "Charitables de St Éloi" go back to a time of plague in 1188. Two local blacksmiths were inspired by a vision to collect and bury the bodies of the poorest victims each night, and thus prevent the malady from spreading. The members of the *confrérie* still attend funerals in the town, wearing black robes and distinctive *bicorne* hats as they accompany the dead to the cemetery. Other villages in the area have similar associations; all join together in late September to take part in a procession to celebrate their patron, St-Éloi. ○ *Procession: late Sept. Starts Rue des Charitables, Béthune; finishes at Chapelle Quinty, Route de la Chapelle-Quinty, off D937 at Naviaux, 1.5km SE of Béthune (tel: 03 21 65 91 15).*

> **Musée de Poche/Maison du Mineur** A wonderful collection of photographs, objects and documents has been gathered to evoke the history of this mining village on the outskirts of Béthune. Next to the *mairie* of Annezin, this charming, "pocket-sized" museum is arranged in sections on history, school, war, the *Charitables* (see above), mining, brick-making and so on, all imaginatively presented on a shoestring budget. A few streets away, a small terraced cottage is being furnished as a "Maison du Mineur", so guides can show visitors a typical interior of a miner's terraced house. ● *Wed 3-5pm; Sat 10am-noon. Closed mid July to late Aug. Place du Général-de-Gaulle, Rue de la Mairie, Annezin, 3km W of Béthune (tel: 03 21 52 39 94). Admission free; donations welcome.* ♿

■ **Fabulous façades: Art Deco in Béthune's Grand'Place.**

■ King coal: mining at Bruay.

>**Musée de la Mine** Alongside a small Art Deco complex that was once a training centre for mine apprentices is a little coal-mining museum with 200 metres of specially-built tunnels. Inside, you embark upon a tour that brings home the conditions of the time. The tunnels are partly equipped with modern techniques of iron props and electricity; partly with old-style wooden pit-props and compressed-air-powered *marteaux-piqueurs* (pneumatic drills). Volunteer guides (former miners or, sometimes, their grandchildren) lead regular hour-long tours through the galleries. Visitors can also go it alone, following a one-way system anticlockwise along the passages and pressing buttons at various points to hear a French commentary. You do have to watch out for bumping your head, or tripping over stuff on the floor, but children relish the chance to creep through a section with headroom of just 90cm. (Taller people can follow a different route!) Near the end of the visit, even adults have to bend double to negotiate a 1.25-metre-high sloping gallery, which takes you past the hydraulic rams that support the roof and the electrically-powered machine called a *rabot* that chewed coal out of the seam. ● *Tours: Mon-Fri, 2pm, 3pm & 4pm. Centre Culturel Georges Brassens, Avenue Guillon (off D937), Noeux-les-Mines, 5km S of Béthune (tel: 03 21 26 34 64/03 21 25 98 58). 5€, children 2€.*

BRUAY-LA-BUISSIERE
ⓘ see Béthune (page 154)

Though just 10km south-west of Béthune, Bruay is a separate town—sixth largest in the Pas-de-Calais. Seeing its surrounding landscape of pit-heaps, you are not surprised to find its heritage largely centred around a mining past. The town had a population of just 500 at the time of the French Revolution. However, once coal was discovered here in 1850 and the first pit began production, the population rocketed. In 1890 it had grown to 11,265 and by 1936, with two other shafts in activity, it reached more than 30,000.

Buay's pit closed in 1966. Its shafts were filled in and towers demolished, and in their place are flowery parks and gardens. The streets of terraced houses (known as *corons*) have been spruced up—a far cry from the days when pit villages were surrounded by walls, to conceal the miners' miserable living conditions from passers-by. However, the mining past is not forgotten. You can visit an interesting *écomusée* that re-creates the atmosphere under ground. There are also monuments to miners around town, and some magnificent stained-glass windows (pictured above) on the staircase of Bruay's grand *hôtel de ville*, or town hall.

>**Écomusée de la Mine** A lamentable lack of signposting makes it hard to find this "mine", built as a training facility, but it's worth persevering. A team of retired Bruay miners put over their way of life with gusto, starting with a 20-minute film (in French) about work in the local pits that once employed 25,000 miners. It explains safety measures such as constant spraying with water to keep coal dust down and monitoring levels of *grisou*, or pit gas. A second, shorter, film shows General de Gaulle, clad in overalls, helmet and lamp, visiting Bruay in 1959 when he delighted the miners with his speech paying tribute to their "courage" and "nobility".

BRUAY EXTRAS

Accommodation/food:
Chartreuse du Val St-Esprit *Luxurious 4-star hotel in a former monastery, with bar, restaurant & brasserie. Rooms from 100€; menus 32-67€. 1 Rue de Fouquières, Gosnay, 5km NE of Bruay, near J6 of A26 (tel: 03 21 62 80 00). www.lachartreuse.com/*
Restaurant: La Médina *Smart North African-style couscous restaurant. Lamb or chicken couscous 22€. Closed Mon. 442 Rue Leroy (tel: 03 21 62 29 98).*
Brocante: **Emmaüs Artois/Le Relais** *Furniture, bric-a-brac, toys, bicycles & clothes. Mon-Fri 2-5pm, Sat 10am-noon & 2-5pm. 1987 Chemin des Dames, Gosnay, 7km NE of Bruay; follow Le Relais sign under railway bridge, & then for 1km (tel: 03 21 52 26 78).*

During your own tour, the guide can run a slightly ponderous English version of the commentary over a loudspeaker. You are shown miners' tools, with holes drilled through them so that each worker could lock his own away at the end of his shift. Then you "descend" in a rattling cage to tunnels similar to those in which children would haul loaded *berlines* (coal-wagons) along to the lift shaft to be carried to the surface, in constant danger of being crushed to death. You see areas just 40cm high where a miner might work in a prone position for his entire 12-hour shift. Machines that the guide occasionally puts into action give a small idea of the noise from pumps, drills and hammers that rendered many workers deaf. Allow a good couple of hours for your visit. (There is no opportunity to arrive late or to leave early once a tour has begun.) Wear sensible shoes and a sweater as, on a summer's day, it can be chillier inside than out. ◑ *1 Apr-late Oct, Sat & Sun 2-5pm (1 July-31 Aug, daily 2-5pm). Cours Kennedy, about two-thirds of the way down, on the E side of the road (tel: 03 21 53 52 33). 4.50€, children 2.50€, under-10s free.* ✆

>Musée de la Mine Jacques Déramaux The 90-minute guided tour here, along 250 metres of tunnels, starts with a 25-minute audiovisual presentation, with live commentary by a retired-miner guide. Drawings show how coal is formed from decomposition of vegetation, and illustrate ways seams are accessed: through geographical faults, vertical sections and open-cast mining. You hear about the tall Boulonnais pit horses—used until the 1950s—that would haul 10 loaded wagons. (If the animal sensed an 11th had been hooked on, it would refuse to budge!)

Down in the dark passageways, the guide keeps up a commentary (a good knowledge of French is vital for this tour) interspersed with lively anecdotes, and at one point turns off the overhead lights to demonstrate the gloom in which miners worked. A shrieking cutting-machine gives a small taste of the constant din from ventilators, conveyor belts, pumps and jackhammers.

Unlike most others, this place does not have models of miners at work. Instead, it concentrates on working conditions, with a strong emphasis on mine safety. You learn how a circle of dust in the roof could mean the presence of a fossilised tree, likely to crash down vertically and kill anyone beneath. You are told about the deadly *gaz carbonique*, or carbon dioxide, released after blasting, which hung about at floor level. And you hear about ways of detecting *grisou*, the explosive pit gas released from within the coal during cutting. A sobering short safety film shows an explosion (under controlled conditions) caused by igniting *grisou*. It is then repeated, using a mixture of *grisou* and coal dust—a typical combination in a mine: the result is one huge fireball. You can only guess how much worse that would be under ground, and look with increasing admiration at your elderly guides, who have faced it all and yet who seem so upbeat about their former way of life.

More up-to-date techniques and equipment show tunnels lined in iron rather than pine, and the modern machine called a *rabot* that ground coal out of the seam. You emerge into a room with a reconstructed miners' kitchen, displays of fossils, and some fascinating maps of the underground galleries that linked the area's pits. Tours usually start before 10am and take a couple of hours. It's as well to telephone the day before, in case the organisers want to give you a specific start time, and to turn up promptly on the day. ● *Thurs 9-10am start. Boulevard de la Paix (D183E), Auchel, 8km NW of Bruay (tel: 03 21 52 66 10). 4€, children 2.50€.* ✆

>Château d'Olhain A miniature medieval fortress, this moated castle stands in the middle of a quiet village. It was built in 1202 by Crusader-knight Hugues d'Olhain and restored in 1407, after the Hundred Years War. It has withstood changing fortunes as well as invasion and occupation by Spanish, French and Dutch. Abandoned in the late 19th century, it is now used as a farmhouse. Bridges lead across successive watery barriers into the *basse-cour* (farmyard), and over a final drawbridge into the courtyard where the crowing of cockerels, cackling of geese and gentle whiffs of manure add authenticity to the old stones. Visitors are allowed to wander through the chapel, bakery, vaulted cellars

■ **Fort over: Olhain's moated castle.**

and guard-rooms. A hundred stone steps lead to the top of one of the towers, from which you have a bird's-eye view through a window, with signs pointing towards various battlegrounds throughout the château's existence: Bouvines, 45km away (a French victory in 1214 over John Lackland of England); Agincourt, 30km (victory of Henry V over the French, 1415; see page 99); and Lorette and Vimy, 10km (French and Canadian victories over the Germans during World War I; see page 168). ◑ *1 Apr-1 Nov, Sun & public holidays 3-6.30pm (1 July-31 Aug, Sat, Sun & public holidays 3-6.30pm). Olhain, 5km SE of Bruay (tel: 03 21 27 94 76). 4€, children under 12 free.*

>**La Table des Fées** One of a few neolithic remains in the area, this dolmen (or covered tomb) on the edge of a hilltop wood is a reminder of the presence of prehistoric man. Locals maintain that the fairies used to sit around it for meals—presumably enjoying the fantastic views towards Arras. ● *Bise-Pierre, signposted off the D57 between Verdrel & Fresnicourt, 6km SE of Bruay.* ◉

>**Piscine Art Déco** A fabulous open-air swimming pool in the purest Art Deco style, beautifully painted in cream and pale blue, lies just off Bruay's Rue de la République. Built in 1936, it is claimed to be the last outdoor pool of this period still in use in France, and was designed—like the adjacent sports stadium—by a Bauhaus-influenced architect, Paul Hanote. If you decide to sunbathe after your swim, note that you are not allowed to sit on the grass. ○ *1 June-mid Sept. Daily 10.30am-1pm & 3-6pm. Rue Augustin-Caron (tel: 03 21 62 43 18). 2.50€, children 1.20€.* ◉

LENS

ⓘ 26 Rue de la Paix (tel: 03 21 67 66 66 fax: 03 21 67 65 66)
www.tourisme-lenslievin.fr
info@tourisme-lenslievin.fr

Tourists who have visited this former mining town would probably have been attending a match at its famous Bollaert stadium. However, a new building, due for completion in 2009, is set to put Lens as firmly on the cultural map of Europe as it already is on the sporting one with the opening of a branch of the Louvre museum, known as the Louvre-Lens.

After the discovery of coal in the area, a group of industrialists formed the Société des Mines de Lens in 1852, which became the most powerful mining company in France. The population grew from 2,200 in 1789 to 220,000 a century later. Along with those of Liévin and Loos-en-Gohelle, the pits of Lens were destroyed on a grand scale by the retreating Germans in 1918, but revived to fuel a post-war industrial renaissance.

The last pit may have closed, but you still feel dwarfed by the famous *terrils jumeaux*, the 150-metre-high "twin peaks" that tower above the A21 motorway, near junction 8. Between 1960 and 1986, 24 million cubic metres of spoil was piled here making these the tallest pit-heaps in Europe. They are now officially historic monuments. Of the two winding-towers associated with them, that of Fosse (or pit) 11 is in traditional, delicate-looking openwork; the taller, less romantic, white tower served the more modern Fosse 19.

Boulevard Émile-Basly is Lens' main shopping street. At its upper end, a wonderful concentration of Art Deco architecture leads the eye to the imposing byzantine-style church of St-Léger. A map from the tourist office will guide you to other, slightly more hidden, treasures of the 1920s. A block north of Boulevard Basly, on Rue Casimir-Beugnet, stands the ornately-decorated Maison Syndicale, once the offices of the miners' union. Another highlight is the magnificent neo-Flemish-style Grands Bureaux des Mines de Lens, in a leafy park on Rue Jean-Souvray. Designed in 1928 by Louis Marie Cordonnier, this former headquarters of the mining company is now part of the University of Artois. Don't miss Lens' fanciful Art Deco railway station; if you give free rein to your imagination, you can see its exterior has the voluptuously rounded form of a steam locomotive.

>**Louvre-Lens** The first provincial branch of Paris's Louvre museum is due to open its doors on the site of Fosse 9, west of Lens town centre. Set in landscaped grounds, the glass and steel

■ Decorative: 1920s style in Lens.

Market: Tues & Fri, both Place Roger-Salengro, N of St-Léger church.

Accommodation/food:
Lensotel *Modern 3-star hotel by a retail park. Rooms from 73€; menus 16-30€. Centre Commercial Lens II, Vendin-le-Vieil , 2km N of Lens, near J10 of A21 (tel: 03 21 79 36 36). www.lensotel.com/*

Restaurants:
L'Arcadie II *Smart place in town centre. Menus 13€-30€. Closed Sun-Wed evg, & Mon & Sat lunch. 13 Rue Decrombecque (tel: 03 21 70 32 22).*

Restaurant du Commerce *Unexpectedly charming modern restaurant, serving refined dishes indoors or out. Menus from 16€. Open Mon-Sat lunch, & Fri evg. 15 Place Jean-Tailliez (near Hôtel de Ville), Courrières, 5km NE of Lens, near J18 of A1 (tel: 03 21 20 02 69).*

Shop: Brasserie Castelain *Huge selection of Ch'ti beers at this brewery shop with a small museum of brewing attached. Mon-Fri 9am-noon & 2-6pm. 13 Rue Pasteur, Bénifontaine, 8km N of Lens (tel: 03 21 08 68 61).*

construction by Japanese architects Kazuyo Sejima and Ryue Nishizawa will house 500 to 600 works from the Louvre's reserves, changed on a three-yearly basis. It will also host temporary exhibitions. ● *Opens 2009. Off Rue Jeanne-d'Arc. Days, times & admission charges not known at time of writing. Information from tourist office (tel: 03 21 67 66 66).* ᗐ

❯**Stade Bollaert** Called after a mine-owner and benefactor of the town, this famous stadium has hosted many international football matches. Its home team, Racing Club de Lens (RCL), known to its fans as "*les sang-et-or*" (the blood-and-golds, for their red-and-yellow strip) was formed in 1906. *Ticket information (tel: 08 25 86 28 62). www.rclens.fr/*

❯**Musée Alexandre Villedieu** In the flower-decorated village of Loos (pronounced "lohss"), just north of the A21, is a museum devoted to the battles fought here during World War I. On this wide plain, all vantage-points were precious, and the Germans were in possession of most of them: "Hill 70" (north-west of junction 10 of today's A21); the "Double Crassier" (two long, flat-topped slag-heaps that were the basis of today's twin *terrils*); and a structure nicknamed "Tower Bridge" (a pair of 50-metre-high pit-head towers). A first attempt, by the French in May 1915 to evict the Germans led to catastrophically heavy losses. In September/October 1915, at what is generally referred to as the Battle of Loos, Scottish regiments managed to recapture Loos itself, but failed to hold the all-important Hill 70. This battle was the first at which the Allies used chlorine gas. The huge Allied casualties (more than 50,000 killed, wounded or captured) have caused this particular encounter to be dubbed "the British Verdun". In August 1917, after months of planning, Hill 70 was secured by Canadian forces. The Allies' troops and equipment had remained hidden for two weeks in specially-dug tunnels, ensuring total surprise for the attack.

The museum is named after a French soldier whose body was found near here in 1996. With it was a Waterman fountain pen that—once refilled with ink—was found still to write perfectly. Another pen, this time engraved by the UK Post Office, helped identify the remains of a Scottish soldier unearthed in 2001 and enabled him, too, to be given a full military funeral. These and other anecdotes are related with passion and enthusiasm by the energetic anglophile president, Alfred Duparcq. During a guided tour (in French) he brings the period to life, describing the trench souvenirs in their glass cases. Grouped by nationality, the French, Allied or German possessions are those of soldiers everywhere: bottles, mugs, cutlery, guns, grenades, spades and picks. In the back room are French uniforms, and several guns—including some used to launch gas canisters.

For a minimum of six people, you can ask for a tour, taking in no man's land, the site of the now-vanished "Tower Bridge", and the plateau alongside today's twin *terrils*. The latter commands a view over the scene of the fighting that is as good as any battle map. From 2008, the museum hopes to have larger premises. ● *Mon-Fri 9-11am & 2-5pm, by appointment; English-speaking guide available on prior request. Hôtel de Ville, Place de la République, Loos-en-Gohelle, 5km N of Lens (tel: 03 21 78 31 29). Museum: 3€, children 2.50€. Visit to battle sites (minimum six people) 6€.*

❯**Musée de la Mine et de l'École** An unexpected find next to a primary school in the centre of Harnes is this museum lovingly created by a retired miner, Monsieur Legrain, and his ex-school-teacher wife. From outside, it looks like any brick-built terraced house. Once through the door, however, instead of the interior of a traditional "two-up, two-down", you find yourself plunged into a veritable mine of information (all in French) on the area's coal industry. Alongside maps of coal-seams, fossils and pieces of glittering coal, a costumed miner waits to descend a shaft in a metal barrel. Drills, chains, ropes, respirators and safety lamps rub shoulders with homelier items such as a coffee canister or a lunch bag.

A grimmer side is apparent in X-rays showing the progression of pneumoconiosis in a miner's lungs. There are articles about the 1906 Courrières pit disaster—Europe's greatest mining tragedy—when 1,099 coal-face workers died in a *"coup de grisou"*, or methane explosion 2km from here. Days after the search had been abandoned, 13 wraith-like survivors struggled to the surface after having spent three weeks groping past rockfalls in subterranean darkness.

After negotiating a dark passageway that makes you feel you have already entered a pit, you are sent off down to the cellar, which Monsieur Legrain has transformed into a mine gallery, complete with pit-props, drilling equipment and coal-wagons. On emerging, and climbing upstairs to the first floor, you find reconstructions of a mining family's kitchen with its tin bath, and of a typical *estaminet* in which miners would stop for one or more thirst-quenching beers. Displays evoke their traditional pastimes of pigeon-racing, cock-fighting, choral-singing and *fanfares (*brass bands).

Right at the back of the house is a recreation of a typical schoolroom of the 1950s in which you may be lucky enough to see Madame Legrain putting a party of visiting French children through some thoroughly old-fashioned dictation, and causing them to gasp with horror when she reveals that not only did miners' houses of the 1920s have no running water, but they also lacked such modern essentials as a television set! ● *Tues & Thurs 2-5pm. 20-24 Rue de Montceau-les-Mines, Harnes, 7km NE of Lens (tel: 03 21 75 38 97). Admission free; donations welcome.* 🪕

❯**Musée Municipal** A solid *"maison bourgeoise"*, also in the centre of Harnes, contains a fascinating collection of photographs and documents on the history of the area, particularly relating to both World Wars. None of it is in English, but much of it is pictorial, so of interest even to non-French-speakers. The first room on the right has photographs of the quiet streets before 1914, when Harnes' 5,600 inhabitants worked either in agriculture or in one of the two local mines.

Fund-raising posters and documents on the French mobilisation of 1 August 1914 evoke the coming war, which took many men away from their town or village for the first time. The invading Germans dug into the stragetic high points, turning the area into a fortified zone. Displays include postcards, embroidered items, and scarves printed with portraits of German leaders, a map of France, and some Allied marching songs. There are British and Canadian insignia, headgear, trench periscope, wire-cutters, bottles, spades, shell-cases and shrapnel. The adjoining room has sketches of German cavalry uniforms, a gas-warning bell, and enamel funerary plaques, each bearing a moving photograph of one of the 200 men of Harnes who lost their lives.

In the hallway, displays move on to the 1930s: the rise of Fascism, the declaration of World War II in September 1939, and the ensuing *drôle de guerre*, or "phoney war". By June 1940 the *départements* of the Nord and Pas-de-Calais had come under German rule once more, and were declared *"zones interdites"* (forbidden areas). Occupation money and newspapers are on show, and there is a section on local people deported to German prison camps.

A back room contains much material on the Resistance, which grew up in response to General de Gaulle's June 1940 broadcast to those who remained in France, encouraging them to resist the enemy. You see mollifying statements issued by the occupiers: ("Have confidence in us"; "Help us to help you"), and newspapers dropped by the Allies to inform the locals of the true situation. There are clandestine newspapers, FFI (Resistance) armbands, official stamps stolen to create false papers, and items parachuted to the Resistance by the RAF to help with sabotage. In the hallway, another *vitrine* illustrates the hardships endured during the Occupation years, with home-made shoes; recipes for cheap, nourishing dishes; and instructions to save copper pans and pork fat. You could spend one or even two hours here, if you are fascinated by the subject (and understand sufficient French). ● *1 Jan-31 July & 1 Sept-31 Dec, Wed 10am-noon & 3-6pm, Sat 3-6pm. Closed 1-31 Aug. 50 Rue André-Deprez, Harnes, 7km NE of Lens (tel: 03 21 49 02 29). Admission free; donations welcome.* ☜

➤ ★ **Centre Historique Minier** Some distance from Lens, on the site of one of the region's many coal-mines, a showcase mining centre gives an excellent idea of life under ground. Evocative guided tours are given by former miners—in French (though the 17 guides are taking English lessons!). Non-French-speakers can use free audioguides; issued at the ticket desk, and switch them on at specific numbered locations during the visit for a good commentary in English.

On arrival you are given a tour number, time and rendezvous point for the 90-minute guided visit. (It's probably as well to encourage everyone in your party to visit the toilets shortly before it starts.) Before or after, you can visit the rest of the site at your own pace. One building shows, with

Black gold

Dug here for 150 years, coal formed the landscape of northern France. Now the mines have closed, there are opportunities to visit tunnels under ground and slag-heaps above.

The discovery of coal in this region around 1850 gave impetus to France's tardy industrial development. A 12km-wide basin—the country's largest coal-producing area—ran from Bruay-la-Buissière 105km east to Valenciennes. Émile Zola's 1885 novel *Germinal* first opened the eyes of the nation to the harsh conditions of miners' lives. Women worked under ground until 1892, and children under 11 until 1906.

Rows of terraced houses, called *corons*, stood adjacent to each *fosse*, or pit. A miner's house usually had a plot for vegetable-growing but until the 1950s few had running water.

The ever-present threat to miners' health was pneumoconiosis, caused by inhaled dust. Other enemies were the explosive

grisou (pit gas), and the asphyxiating *gaz carbonique* (carbon dioxide).

At the end of World War I, the departing Germans destroyed factories and flooded the mines. In view of the death and disablement of so many Frenchmen in the war, thousands of workers were imported from Poland to restore output, establishing a community that endures to this day.

In 1944, the pits were again destroyed. The rebuilding programme introduced electricity and new technology, boosting production, but demand eventually declined, and the last pit closed in 1990. Today, former miners share their experience with visitors at Lewarde (the largest site), at Bruay, Auchel and Noeux-les-Mines.

Twenty-six pit-head

towers have been preserved, as have 400 of the black, mostly conical *terrils*. Some of these former blots on the landscape are now grassed over and used for dry-skiing or para-gliding. Wildlife and surprisingly exotic flora are colonising the slopes, and forgotten strains of apple and pear trees have sprung up from pips discarded from the lunchboxes of generations of miners.

Disused *terrils* can present dangers from landslip or smouldering, so access is strictly controlled. An environmental group, Chaîne des Terrils, organises nature walks (brochures from the area's tourist offices). *Mid Feb-early Dec, usually Sat, Sun; venues vary (advance booking essential). CPIE Chaîne des Terrils (tel: 03 21 28 17 28). http://chaine.des.terrils.free.fr/*

wall panels and a well-made animated film, how coal was formed 300 million years ago. You look at offices and the infirmary; read about St Barbe, patron saint of miners; and see pictures of family life, as well as equipment associated with favourite pastimes: skittles, bowls, giant feathered darts called *javelots*, and cock-fighting (still not illegal in this area). Alongside an interesting timeline are models of mines of the 18th, 19th and 20th centuries, and displays of miners' tools and their *barettes*, the stiff leather hats that for many years were their only protective clothing. Village life revolved around the mine, and every member of the family was expected to work there in some capacity, otherwise the family would lose the house.

You meet your guide in the "*salle des pendus*", the high-ceilinged room where miners coming on shift would change into their working gear and winch their clean clothes up to the ceiling to clear floor space for those coming off shift to have their showers. The guides spew forth explanations, and even those with good French will probably not grasp each statistic or every bit of jargon. However, the whole visit is incredibly atmospheric, and the audioguides fill in the gaps.

You are shown the history and evolution of the safety lamp, which would be handed to miners before their descent. Then you are issued with a plastic helmet and led outside to a little yellow train that trundles you round part of the site. On arrival at the pit head, you climb two flights of metal stairs and are shown a short 1950s' film about life in the pit, before stepping into a (relatively modern) lift for a speedy descent.

You emerge into a different world, picking your way over rail tracks and into galleries lined with pit-props. At times, the guide puts bits of equipment into action so you can appreciate the deafening noise to which miners were subjected. Dummies dressed as miners crouch alongside seams, from which children as young as nine would have shovelled away the coal as fast as the men cut it. A series of galleries show equipment from the 1930s to 60s, when hydraulic rams replaced pine pit-props. This is one visit where you are delighted to tip the guide a euro or so; it slightly salves your conscience for his having had to do such a terrible job.

There is plenty to see in the outbuildings around the site, from stables to steam-engines. If you think of eating here, you will find a bar behind the admissions desk, a picnic area near the far end of the site, and even a proper restaurant: Le Briquet, named after the word for the miner's packed lunch (tel: 03 27 95 82 80). Allow at least three hours for the whole experience. ● *1 Feb-31 Dec. Mon-Sat 1-7pm (last admission 5pm); Sun, school-holiday periods & public holidays 10am-5pm (1 Mar-31 Oct, daily 9am-7.30pm; last admission 5.30pm). Fosse Delloye, on D132 30km E of Lens, 8km SE of Douai & 1km S of Lewarde (tel: 03 27 95 82 82). 9.90€, students & children 4.90€ (1 Mar-31 Oct 10.90€ & 5.90€). Closed 1-31 Jan, 1 May & 25 Dec.* ♿ ☈ ☯

■ **Pit stop: retired miners at Lewarde give a flavour of life under ground.**

LILLERS

ⓘ 4 Place Roger-Salengro (tel: 03 21 25 26 71 fax: 03 21 25 10 88)
www.tourismelillerois.com
tourismelillerois@wanadoo.fr

Formerly one of the shoe-making capitals of France, Lillers has some attractive old houses—including the 1631, stepped-gabled Maison de l'Argentier.

Today, the town has one of the largest sugar refineries in the Pas-de-Calais, its billowing smoke visible from the busy N43. It processes almost 14,000 tonnes of beet a day; most of its output is distilled into sugar alcohol, for making spirits, perfumes, medicines, cleaning products and solvents.

Lillers is also known for its artesian wells, holes bored through impermeable rock to a water source below. Pressure on the water-table from above causes water to come gushing up to the surface, a phenomenon first recorded by monks from this area, the Artois, in the Middle Ages. Since then, the adjective "*artésien*" (meaning "of the Artois") has been used to denote any well of this type.

For some magnificent scenery, drive along the D341, 5km west of Lillers. This ancient Roman road, called "Chaussée Brunehaut" (see page 32), links Arras and Thérouanne across plateaux, down into valleys and past grassed-over slag-heaps. Close to Lillers, near Rely, curious clusters of brick in the fields are vestiges of hangars from a World War II airfield, a base for Luftwaffe bombers.

❯ **Maison de la Chaussure** The region's shoe industry, which flourished here from 1827 to 1996, is shown off at this small museum. In the 1920s a tenth of the town's population worked at shoe-making. Displays show the weird-shaped bits of hide that make up the *tige* (or upper). Cutting was done by men; stitching was women's work. Items on view include buttonhooks, sewing-machines, photographs of the workforce, and a giant shoe that won a place in the French version of the *Guinness Book of Records*. Eventually machines outstripped men, cutting 20 pairs of soles a minute compared with the four that a human worker could manage. ● *Place du Capitaine-Ansar, Lillers, 12km NW of Béthune. For opening days & times, contact tourist office (tel: 03 21 25 26 71). Admission free.*

❯ **Son-et-lumière: *La Légende des Princes Irlandais*** In these open-air performances, 40 horsemen and more than 1,000 costumed locals re-enact the story of Lugle and Luglien, two 7th-century Irish princes who set off on a pilgrimage to Rome. Passing through this area of France, they were set upon by bandits. The princes' servants fled, but one called Erkembode returned to the scene, where he, too, was beaten and left for dead. Coming to, as he later told the bishop of Thérouanne, he found his masters decapitated, but witnessed angels descending and restoring the severed heads to the bodies. Sensing a miracle, the bishop collected the bones of the two men, and today

LILLERS EXTRAS

Market: Sat.

Specialities: Watercress. Sugar. Shoes. Shallots.

Accommodation/food:

Château de Beaulieu Michelin-starred eating at Marc Meurin's 4-star country-house hotel. Rooms from 140€; menus from 55€. Closed Sat lunch, Sun evg & Mon. Route de Lillers, Busnes, 4km NE of Lillers (tel: 03 21 68 88 88). www. lechateaudebeaulieu.fr/

Les Cohettes Warm welcome to this B&B in a traditional Artois house. Rooms from 50€; convivial suppers (on reservation) 20€. 28 Rue de Pernes, Auchy-au-Bois, 6km W of Lillers (tel: 03 21 02 09 47). www. chambresdhotes-chezgina.com/

Restaurant:

Les Marronniers Delicious meals & quirky decor in old farmhouse; game dishes in season. Menus 26-30€. Closed Sun evg. 343 Rue de Busnettes (D187), 4km E of Lillers (tel: 03 21 54 27 14).

Festival: **Fête St-Crépin** Special events in honour of St Crispin, patron saint of shoemakers, late Oct.

■ **Booting up: footwear at Lillers' shoe museum.**

these relics are still venerated at Lillers, Montdidier and Ferfay. Erkembode himself was made a saint; his large stone sarcophagus can be seen in the cathedral of St-Omer (see page 82). O *Early June, 10pm. Parc Trystram, Rue des Promenades (tel: 03 21 25 26 71). 12€, children 6€. http://lesprincesirlandais.free.fr/*

■ St Benoît: humble birthplace.

➤**Maison Natale de St Benoît Labre** At the bottom of a steep, grassy slope opposite a village church is a charming whitewashed cottage that was the birthplace of the Pas-de-Calais' most famous saint. The eldest of 15 children, Benoît-Joseph Labre was born on 26 March 1748 and at the age of 21 decided to spend his life in wandering and prayer. Filthy and unkempt, he was endlessly turned away from religious establishments. He covered thousands of kilometres in his search for God before reaching Rome, where he lived in abject poverty and died at the age of 35. He was canonised in 1881, and is revered as the patron saint of beggars and down-and-outs. (See also page 98.)

The pretty little grey-shuttered house contains a statue of St Benoît, and a few items of furniture that date from his time. Under the eaves, illuminated by shafts of light shining through chinks in the tiles, the room of the saint's birth is now a shrine. You can leave a prayer or a word of appreciation, and a donation in the box. A pilgrimage takes place here each year in late August.

Inside the village church is the font in which the future St Benoît was baptised and some panels describing his life. Numerous relics include a board from the saint's bed, books he was carrying when he died, and his death mask. His parents are buried in the churchyard. ● *Sat, Sun 9am-6pm. 2 Rue de l'Église, Amettes, 8km SW of Lillers (tel: 03 21 25 26 71). Admission free.* ♿ *(ground floor only, via a driveway opposite 27 Rue d'en Bas, at the bottom of the hill.)* ⓢ

MERVILLE

ⓘ **6 Place de la Libération (tel: 03 28 43 67 96 fax: 03 28 43 67 96)**
www.ville-merville.fr
tourisme@ville-merville.fr

Straddling the junction of the Lys and the Bourre rivers, 15km north of Béthune, Merville is endowed with no fewer than 17 bridges crossing its waterways. On the historic borders of France and Flanders, this former cloth-making town has been ravaged by war through the centuries and destroyed 11 times—most recently during World War I. Totally rebuilt since then, it has some interesting buildings including an imposing town hall and a vast church (with byzantine-style onion domes), both designed by the ubiquitous post-war architect Louis Marie Cordonnier.

True to the traditions of the Nord *département*, Merville's annual Easter carnival is based around its giants: St Antoine (St Anthony) and, bizarrely, a 5-metre-tall cat called "Le Caou".

➤**Station Bac-St-Maur** The jovial proprietor of this restaurant, located in a small railway station, dons a stationmaster's uniform for his self-styled role as *chef de gare*. The décor features posters, guards' lamps, model trains and battered railway trunks—you might even see a (real) goods train rattle past. Menus have names of railway tickets: the 8.50€ is *"Billet 2ème classe"*. Snack dishes served by dungaree-clad staff include Maroilles cheese flan, a *planche* (a substantial sandwich), and a *welsh* (ham and cheese on toast). Full-blown menus feature steak, duck and fish.

■ The right lines: lunch in an old railway station.

MERVILLE EXTRAS
Market: Wed.
Restaurants:
Le Cerisier *Eric Delerue's Michelin-starred restaurant. Menus 29-66€. Closed Sat lunch, Sun evg & Mon. 3 Rue de la Gare, Laventie, 11km SE of Merville (tel: 03 21 27 60 59).*
Station Bac-St-Maur
Eat lunch in a former railway station (see left). Menus 8.50-26€.

Leave room for the heavenly ice-creams, or for the *rabotte du Nord* dessert (apple with brown sugar). Real train-buffs will appreciate the chance to spend a night in a marquetry-lined, 1930s, first-class sleeper in a siding next to the restaurant. ● *77 Rue de la Gare, Sailly-sur-la-Lys, 7km NE of Estaires (tel: 03 21 02 68 20). Open daily for lunch; closed Sun-Thurs evenings & 23 Dec-5 Jan. B&B in railway wagon (weekends only) 35G. www.stationbacsaintmaur.com/*

➤**Massacre du Paradis** On 27 May 1940, 97 officers and men of the Royal Norfolk Regiment who had been ordered to hold back German forces to facilitate the Dunkirk evacuation, surrendered to an SS battalion at the village of Le Paradis. Against all the rules of war, they were disarmed and killed by machine-gun fire, revolver shots and bayonet thrusts. Miraculously two survived to see the SS commanding officer brought to justice after the end of the war. A memorial stone stands outside the church; the dead lie in the cemetery behind it. ● *Le Paradis, 6km S of Merville.* ⬣

ST POL-SUR-TERNOISE

ⓘ Place de l'Hôtel-de-Ville (tel: 03 21 47 08 08 fax: 03 21 47 50 33) www.ville-saintpolsurternoise.fr/ www.ternois-tourisme.com ot-saintpol@wanadoo.fr

The market town of St-Pol takes its full name from the small river that flows through it. On the north side, a few old buildings and some crumbling stone walls from the stronghold of the once-powerful Counts of St-Pol are witness to an ancient past. Targeting of the town's railway lines during both world wars resulted in large-scale destruction—and some interesting modern buildings that include a church with a dramatic openwork bell-tower.

A fertile soil has made St-Pol the focus of a large agricultural industry. The Monday-morning market fills the streets around church and town hall with shoppers and farmers—chatting, often in *patois*, over the fruit, vegetables and live poultry. Unusually, most shops are open on Monday (and closed on Tuesday). The growing conditions have also favoured the setting up of nurseries in the area, some specialising in rare plants. In addition, during early summer a number of private gardens open at weekends to show off their roses and other delights (see page 15).

An unexpected feature is a motor-racing circuit at Croix-en-Ternois, 3km west of town, venue for regular car- and motorcycle-racing events. (Details on www.circuitdecroix.com/)

➤**Musée Bruno Danvin** The town's small museum is in the chapel of an 18th-century former convent alongside the church. Its echoing hallway contains stone sculptures retrieved from the original façade. Upstairs is a haphazard collection of pottery, old postcards, a few neglected *coiffes* (head-dresses), a gloomy painting of Hell (*L'Enfer*) by Brueghel the Younger, slightly dingy 18th- and 19th-century canvases, and a few, more modern works. Most interesting is the archaeological collection on the platform at the end featuring items unearthed during recent road-building: flint tools, polished axe-heads, Roman coins, Gallo-Roman glass, some beautiful funerary urns, and a well-preserved 7th-century skeleton. Sadly, there is little on the town's more recent history, just a few medieval floor-tiles excavated from the site of the feudal castle. ● *Mon 11am-1pm, Wed 3-6pm; Sat, Sun 11am-12.30pm & 3-6pm. Rue Oscar-Ricque (tel: 03 21 47 00 10). Admission free.* ⬣

➤**Donjon de Bours** Since 1982 this extraordinary little 12th-century castle keep has served as the *mairie* for a small village of 500 souls. The castle itself, once surrounded by a moat and sturdy outer walls, was burnt down by French troops in 1543. However, this part, a fine example of a medieval lordly

■ Keep up: remains of Bours castle.

dwelling still stands proudly above the green meadows beside the old village church, its pointed towers resembling a cluster of giant candles. A local historian gives an hour-long tour of its stone-walled rooms and takes visitors up into one of the towers for a great view over the countryside. ❶ *Mid Mar-late Oct: Sat, Sun & public holidays 2-6pm. Place du Donjon, Bours, 12km NE of St-Pol (tel: 03 21 04 76 76). Admission free; donations welcome.*

➤**Abbaye de Belval** At their modern, brick-built convent in a wooded valley, a Cistercian order of nuns has been making and selling renowned cheeses since 1893. From a shop alongside the convent's farmyard, you can buy the three different types made here, as well as honey, books, rosaries, and souvenirs with a religious theme made at 30 other

■ **Big cheese: made by nuns at Belval Abbey.**

monasteries. ● *Mon-Fri 2.30-5.30pm; Sat 9.30-11.30am & 2.30-5.30pm; Sun 2.45-5.45pm. Vespers: daily 6pm. On D87, Belval, near Troisvaux, 5km N of St-Pol (tel: 03 21 04 10 10).* ❐

➤**La Méridienne Verte** In the car park near the convent shop stand three young trees, beside a concrete bollard topped with a metal badge. If you have been mystified as you zip along the motorways by signs proclaiming that you are crossing *"la méridienne verte"*, this is your chance for a close-up look. To celebrate the millennium, groups of trees were planted to form a "green meridian" along the longitude of Paris (2° 20' E). This line runs 1,000km—from Dunkerque to Barcelona—passing through 20 French *départements*. ● *D87, Belval, 5km N of St-Pol.* ❐

SOUCHEZ

ⓘ Centre Européen de la Paix, 100 Rue Pasteur (tel: 03 21 72 66 55 fax: 03 21 72 66 51)
www.tourisme-lenslievin.fr
info@tourisme-lenslievin.fr

"Soldiers' graves are the greatest preachers of peace," said French theologian and missionary surgeon Albert Schweitzer, and nowhere does this seem more true than around Souchez, 8km south-west of Lens. A modern *monument départemental* in the village centre pays tribute to the 700 young men of the Pas-de-Calais who lost their lives in North Africa between 1952 and 1964 during the Algerian war of independence.

But beyond this lie many thousands more soldiers—French, German, British, Canadian and others—killed in the battles of World War I. Along the D937 south of Souchez are the Allied cemetery of Cabaret Rouge with its Indian-style pavilions; memorials marking Czechoslovakian and Polish losses; Maison Blanche—largest German cemetery in France—whose slender black crosses commemorate 44,833 dead; and a French cemetery near La Targette holding 12,210 soldiers of both World Wars. In the centre of La Targette village an outsized sculpture of a hand holding a flaming torch symbolises the rebirth of neighbouring Neuville-St-Vaast, which was obliterated during World War I.

However, the main reason to visit Souchez is to pay homage to 42,000 French dead at the vast, and moving, French national cemetery of Notre-Dame-de-Lorette. The ridge on which it stands was the site of a battle that lasted from October 1914 to October 1915.

➤**Centre Européen de la Paix** The uncluttered modern museum on the lower floor of Souchez's tourist office makes an excellent introduction to this war-torn area. Behind an Art Deco frontage, opposite the road up to Notre-Dame-de-Lorette, it has three rooms of material presenting a small selection of World War I uniforms—French, German, Scottish, Russian, Indian and others. French soldiers began the war in dark blue jackets and conspicuous scarlet trousers, modified to all-over pale "*bleu horizon*" in 1915. (The British had already discovered the advantages of more discreet khaki during the Boer War of 1899 to1902.) Notice the metal skull-caps, known as *cervelières*, that French *poilus*, or infantrymen, wore under their soft *képis*, before the "*adrien*" helmet was introduced in May 1915. Before then, no soldiers of any side had steel head-protection: British troops were issued with the familiar "Brodie" helmet between autumn 1915 and spring 1916; German soldiers obtained their distinctive "Stahl" headwear in 1916. In the glass cases are identity tags, anti-flash masks and a Prussian bugle; above them, some printed panels—in French only—bear ghastly recollections from war writers of red-trousered bodies scattered over fields like poppies.

Rusty support posts for barbed wire show the curly shape that allowed them to be screwed silently into the ground. Nearby lie objects, collectively known as "trench art", crafted by soldiers from redundant bits of ammunition. They created paperknives from scraps of copper, decorated brass shell-cases with *repoussé* designs and whittled helmets out of wood. Also on display is one of the gift-boxes sent by Princess Mary to every British soldier for Christmas 1914. An informative 50-minute documentary (commentary in French) uses archive film to explain World War I, from the assassination of the Archduke to

The forgotten front

Most people think of Allied involvement on the Western Front in terms of Ypres and the Somme. However, fighting on the area in between, generally referred to as the Battles of the Artois, cost almost as many lives. From 1914, the Germans had occupied, and strongly fortified, the ridges of Aubers, Vimy and Lorette, and other vantage-points. The Allies' aim was to prevent the enemy advancing to take either Paris (and, hence, France) or a seaport (cutting British supply lines), and to recapture the city of Lille. Below are the main battles fought in the area, with related visitor centres and museums.

1914
Oct 1914-Oct 1915
Notre-Dame de Lorette
French take Lorette ridge after a year's fighting. During 1915 alone, French losses in Artois reach almost 250,000.
Notre-Dame-de-Lorette basilica & tower; Musée Vivant; Centre Européen de la Paix; Souchez (p166-168). Musée Militaire, La Targette (p169).
25 Dec
Christmas Truce
at Fromelles, Neuve-Chapelle & smaller places on this front.

1915
10-13 Mar
Battle of Neuve-Chapelle
British and Indians achieve a small advance.
Indian Memorial, Neuve-Chapelle (p154).
9-10 May
Battle of Aubers Ridge

British and Indian regiments lose 11,500 men.
Musée 14-18, Fromelles (p153).
25 Sept-19 Oct
Battle of Loos Scots take Loos village. Hill 70 taken by Guards Division, but later lost. Casualties in first two days: 50,000 killed and wounded, and 22,500 missing. First Allied use of gas.
Musée Alexandre Villedieu, Loos-en-Gohelle (p159).

1916
(Elsewhere: 21 Feb-6 Dec, Battle of Verdun; 1 July-20 Nov, Battle of the Somme.)
19 July
Attack at Fromelles The Australians' first, and most disastrous battle on the Western Front; 5,000 men lost in this diversion for the Battle of the Somme.
Musée 14-18; VC Corner;

Parc Australien; Fromelles (p153).

1917
9 Apr
Vimy Ridge Canadians capture ridge called Hill 145.
Canadian memorial & visitor centre, Vimy (p168).
Battle of Arras British attack Hindenburg Line, from Arras.
Carrière Wellington, Arras (p135).
15-23 Aug
Battle of Hill 70 Canadians take Hill 70, near Loos.
Musée Alexandre Villedieu, Loos (p159).

1918
9-29 Apr
Battle of the Lys Fought between Armentières and La Bassée. Portuguese lose 7,425 on first day.
Portuguese cemetery, Neuve-Chapelle (p154).

the Armistice. It touches on the changing role of women in the workplace, and on the way life in Paris and other big cities went on as normal. It also shows war-time inventions, such as tanks, poison gas, aerial surveillance and submarines (as well as a few less successful ideas).

The well-stocked tourist office has interesting leaflets, and offers a fantastic view towards the twin *terrils*, near Loos, that look like a piece of landscape art. If you stay for the film, you could easily spend a couple of hours here. ● *Mon 2-6pm; Tues-Fri 10am-noon & 2-6pm; Sat 2-6pm; Sun 3-6pm. 100 Rue Pasteur (D937), 1km N of Souchez (tel: 03 21 72 66 55). Admission free.* ♿ ☎

❯**Notre-Dame-de-Lorette** Visible from afar, the tower above the French national memorial for the fallen stands proudly on a 164-metre-high ridge. The sombre, 13-hectare site contains the graves of almost 20,000 French dead, plus the bones of 22,000 unknown soldiers. Known as the Battle of Lorette, the struggle to recapture this ridge raged for 12 months, from October 1914. The French retook the hill in 1915, though not the coalfields to the north-east.

Around the 1930s Byzantine-style basilica, a forest of white crosses stretches into the distance. Wall-tiles inside bear the names of thousands who died in World War I with no known grave. On the north side of the aisle is a memorial to the French spy Louise de Bettignies, who worked for British Intelligence, running an information network in northern France. Arrested in 1915, and refusing to talk in spite of torture, she was condemned to forced labour and died of tuberculosis in 1918.

The slender, 52-metre-high lantern-tower outside marks the ossuary where the bones of many unknown French soldiers—also from World War II, Indo-China and Algeria—are gathered. You are asked to stay silent as you step inside to view the top layer of black and gold coffins. In front of them, on a ledge, a smaller casket contains the ashes of French concentration-camp victims. On the first floor, a small museum presents a collection of newspaper-cuttings and militaria and a large wall-map shows locations of military graveyards in the area. ● *Lantern-tower & basilica: daily 9am-8pm. Museum: daily 9am-noon & 2-6.30pm. Colline de Notre-Dame- de-Lorette, 3km NW of Souchez. Admission free.* ◐

❯**Musée Vivant 1914-1918** On Lorette hill, round behind the cemetery, is an interesting museum that ingeniously re-creates a series of sandbagged dugouts. After passing the large glass cases containing hundreds of uniforms and regimental insignia, you enter a dimly-lit, wood-lined tunnel containing good life-sized tableaux of the French army, with commentary. (Push the lower button to hear it in English.) Look carefully, and you may see some of the figures move!

An adjacent building contains a series of stereoscopic viewers, showing 3D war images. You need 40 centimes to view each batch of 16; change is obtainable at the museum's desk. (The machine entitled *The Horrors of War* is not recommended for children, or for the squeamish.) Beyond this, through a coin-operated turnstile, is an area of battlefield with visible trenches, where sheep graze among rusting field-guns and barbed wire. It's chilling to see French and German front lines were so close that soldiers could have shaken hands across them. ● *Daily 9am-8pm. Notre-Dame-de-Lorette, 3km NW of Souchez (tel: 03 21 45 15 80). Museum: 4€, children 2€. Battlefield: 1€.* ◐

❯ ★ **Mémorial Canadien/Vimy Ridge** As you drive along the A26 motorway, your attention is caught by a brown sign indicating "Vimy: Mémorial Canadien". Swivel your eyes in the direction of the arrow to see the dramatic silhouette of a tall white monument commemorating all Canadians who fought in France during World War I.

At this point, on 9 April, 1917, the Canadian Corps succeeded in taking Hill 145 (Vimy Ridge), a 14km-long crest that had been in German hands for three years. From junctions 6 or 7, follow signs through sheep-nibbled grassland to the visitor centre, set away from the memorial among a silent army of Douglas firs. From the car park it is a short walk to the sandbag-lined trenches (see picture, page 36), clearly labelled to show German and Canadian front lines. Visitors move about the gravel paths in stunned silence, taking in the close proximity of the two sides and, especially, the shell-holes—now softened by grass—and massive craters resulting from the explosions of mines.

The visitor centre has good displays (in English and French) showing the progress of the war overall, and the execution of the 1917 attack on Hill 145 by four Canadian divisions. Meticulous planning included the creation of a detailed three-dimensional map to familiarise officers with the

■ Killing fields: Notre-Dame-de-Lorette cemetery.

SOUCHEZ EXTRAS

Restaurant:
Estaminet de Lorette
Drinks & meals served all day at this large 1930s-style bar/café/restaurant on Lorette ridge, behind the French military cemetery. Menus from 14€; pub games to play. Closed Sun-Thurs evgs. Notre-Dame-de-Lorette, 3km NW of Souchez (tel: 03 21 45 29 07).

Brocante: Le Jardin de Jadis *Garden gazebos & statues outside; choice furniture, ceramics & other objects within. Wed-Mon, & public holidays 3-7pm. 4 Rue Carnot (D937), near Cabaret-Rouge cemetery, 1km S of Souchez (tel: 06 12 99 81 25).*

Shop: Brasserie St Germain *Local brewery producing beers flavoured with rhubarb, honey or roasted chicory, plus special Christmas & spring brews. Shop: Wed-Fri 3-7pm; Sat 9am-noon & 2-6pm. Brewery visits: Fri 2pm, 3€. 26 Route d'Arras, Aix-Noulette, 3km N of Souchez (tel: 03 21 72 24 24).*

terrain; the boring of a 10km network of tunnels to protect Allied troops and to ensure supplies could be maintained; and the laying of mines below German positions to be exploded on the morning of the attack. Glass cases display weapons and equipment; panels tell you about the supplies of weapons, ammunition, food and fodder needed to keep the army viable. In a small sandbagged enclosure, a multi-media presentation recounts the battle, with archive footage (commentary in English, French or German). Further panels look at the aftermath of war: cemeteries, hospitals and limbless soldiers. Information boards near the door describe tunnelling techniques. At the desk you can book a free tunnel tour. Canadian students acting as guides explain the preparations under ground, and show some World War I artefacts. Almost 4,000 soldiers died in the attack, which had the unsought effect back home of uniting Canada's different provinces and welding the young nation into a single entity.

A little farther north stands the impressive limestone monument, its two 45-metre-high columns representing France and Canada. From here, a cleared avenue through the trees gives an unimpeded view of the jagged ruins of St-Éloi abbey, 9km to the south-west, left in their shell-blighted state as a constant reminder of the devastating effect of war ● *Trenches: open at all times. Visitor centre: daily 10am-6pm (1 May-30 Nov, also tunnel tours). On D55, 2km E of Souchez (tel: 03 21 50 68 68). Admission & tours free; donations at desk welcome.* ♿ *(except tunnels).* ⦿

❯**Musée Militaire de La Targette** A realistic-looking mannequin by a crossroads near Neuville-St-Vaast usually marks the entrance to this vast collection of World War I memorabilia. Its long, dark corridors (sensors cause each section to light up as you approach) are lined with countless cases of uniformed dummies, military musical instruments, Canadian machine-guns, a despatch-rider's motorbike and many other items. There are recreations of an Allied first-aid station, and of a German trench (illustrating how troops could fire through a hole in the roof of their sophisticated dugouts). Grenades lie alongside a block of TNT, rusty guns, spiked Prussian helmets, body armour, sabres, bayonets, saddlebags and magnificent crested helmets of the *dragons* (French dragoons, or cavalrymen). Other Allied memorabilia includes cigarettes and pipe tobacco, Princess Mary's 1914 Christmas boxes, grooming-brushes, officers' whistles and sturdy Sheffield-steel penknives. There are some stereoscopic viewers—unfortunately mostly out of order—for looking at 3D photographs. Upstairs, you find re-creations of a rifle store and of a British dugout, plus homely tins of Camp coffee, peppermint snuff, Andrew's Liver Salts and Mackintosh's toffees. The few captions are in French only. Depending on your degree of interest in the subject, you could spend anything from 30 minutes to two hours here. ● *Daily 9am-8pm. Closed 25 Dec & 1 Jan. 48 Route Nationale (junction of D937 & D49), La Targette, Neuville-St-Vaast, 4km S of Souchez (tel: 03 21 59 17 76). 4€, children 2€.* ⤳ ⦿

Suggested reading

ACCOMMODATION AND RESTAURANTS
Some useful guides and websites are given on pages 11 and 16.

PHRASE BOOKS
Berlitz French Phrase Book & Dictionary Pocket-sized companion for travelling, shopping, restaurant, hotel and roadside.
Collins Gem French Phrasebook: The Right Word in Your Pocket Small-format book on motoring, medical, food and other topics.
AA Essential French for Kids Fun to read, and good for helping children enjoy France.

WORLD WAR I PUBLICATIONS
Battlefield guides:
Before Endeavours Fade Rose Coombs' classic battlefield guide details motoring routes around sites along the Western Front.
Major and Mrs Holt's Battlefield Guides A book on the Somme and another—*Western Front (North)*—for the Artois give itineraries for driving around the cemeteries and memorials.
Walking the Somme/*Walking Arras* Paul Reed provides step-by-step commentated circuits along the Somme and Artois fronts.
Circuit of Remembrance Free leaflet from Somme Tourist Board (see page 11), widely available in the area, illustrates a 40km signposted route around significant war sites.
Scene-setting books:
Birdsong Sebastian Faulks' 1993 novel set in 1910 Amiens and among the WWI trenches.

Horrible Histories: The Frightful First World War Good preparation for visiting with children.
First-hand experiences:
Poetry and autobiographical accounts by Edmund Blunden, Frederic Manning, Wilfred Owen, Siegfried Sassoon and others. German perspective from Erich Maria Remarque; French views by Henri Barbusse and Roland Dorgelès.
Forgotten Voices of the Great War Interviews with survivors, arranged chronologically, bring home the horror and futility of the war.

WORLD WAR II PUBLICATIONS
Forgotten Voices of the Second World War Gripping interviews with servicemen and women describing war on land, sea and air.
Dunkirk: Fight to the Last Man Hugh Sebag-Montefiore's description of the May 1940 evacuation and of the days leading up to it.
Horrible Histories: The Woeful Second World War Excellent digest of the war's causes and events, for parents and children.

WAR-RELATED WEBSITES
Commonwealth war graves www.cwgc.org/
French war graves www.sepulturesdeguerre. sga.defense.gouv.fr/
German war graves www.volksbund.de/
Somme Battlefields website The Somme Tourist Board's useful website in English for battlefield visitors includes accommodation advice and downloadable brochures www.somme-battlefields.com/en/

Glossary

A good phrase book (see above) should help you through most situations. Below are a few more unusual French words—some specific to the area—that you may read, hear or need to use:

ficelle picarde	Snack dish: pancake stuffed with ham and mushrooms, in cheese sauce.
fosse	Pit (in coal-mining context).
hôtel	As well as "hotel", this can mean a town mansion.
hôtel de ville	Town hall.
interdit	Forbidden. (*Pêche interdite* means "No fishing".)
Je suis allergique à...	I am allergic to...
location	Rental. (As in *location de vélos*, cycle rental.)
mairie	Council offices in village.
marais	Marsh, fens, marshland.
mel	Email. (*Arobase* = @ sign; *tiret* = hyphen; *point* = dot.)
occasion	Second-hand (usually *d'occasion*); can also mean bargain.
planche	Snack dish: bread with ham, cheese or pâté, like a ploughman's.
poilu	French infantry soldier of World War I.
potjevleesch	Local dish: mixture of chunky cold meats in aspic, served with hot chips.
terril	Slag-heap.
respectez	Keep off. (*Respectez les pelouses* means "keep off the grass".)
touche étoile/dièse	Telephone star/hash button.
vélo/VTT	Bicycle. *VTT* (pronounced "vay-tay-tay") is a mountain bike.
welsh	Snack dish: toasted cheese and ham.

Index

Where relevant, bold type is used to indicate main entries.

Picture credits